Buy-Sell Agreements

Ticking Time Bombs or Reasonable Resolutions?

Buy-Sell Agreements

Ticking Time Bombs or Reasonable Resolutions?

Z. CHRISTOPHER MERCER, ASA, CFA

Published by Peabody Publishing, LP

Buy-Sell Agreements

Ticking Time Bombs or Reasonable Resolutions?

ISBN: 978-0-9700698-9-4

Peabody Publishing LP
5860 Ridgeway Center Parkway, Suite 400
Memphis, Tennessee 38120
Tel: 800.769.0967
Fax: 901.685.2199

To the memory of Nellie

and to Zeno, where the Z comes from.

Thanks, Mom and Dad, for the solid foundation.

Other Books by Z. Christopher Mercer

Valuing Shareholder Cash Flows:
Quantifying Marketability Discounts (2005 e-book)
www.mercercapital.com

Valuing Enterprise and Shareholder Cash Flows:
The Integrated Theory of Business Valuation (2004)
www.mercercapital.com

Quantifying Marketability Discounts (1997, 2001)
(out of print)

Valuation for Impairment Testing (2001) (contributing author)
(out of print)

Valuing Financial Institutions (1992)
(currently offered as an e-book)
www.mercercapital.com

Acknowledgements

How can an author properly acknowledge the help of so many people who have helped make a book possible? In my case, any attempt will prove inadequate because the help has been so immense. This book is truly not the result of one man's efforts, but of many people who have played a very instrumental role in bringing it to completion.

Everything begins with the wonderful folks at Mercer Capital, where I've had the privilege of working since 1982. Work does not really feel like work there for me – at least most of the time! The ability to have an idea and to walk down the hall or across the floor to talk with just the right person about it is wonderful. Participating in intellectual conversation about other topics and triggering additional ideas is icing on the cake. Watching others develop their own ideas is stimulating and gratifying, as well. My thanks to everyone at Mercer Capital for providing the intellectual incubator that makes books like this possible. My thanks, also, for helping me to pursue this buy-sell agreement book project – and many others!

This book had its beginnings almost a decade ago. By the mid-1990s, we had seen hundreds of buy-sell agreements and had participated in many buy-sell agreement valuation processes. In fact, we recently discovered an initial outline for a book on buy-sell agreements from 1997. Apparently other projects got in the way. We did begin to compile research on buy-sell agreements as a prelude to this book in early 2005 and James E. Graves, ASA, CFA, Laura O. Matthews, and Glenda A. McNeal all worked diligently to develop the information base which has been so critical to developing this text.

In the fall of 2005, I wrote an article entitled "Your Corporate Buy-Sell Agreement: Ticking Time Bombs or Reasonable Resolutions?" and readers reacted to it with enthusiasm. Based on that article, I was asked to speak at several regional and national conferences which served to further our work on this book. Therefore, my thanks to Parnell Black, MBA, CPA, CVA and Brien K. Jones (National Association of Certified Valuation Analysts), Rick Schwartz (Business Enterprise Institute), Harold G. Martin, Jr., MBA, CPA, ABV, ASA, CFE (Virginia Society of CPAs), Line Racette, CA, CBV, CA-IFA, CFE, ASA (Canadian Institute of Chartered Business Valuators and the American Society of Appraisers), and Ronald L. Seigneur, CPA/ABV, MBA, CVA and James R. Hitchner, CPA/ABV, ASA (AICPA), among others for asking me to speak during 2006 on this important topic. There's nothing like the challenge of the platform to help me develop ideas.

Now, moving on to several very helpful people at Mercer Capital:

- *Barbara Walters Price.* Barbara has been a real driver for this book project. She encouraged me to write chunks of text on my blog, www.merceronvalue.com, and this challenge helped me with the discipline of regular writing in small doses. Without the blogging idea, this book might still be in the "that's a good idea" stage where it lingered for so long! I can't say enough about how important Barbara's help and encouragement have been with this project and all the books that have preceded it. She is this book's real publisher.

- *Kenneth W. Patton, ASA.* Ken and I have worked together for over twenty years. He has encouraged and supported this project from the outset. He has also spent many hours in the role of reviewer/editor, bringing fresh insights to each succeeding draft. His help and insight have been invaluable.

- *Matthew R. Crow, ASA, CFA.* Matt has pushed this project and encouraged me greatly. He has also applied his advanced degree in English to the draft tightening the text. He is a terrific sounding board and a respected colleague.

- *Timothy R. Lee, ASA.* Tim has also pushed and encouraged this project. He worked hard as a reviewer and contributed greatly to my thinking as well as to the book: some of the "war stories" found in Chapter 22 were provided by Tim. Like Matt, Tim is a wonderful sounding board and a respected colleague.

Ken, Matt and Tim have also taken the "buy-sell presentation" on the road to law firms and other groups. Their efforts further helped with the development of this book. With support from Tim, Matt, Barbara and Ken (who constitute 80% of Mercer Capital's board of directors), this book had to come together!

Three other people also contributed greatly to this book. Matthew G. Washburn brought his considerable design skills to this project by designing the cover, the interior layout, and graphics. V. Todd Lowe, my Executive Assistant, kept things moving on this book in many ways, as he does for so many other projects. Tammy Ford Falkner, previously my E.A. and now our Sales Coordinator, is always willing to nudge things along when I need her.

Again, my thanks to all the professionals of Mercer Capital who are a constant source of inspiration to me. I couldn't do what I do without them. They work diligently to provide the highest level of quality and service to our clients. It is my privilege to work with so many talented, bright, driven and creative individuals.

My family has also been a constant source of encouragement to me as I have worked on this project. My thanks to them – my wife, Ashley, my grown daughter, Amanda, and my kids, Zeno III, Katherine, Margaret, and Katherine for supporting me while this book came into being.

I also want to thank the many clients who provided the experiences that made this book possible. They will, of course, remain nameless for reasons of confidentiality. I hope we have helped them get through some nasty situations with buy-sell agreements gone bad, and have helped others develop agreements that will be workable for a long time to come.

Z. Christopher Mercer, ASA, CFA
December 2006

Table of Contents

Section Three
PROCESS BUY-SELL AGREEMENTS

Section Five
WAR STORIES

Section Six

ACTION ITEMS

APPENDICES

FOREWORD

For most owners, their business has been an inseparable part of their lives for many years – probably decades. The very thought of transferring that business interest is consequently rife with emotion and the uncertainty of its financial consequence. Carefully crafted buy-sell agreements provide an objective means of transferring ownership under difficult circumstances, as well as protecting all parties should trigger events occur.

As Chris Mercer discusses in great detail throughout this book, it is essential to view a business continuity (buy-sell) agreement as a live document that is updated on a regular basis to reflect changing owner objectives and company dynamics, as well as current business valuations. Failure to do so invites conflict.

I emphasize the likelihood of a lifetime transition of ownership for a number of reasons. First, a lifetime transfer is the most likely event to happen. Second, lifetime transfers are not funded – unlike death or disability caused transitions. Therefore, you are dealing with "real" money in lifetime transfers that the buyer must pay – unless carefully designed as part of an Exit Plan – with after tax dollars. Lifetime sales, consequently, are "arms-length" in nature with the seller wanting as much as possible and the buyer wanting to pay as little as necessary. A well-drafted buy-sell agreement must fairly address this most likely of business transfer scenarios. Lastly, it is important to consider the complexities associated with third-party sales to unrelated parties. In drafting a buy-sell agreement, advisors must consider at least some of these complexities – chief among them is the price to be paid. In a true arms-length scenario, the price is always negotiated between a willing buyer and willing seller, which is the classic definition of value, as outlined in the IRS Revenue Ruling 59-60. If you don't have (or want) the negotiation element in a buy-sell agreement, the alternative is a fairly determined value for the ownership interest being transferred – and this critical element is at the heart of Chris' book.

Fortunately, Chris thoroughly explains the significance of valuations to ensure effective buy-sell agreements. I suspect that Chris asked me, as an attorney and president of BEI, to write this foreword because a reliable business valuation also is the bedrock of BEI's entire Exit Planning Process™.

As discussed in Chris' book, the most viable method of determining value is a process method that provides periodic valuations by a single appraiser. We've found that this type of method is applicable not only to buy-sell agreements, but also to the periodic use of appraisals in Exit Planning. It is important to note that the suggestions Chris offers in his book are based not on abstract tax or legal theory, but on practical experience that advisors can start using today with their business owner clients. The practical nature of Chris' suggestions also is easy to incorporate into the Exit Planning Process™ because owners need to execute accurate business valuations in order to meet their overall exit objectives.

A most valuable discussion in this book centers on the need to perform not only periodic valuations, but also regularly scheduled "buy-sell audits." These audits serve the purpose of ensuring that a company's buy-sell agreement continues to fairly reflect the owners' objectives (wishes and desires), in accordance with good business practices. As such, Chris' suggestions for a buy-sell audit include asking forward-looking questions such as the following:

- Is there a reasonable probability that the agreement will operate to effectuate a reasonable transaction when trigger events occur?
- Are all shareholders who should be subject to the agreement parties to it?
- Do the shareholders who are parties to the agreement understand how the agreement will operate to determine prices and terms for future transactions?
- Has the agreement been reviewed by counsel to ensure compliance with applicable laws and statutes?
- Are the six defining elements of value as developed in Chris' book clearly specified?
- Will the pricing mechanism provide a reasonable value if and when trigger events occur in the future?
- Is the funding mechanism in place and workable?

After you read this book, I think you will agree that many – too many – existing buy-sell agreements are "boiler plate," outdated or simply don't fully deal with the fundamental goal of ensuring that both the buyer and seller engage in the sale process using an accurate valuation. Otherwise, one party will benefit and one will feel (and be) aggrieved. None of us, I submit, would find that result acceptable.

This book is a great resource for business owners and their advisors because Chris is a businessman himself and he uses real-world scenarios in extensive case studies throughout the book. These case studies illustrate the importance of "practicality" when designing buy-sell agreements.

Finally, there is a fascinating and informative discussion on the "level of value," which alone is worth the cost of this book for every lawyer and other business planning professional.

John H. Brown
President
Business Enterprise Institute

For inquiries into The Seven Step Exit Planning Process™ developed by the Business Enterprise Institute and practiced by business owner advisors nationwide, contact John H. Brown at (888-206-3009) or via e-mail at (jbrown@exitplanning.com).

Introduction

Buy-sell agreements are prevalent throughout the corporate world. They are common when businesses have multiple shareholders, partners, or joint venture participants. At the outset, let's be clear that this book is applicable to a broad range of businesses, regardless of their corporate form of organization or their size.

This book provides business and valuation information for enterprises ranging from:

- Corporations, whether organized as S corporations or C corporations
- Limited liability companies
- Partnerships, whether between individuals or between entities such as corporate joint ventures
- Not-for-profit organizations

This is *not* a book on how to draft buy-sell agreements, although the *Buy-Sell Audit Checklist* in Chapter 23 may provide assistance to counsel. This is a book about buy-sell agreements written by a business appraiser and businessman. It is a book calling for appropriate utilization of valuation expertise in the process of examining existing buy-sell agreements *from business and valuation perspectives*, as well as in the drafting of buy-sell agreements currently – from those same perspectives.

For purposes of simplicity, we typically refer to business enterprises as "the company" or "the corporation" in the text. All owners will be referred to as "shareholders."

Who Should Read this Book?

The book is written for:

- Legal counsel
- Business owners
- CPAs & accountants
- CFOs and other management team members
- Fiduciaries of business owners
- Estate planning counsel
- Insurance professionals
- Corporate directors

The book is appropriate for owners and managers of companies of all sizes, ranging from small general partnerships, to the largest corporations in the world. The examples discussed throughout this book are based on our experience with corporate buy-sell agreements but are modified to ensure confidentiality.

Why This Book Is Important

Buy-sell agreements are *legal contracts*. What is not clearly understood, however, is that they are also *business and valuation documents*. We refer to buy-sell agreements as business and valuation documents because they represent contractual agreements between the respective parties concerning:

1. The *business objectives* they are designed to facilitate; and,
2. How the pricing and terms will occur. In other words, buy-sell agreements determine how the *valuation* of businesses (or business ownership interests) will be determined in future transactions that may or will occur.

Again, this book is written from the perspective of a businessman and a business valuation expert. It is based on personal experiences spanning some thirty years and, since 1982, on the experiences of the professionals at Mercer Capital. During the course of providing valuation and investment banking services to thousands of companies, we have reviewed many buy-sell agreements.

This book does not replace legal counsel. If anything, we strongly urge you to listen more carefully to your attorney when agreements are prepared. Our intent is to assist lawyers, professional advisors to corporations, and owners, in accomplishing their desired business objectives.

Buy-sell agreements often offer proof of the law of unintended consequences. Yes, we have seen some buy-sell agreements accomplish their goals. We have also seen agreements that have not worked anything like the parties anticipated or desired when their terms were invoked (see Chapter 22 for "war stories" from our files).

INTRODUCTION

Definition

A general definition or description of buy-sell agreements offered from a business perspective follows:

> Buy-sell agreements are agreements (contracts) by and among the shareholders (or equity partners of whatever legal entity) of a business and, perhaps, the business itself. They establish the mechanism for the purchase of equity interests following the death (or other adverse or significant changes) of one of the owners. In the case of corporate joint ventures, they also establish the value for break-ups or for circumstances calling for one corporate venture partner to buy out the other partner.

Buy-sell agreements are important because they represent agreement between a corporation and its shareholders regarding how the future transactions contemplated by the agreements will occur. It is important to note that at the time most buy-sell agreements are initiated, either the interests of the corporation and the shareholders are aligned, or they are not sufficiently misaligned to prevent agreement from taking place. Perhaps, because of this, despite the best efforts of a corporation's counsel, the shareholders often do not, prior to the initiation of a buy-sell agreement, take sufficient time to understand the exact nature of the agreement, how it will work in the future, and the implications for them (whether they will be a buyer or seller in future transactions).

A brief focus on the term itself is instructive:

1. *Buy.* A buy-sell agreement specifies the conditions under which one party, or the company, will purchase the equity interest of another party upon the occurrence of specified trigger events.

2. *Sell.* A buy-sell agreement specifies the conditions under which one party, or the company, will sell its equity interest upon the occurrence of specified trigger events.

3. *Agreements.* Buy-sell agreements are legal agreements. They are signed by parties, often at the beginning of a business relationship, and represent collective agreement, or at least contractual acquiescence, to their terms.

Buy-sell agreements are necessary because no one knows, at the time of signing, who will be the buyer and who will be the seller. No one can predict the future. As

Yogi Berra says: "The future is hard to predict. It hasn't happened yet." It is, therefore, important that agreements be satisfactory from a business standpoint to all parties, whether ultimately they will be future buyers or sellers pursuant to their particular buy-sell agreements.

Key Aspects of Buy-Sell Agreements

From a valuation and business perspective, buy-sell agreements generally incorporate several important aspects defining their operation. Specifically, buy-sell agreements that have reasonable prospects for working successfully:

1. **Require agreement** *at a point in time* among shareholders of a company and/or between shareholders and the company.

2. **Relate to transactions** that may or will occur *at future points in time* between the shareholders, or between the shareholders and the corporation.

3. **Define the conditions** that will cause the buy-sell provisions to be "triggered." For example, trigger events involving corporations, partnerships and joint ventures relate to circumstances such as bankruptcy or change of control of a corporate partner, an outside offer for the joint venture (or a partner's interest in it), the inability to meet capital calls, and other events that may be considered by the parties to be disruptive to the continuing nature of the business. Trigger events involving individuals include situations when an employee-shareholder subject to the agreement quits, is fired, retires, dies, or is disabled ("QFRDD"). Trigger events can also include the divorce, bankruptcy, insolvency, or any other event to which the shareholders and the corporation agree. The quitting or firing or retiring would obviously not relate to a non-employee shareholder.

4. **Determine the price** (per share or per unit or per member interest) at which the identified future transactions will occur. This is one of the hardest parts of establishing effective buy-sell agreements.

5. **Provide a funding mechanism** so that the contemplated transactions can be affected on terms and conditions satisfactory to both selling owners and the corporation (or other purchasing owners). This element is important and often overlooked. Given its vital importance, we mention it from a business perspective.

6. **Satisfy the business requirements** of the parties. While buy-sell agreements have much in common, each business situation is different and unique parties are involved. In the end, legal counsel must draft buy-sell

agreements to address the business issues that are important to the parties. Clearly, establishing and agreeing on the key business issues and having them reflected in the agreement is often difficult.

7. **Provide the potential for estate tax planning** for the shareholders, whether in family companies or in non-family situations. The Internal Revenue Service has rules to determine whether the price determined in a buy-sell agreement, even if binding on the parties, is also determinative of fair market value for estate tax purposes. Recent court cases have also addressed the issue. If a buy-sell agreement is expected to be used as an estate planning tool, it is essential that tax advisors work with legal counsel and valuation advisors to ensure that the agreement will meet both business and estate planning objectives.

8. **Satisfy legal requirements** relating to the operation of the agreements. Buy-sell agreements must be drafted such that they are legally binding on the parties to them. In addition, agreements must be drafted to comply with laws and/or regulations that may be applicable to their operation. Business owners must rely on legal counsel regarding such matters.

How to Read this Book

This book cannot possibly illustrate every possible problem or unique issue with every buy-sell agreement. It does, however, provide a roadmap for attorneys or other advisors who are thinking about buy-sell agreements generally and for shareholders, investors and corporate officers.

There are several pages for your notes at the end of the book. We recommend that readers read aggressively.

- Highlight relevant facts or issues for further study.
- Raise questions or make comments in the margins to focus your thinking about buy-sell agreements generally or about your agreement specifically.
- If you have an existing buy-sell agreement, read it in conjunction with this book. Raise questions in your agreement and add to your notes. Then, consult the *Buy-Sell Audit Checklist* in Chapter 23.
- If you are initiating a buy-sell agreement at the time you are reading this book, make notes relating to your situation. Then, consolidate your notes on the *Buy-Sell Audit Checklist* in Chapter 23 before discussing them with legal counsel or other business advisors.

In the final analysis, we hope you will use this book as an active tool to help you, your lawyers and other advisors craft workable agreements. Is your buy-sell agreement a ticking time bomb? Or will it provide a reasonable resolution to the future transactions it contemplates?

SECTION ONE

An Introduction to Buy-Sell Agreements

CHAPTER 1

How Buy-Sell Agreements Come Into Existence

Business lawyers and business persons with any experience know that corporations and their owners need buy-sell agreements to protect the interests of the corporation and their shareholders. However, as important as buy-sell agreements are, many are created almost as an afterthought, particularly from the viewpoint of shareholders/investors in private businesses. When transactions are consummated or companies are created, the shareholders/investors tend to think that the job is done. After all, they have agreed on the economics of the investment and their relative ownership positions. They should be able to get down to business.

At this point, an experienced business attorney says to the shareholders/investors, "Now, we have to put a buy-sell agreement into place. You do want to take care of things appropriately if one of you should die, don't you? You need to agree on a buy-sell agreement to determine what happens if one of you quits, is fired, retires, dies, or is disabled. These are things that can happen."

The attorney goes on to say, "And you do want to control who you do business with in the future, don't you? The most likely way to do that is to prepare a right of first refusal agreement. So let's talk about the important issues this raises for your consideration and agreement."

At this moment, the pace of communication between the attorneys and the owners frequently begins to slow. Investors are weary of negotiations and ready to move on with their business proposition. They typically don't want to spend any more money on legal fees and many definitely don't want to talk about their own mortalities, the potential of future fall-outs, retirements, or disabilities. They also know that a real discussion of a buy-sell agreement would be difficult and potentially divisive based on one or more actual or potential opposing characteristics among shareholder group.

POTENTIAL OPPOSING SHAREHOLDER CHARACTERISTICS THAT MAKE DISCUSSING BUY-SELL AGREEMENTS DIFFICULT

Characteristic	Shareholder 1	Shareholder 2
Age	Younger	Older
Ownership	Non-controlling	Controlling
Involvement	Active	Inactive
Investment Type	Sweat Equity	Real Money
Investment Amount	Smaller	Larger to Much Larger
Personal Guaranties	None	Substantial

FIGURE 1

Then, someone volunteers to the attorney and other owners, "We've all been in business and we know what buy-sell agreements are all about. You have one in your word processor, don't you?"

The attorney replies, "Yes, we have several templates that provide a basis for discussion about the particular needs and circumstances of your business and its ownership. But we need to adapt the template to this situation." The attorney is attempting to deliver an extremely important message.

Nevertheless, the investor replies, "You've been here the entire time we've been putting this deal together and you know us, so just give us a basic buy-sell agreement so we'll have one." And then, he utters these fateful words: "There'll never be a problem, anyway!"

Your attorney drafts an agreement (or agreements if there is an accompanying right of first refusal to be put in place) subject to the review and approval of all of the parties. The shareholders/investors glance at them and sign them. The agreements go into the corporate records and personal lock boxes until trigger events happen – and trigger events will almost certainly occur.

The Use of Templates

Templates are forms used by many professionals to facilitate the initial drafting of documents. We use a variety of them at Mercer Capital. Like valuation professionals, attorneys also use templates. It is important to recognize that a template is nothing more than a framework for answering and documenting the answers to important questions. Templates also have to be updated regularly because of legal and valuation changes which render the current forms unusable.

The problem with out-of-date definitions is far greater than definitions embedded in current templates. Many thousands of buy-sell agreements created over the last fifteen or twenty years (or more) contain language that has not been updated. Given recent changes in valuation theory and practice, which we will discuss at length in Section Four, the valuation-defining language used in older agreements could be clear only by chance. *And chance is not good enough!*

Initial Recommendations

It is appropriate to highlight just a few of the recommendations of this book in this initial chapter:

1. If you have a buy-sell agreement, consider having it reviewed from both a business and a valuation perspective. We introduce the concept of the *Buy-Sell Audit Checklist* in Chapter 23. At the very least, read this book in its entirety before deciding not to engage in such a review.
2. If you know there are problems with your buy-sell agreement, do not stop until you are satisfied that they are resolved and your agreement reflects a consensus understanding of its future operation. The *Buy-Sell Audit Checklist* can provide a helpful roadmap for your discussions. Again, reading this book in its entirety should assist you, whether you are a business owner or advisor, as you attempt to develop this consensus understanding.
3. If you are currently drafting a buy-sell agreement, consider obtaining valuation expertise to ensure that the valuation aspects of the agreement are clearly understood in the context of current financial and valuation theory. The *Buy-Sell Audit Checklist* in Chapter 23 can assist in this process. To repeat once more, it is important that you read this book in its entirety before completing your buy-sell agreement.

Questions to Consider

1. **Business.** Will the existing design and operation of your buy-sell agreement accomplish your business objectives? Only you can answer this question, hopefully working with your lawyer(s) and other advisors. This analysis requires that you understand what the objectives of your agreement are and how the "words on the page" will be implemented upon the occurrence of some stressful future event.

2. **Legal.** Does your buy-sell agreement comply with all applicable laws, and does the legal language reflect your business intentions? Your lawyer will have to address legal compliance issues, and you will have to explain your business intentions clearly.

3. **Valuation.** If a trigger event occurs, will the valuation mechanism in your buy-sell agreement accomplish the objective of providing a then-current price for the company's stock at the level (the kind of value) you and your partners/shareholders/investors agree to be reasonable? We will discuss these issues at length, but your valuation professional may have to help you and your lawyer address this question.

ACTION STEPS

Business owners. If you are a business owner or shareholder and your buy-sell agreement has not been updated within the last year (or if you don't understand it if it has), run, don't walk, to your attorney to talk through these issues. If you or your attorneys don't understand the valuation nuances of your buy-sell agreement, don't hesitate to bring in a qualified business appraiser to read the agreement from a valuation perspective and to tell you what he or she thinks it means and what aspects of the document may represent legitimate room for misunderstanding between appraisers. Find out what needs to be done, make the necessary decisions, and fix the document(s). It will never be easier than right now (see the *Buy-Sell Audit Checklist* in Chapter 23).

Corporate attorney. If you are a corporate attorney for businesses having buy-sell agreements, and this chapter (or the rest of the book) creates uncertainty about the potential operation of any of those buy-sell agreements, call your clients and encourage them to address the issues immediately. This move is not about "mistakes." It is about improvement and clarification for your clients' benefit.

Certified public accountants and other business advisors. If you are a trusted advisor to a business owner or significant shareholder, you will provide excellent client service by making immediate contact for the explicit purpose of discussing the buy-sell agreement and subjecting it to formal review and/or revision.

Business directors. If you are a director of a private company with one or more buy-sell agreements in place, take the time to investigate the agreements and encourage management and the shareholders to review and update their agreements, if appropriate. If you are a director of a private or public company with multiple joint ventures involving substantial resources, you can bring great value to your company by requesting a review, from legal, business and valuation viewpoints, of all existing buy-sell and/or put agreements with appraisal-type pricing mechanisms.

THEY DID IT RIGHT THE FIRST TIME

We have rarely been consulted regarding how the valuation mechanism in a buy-sell agreement would or should work before the agreement was finalized. Remember the old saying "there is never enough time to do it right, but there is always time to do it over." Make time to do it right the first time and you won't have to do it over.

For example, in one instance, we were contacted by a key shareholder in a company with revenues of approximately $100 million. The draft buy-sell agreement called for the appraiser to be a licensed general appraiser in the state where the company was domiciled.

Licensed general appraisers are real estate appraisers. Such credentials are not sufficient nor are they appropriate for the valuation of a business enterprise with $100 million in sales. Upon our review of the draft agreement, we identified this issue for the client and the agreement was changed. The final agreement specified the credentials and qualifications of business appraisers who might be retained to provide valuations for future trigger events.

CHAPTER 2

What Are Buy-Sell Agreements Designed To Accomplish?

We use "QFRDD" to denote common trigger events for buy-sell agreements. The term "trigger" can have a benign connotation. If A happens, then B is triggered, or set in motion to happen. However, the majority of trigger events related to buy-sell agreements have less benign connotations. While it is easy to think of these events in personal terms, analogous situations also happen to companies. "Quits" equates to withdrawal from the venture; "disabled" could mean inability to answer a capital call; and, "dies" represents bankruptcy of a participant.

If you think about the events suggested by QFRDD, none of them are very pleasant to talk about, particularly to a group of shareholders who may have just come together for a common business purpose. In fact, circumstances could be such that the shareholder most affected by a trigger event has a proverbial gun to his or her head! In the alternative, the company may perceive that it has a gun to its head in order to fulfill the repurchase requirements of a buy-sell agreement.

Buy-sell agreements are designed to accomplish one or more of the following objectives from one or more of several viewpoints: the corporation, the employee-shareholder, the non-employee shareholder, and any remaining shareholders. Think of QFRDD to remember.

Q – Quits. A buy-sell agreement may provide a mechanism for shareholders who leave a business to sell their shares to the corporation or other shareholders. From the corporation's viewpoint, the agreement may prevent the departing shareholder from retaining his shares. By requiring a shareholder who quits to sell his or her shares to the corporation upon departure, the corporation and remaining shareholders eliminate any potential for conflict over future corporate policies with the departed shareholder. They also eliminate the potential for the departed shareholder to benefit from future success of the business created by the remaining shareholders. Finally, the agreements prevent a shareholder (or his or her estate) from selling shares to "undesirable" parties, enabling the remaining shareholders to decide who will be the next shareholder, if any. These reasons for buy-sell provisions apply to virtually all trigger events.

F – Is Fired. When an employee-shareholder is terminated, most corporations desire to retain control over the shares. Terminations generally result in diverse, or more likely, adverse interests between the fired shareholder, the corporation, and remaining shareholders. From the employee's viewpoint, the buy-sell agreement assures that his or her shares can be sold at the buy-sell price and creates a market for the shares. From the corporation's viewpoint, buy-sell agreements create the right, or the obligation, to purchase the departing employee-shareholder's shares. They also eliminate the potential for the terminated shareholder to benefit from any future success of the business created by the remaining employees and shareholders. Some agreements call for a penalty to the valuation in cases of termination, particularly for cause.

R – Retires. The retirement of an employee-shareholder creates a potential divergence of interests between the shareholder and the corporation. The shareholder may desire current liquidity over the uncertain future performance of the corporation, and the corporation may desire not to have potential interference or disagreement with corporate policy, or to have the retired shareholder benefit from future appreciation in value.

D – Disabled. After a defined period of time, the corporation may have the right (from its viewpoint) or the obligation (perhaps, from the employee's viewpoint) to purchase the disabled employee's shares. The other features related to fired employees also relate to disabled ones.

D – Dies. The death of a shareholder creates issues that are often resolved by buy-sell agreements. If a shareholder dies owning a minority interest in a corporation for which there is no market for its shares, the illiquidity of the stock can create estate tax issues. The shares must be valued for estate tax purposes, and the appraisal amount will add to the estate's value. To the extent

> that the estate is taxable, there may be no liquidity to pay the estate taxes. Buy-sell agreements provide a mechanism for determining the value of shares for estate tax purposes and for monetizing that value for the estate, generally in cash or in a term note. Therefore, the shareholder's estate realizes liquidity and can pay taxes due and does not face the combination of uncertainty of independent valuation and the certainty of payment of taxes in the absence of liquidity. From the corporation's viewpoint, the buy-sell agreement eliminates the need to address uncertain ownership dictated by the deceased shareholder's will and can create the requirement for funding.

If the parties agree, buy-sell agreements also operate in the event of the divorce, declaration of insolvency, or bankruptcy of one or more shareholders (or even the corporation). In the event of the divorce of an employee-shareholder, the buy-sell agreement will most likely be designed to prevent the non-employee spouse from realizing any ownership in the stock of the corporation. If an employee declares bankruptcy or becomes insolvent, the corporation may exercise its right to purchase the shares to prevent their dispersion to creditors.

It should be clear from the above that buy-sell agreements *can be* favorable from the viewpoints of employee-shareholders, non-employee shareholders, the corporation, and any remaining shareholders in many diverse situations. The emphasis is on "can be" because the operation of a buy-sell agreement can go awry despite the best intentions of its creators.

In conclusion, buy-sell agreements are designed to provide objective means of transferring ownership under difficult circumstances. In the absence of a workable buy-sell agreement, the remaining shareholders and the corporation may be placed in the unenviable position of negotiating under adverse circumstances with former friends, their families, or their estates. At best, this can be difficult for all parties involved.

CHAPTER 3

Business Factors to Consider With Buy-Sell Agreements

An Estate Planner's Guide to Buy-Sell Agreements for the Closely Held Business, by Louis A. Mezzullo, provides a list of factors to consider when creating buy-sell agreements.[1] The structure of the following discussion borrows from Mr. Mezzullo's, however, unless otherwise indicated, the comments are ours based on our experience.

1. *Nature of the entity.* S corporations and certain professional corporations may need to restrict ownership to appropriate classes of shareholders.

2. *Size of the entity.* Often, complexity in ownership develops as companies increase in size and value. While companies are small, remaining shareholders may agree to purchase the shares of departing shareholders in cross-purchase agreements, often funded by life insurance. As the number of owners and value increase, such agreements become cumbersome or unworkable.

3. *Valuation of the entity.* Addressing this question is a primary focus of this book.

4. *Relative ownership* If a company has a dominant shareholder and one or more owners with relatively small interests, the operation of a buy-sell

---

1 Mezzullo, Louis A., *An Estate Planner's Guide to Buy-Sell Agreements for the Closely Held Business* (American Bar Association, 2001), pp. 11-15.

agreement can place hardships on the minority owners who may be required to purchase the shares of the majority shareholder. In such cases, it is helpful to have a corporate buy-sell agreement in place that is funded, hopefully, by life insurance.

In smaller companies, shareholders may be given the right to purchase a departing owner's shares on a pro rata basis in order to maintain relative ownership percentages. Occasionally, companies are owned by "groups" of shareholders, for example, by the descendants of two families. The buy-sell agreement may be structured to maintain the relative ownership of the two groups, with individual shareholders within the groups making the necessary decisions to maintain their relative ownership positions.

5. *Ages of the owners.* While even young owners can die or have change-of-life experiences, the issue of aging needs to be considered when structuring buy-sell agreements. This is true for the estate planning issues mentioned previously. It is also true for owners nearing normal retirement age. Buy-sell agreements can provide for a structured purchase of a retiring owner's interest, and life insurance in the event of an unexpected death. If life insurance is not available or its cost is prohibitive, it may be necessary to provide for a purchase of the departing owner's shares over time. It is far better to agree on or anticipate these issues before adverse circumstances force their consideration.

6. *Relative financial positions of owners.* Some corporations are financed by highly affluent individuals, other companies, private equity groups, or other institutions. Such companies often have managers with ownership interests in the business. Buy-sell agreements need to consider the relative inequality of wealth of the various owners. Neither any owner nor the corporation should be placed in the position of engaging in transactions they are not financially capable of handling.

7. *Health and insurability of owners.* In the event of the ill health of an owner, it is essential to establish agreement as to how the transition of ownership will occur. For example, what will happen if the shareholder is unable to continue working or in the event of death? If a shareholder is not insurable for health reasons, this factor will need to be addressed in the buy-sell agreement, because funding options may be limited.

8. *Commitment of owners to the business and importance of their participation in the business.* Over time, companies often develop groups of "inside" shareholders who are active in a business and other shareholders who are passive owners. It may be appropriate when structuring a buy-sell agreement to provide for the ability of "inside" shareholders to benefit disproportionately from the purchase of a passive owner's shares. Rights of first refusal are common in such circumstances, because "inside" shareholders want to ensure that new passive owners are acceptable to them.

9. *Availability of assets for redeeming the interest.* If it is anticipated that there will be insufficient assets for a company to redeem an interest, or life insurance is not available, it may be appropriate for the shareholders to have cross-purchase agreements in place to handle the transfers outside the corporation. This could be problematic in the event that one or more shareholders lack the capacity to make such a purchase and may become impracticable as the number of shareholders grows beyond a small number.

10. *State law with respect to stock redemptions in the case of a corporation or distributions to members of an LLC.* Mr. Mezzullo cites certain Virginia statutes and notes as follows: "Most states prohibit a corporation or LLC from making a redemptive distribution to a shareholder or member if doing so will leave it unable to pay its debts when due in the usual course of business, or if as a result its assets will become less than the total of its liabilities plus any amounts needed to satisfy any preferential distribution rights held by shareholders or members that are superior to those of the distributee if the corporation or LLC were to be then dissolved."[2] In other words, drafters of buy-sell agreements must be concerned that their operation will not render a corporation insolvent.

11. *Existence of restrictions under loan agreements.* Lenders often place restrictions on the ability of companies to utilize corporate assets for purposes of share repurchases if so doing would diminish creditworthiness below threshold levels. These matters are often negotiated in the context of loan agreements and the impact of such covenants should be considered in the structure of buy-sell agreements.

---

2 Ibid, p. 13.

It is clear that there are a number of important factors to be taken into account when preparing a buy-sell agreement, some of which will be of relatively more importance to particular shareholders. A number of these factors are included in the *Buy-Sell Audit Checklist* in Chapter 23 for your consideration.

SECTION TWO

Categories & Types of Buy-Sell Agreements

CHAPTER 4

Categories of Buy-Sell Agreements

There are three general categories of buy-sell agreements which are defined by the relationships between the corporation and the shareholders who are subject to the agreements.

1. **Cross-Purchase Agreements.** Cross-purchase agreements are agreements between and among the shareholders of a corporation calling for the purchase by the other shareholder(s) of the shares subject to the buy-sell agreement. Cross-purchase agreements are often funded by life insurance owned by shareholder(s) on the lives of other shareholders. Cross-purchase agreements quickly become unworkable as the number of shareholders and market value increase. See the discussion and table below for an illustration of the growing complexity of cross-purchase agreements.

2. **Entity-Purchase Agreements.** Entity purchase agreements call for the corporation to purchase the shares upon the occurrence of trigger events. The entity is then responsible for defining or providing the funding mechanism. The funding mechanism may be the purchase of life insurance, financing by a third party or the selling shareholders, or cash on hand, or a combination.

3. **Hybrid Agreements.** Hybrid agreements generally call for the entity to have the right of first refusal to purchase shares upon the occurrence of trigger events. In the event that the corporation declines to purchase, it may have the right to offer the shares to the other shareholders pro rata, or to selected shareholders. Finally, hybrid agreements often give the corporation a "last look" if shares are first refused and other shareholders do not

purchase the stock. For the hybrid agreement to be effective, the corporation's "last look" must be binding as to the purchase of the shares.

Hybrid agreements can be used to create non-pro rata changes in relative ownership if that result is desired for business reasons. Funding may be through a combination of self-financing by the corporation, notes from selling shareholders, and life insurance.

For larger corporations, most buy-sell agreements are entity purchase agreements, or they are hybrid in nature if the corporation has the right to allow individual shareholders to stand in its place. For substantial corporations with more than a few shareholders, the preponderance of buy-sell agreements are entity purchase agreements, some of which may allow the redirection of purchases to some or all shareholders.

CROSS-PURCHASE COMPLEXITY

Cross-purchase agreements are often used in relatively small businesses with two or three shareholders, although there are exceptions to this statement. On the first line of the table below, assume A and B each own 50% of the business:

- There are two shareholders
- There is one relationship
- If life insurance funds their buy-sell agreement, two policies will be required (A buys a policy on B's life and B buys a policy on A's life)

Growing Complexity of Cross-Purchase Agreements Limits Their Usefulness

# Shareholders	Shareholder Relationships	# Relationships / # Policies
2 (A and B)	AB	1 / 2
3 (A, B and C)	AB BC AC	3 / 6
4 (A, B, C and D)	AB AC AD BC BD CD	6 / 12
5 (A, B, C, D and E)	AB AC AD AE BC BD BE CD CE DE	10 / 20
6 (A, B, C, D, E and F)	You get the picture!	15 / 30

As the table above illustrates, the number of relationships increase as the number of shareholders increase. The number of required insurance policies increases even faster. At some point, cross-purchase agreements become too cumbersome for reasonable operation.

CHAPTER 5

Types of Buy-Sell Agreements

The three categories of buy-sell agreements are cross-purchase agreements, entity agreements and hybrid agreements. Buy-sell agreements can also be placed into five general types based on the nature of the valuation mechanism:

1. **Fixed Price Agreements.** These agreements fix the price of future purchases at a specific dollar amount by stating a value for the equity of the enterprise, either in dollars or a per share value.

2. **Formula Agreements.** Formula agreements establish value by providing a formula for determining value. Examples of formulas include a multiple of book value or earnings, or the agreement may call for an averaging of valuation indications developed using two or more formulas.

3. **Shotgun Agreements.** Shotgun agreements outline a process whereby one party offers to purchase (or sell) shares to another and the other party has the right (or the obligation) to sell (or purchase) the shares at the offered price.

4. **Rights of First Refusal.** As we will see, rights of first refusal (ROFRs) are sometimes considered to be a form of buy-sell agreement. More often, they are used in conjunction with buy-sell agreements.

5. **Process Agreements.** Process buy-sell agreements outline a process by which future transactions will be priced, i.e., they define valuation processes. In nearly all cases, process agreements call upon the use of one or more business appraisers in (the process of) determining the price at which contemplated future transactions will occur. We sub-divide process

agreements into two categories, because of important differences in how they operate:

a. **Multiple Appraiser Agreements.** Multiple appraiser buy-sell agreements outline processes by which two or more appraisers are employed to determine value.

b. **Single Appraiser Agreements.** Single appraiser buy-sell agreements outline processes by which a single appraiser is employed to determine value.

Each type of agreement has advantages and disadvantages which are of sufficient importance to warrant specific elaboration as our discussion continues.

CHAPTER 6

Fixed Price Buy-Sell Agreements

Fixed price buy-sell agreements do exactly what their name suggests. They fix a price today for transactions that will occur at future dates. Fixed price agreements are often found in smaller corporations, partnerships and LLCs.

Fixed price agreements:

1. **Require agreement** *at a point in time* between shareholders of a corporation and/or the corporation. With a fixed price agreement, the shareholders simply (or not so simply) agree on a price, which is memorialized in the agreement. The shareholders also agree on the other terms of its operation.
2. **Relate to transactions** that may or will occur *at future points in time* between the shareholders, or between the shareholders and the corporation.
3. **Define the conditions** that will cause the buy-sell provisions to be triggered. These are the business and/or personal events that will trigger the operation of the buy-sell agreement.
4. **Determine the price** (for example, per share or per unit or per member interest) at which the identified future transactions will occur. Fixed price agreements often state that the agreed upon price will be updated periodically and that the agreed upon price will be determinative of value until the time of the next updating.

Advantages

There are advantages to fixed price agreements.

1. **Easy to understand.** Once the price is agreed upon, everyone knows what the buy-sell price will be.

2. **Easy to negotiate**. When fixed price agreements are installed, there is generally a common belief about the then-current value of the business (or business interest) among the shareholders.

3. **Inexpensive**. Fixed price agreements require less legal documentation than more complex agreements and other professionals, such as accountants and business appraisers, are utilized less frequently.

Disadvantages

The primary disadvantage of fixed price agreements is that *they are out of date shortly after they are inked*. While the parties almost always intend to update the price, they seldom do.

It is often easy for the parties to agree on the initial price for a fixed price agreement; however, it can become increasingly difficult and confrontational to discuss price at later dates. Such discussions force shareholders to consider their potential disabilities, firings, retirements, and even deaths. Further, the range of shareholder characteristics tends to widen with the passage of time. Most business owners, at least in our experience, will go to extremes to avoid such discussions (see Figure 1 showing potential opposing characteristics).

If there is a controlling shareholder and the remaining shareholders hold minority interests, it can become awkward to discuss valuation. The minority shareholders are often thinking in terms of the value of the enterprise as a whole, and not in terms of illiquid, minority interests in the corporation. The controlling shareholder may consider the minority shares to be worth proportionately less than his shares.

We have seen agreements where the "out-of-date" problem is cured by calling for an appraisal in the event that an agreed-upon price is more than, say, one year old. This cure, however, just opens up the potential problems associated with process agreements (discussed in Section Three).

At times, fixed price agreements become examples of potentially expensive bets on the part of shareholders. If the price is fixed and they know that price is substantially below the current value of the business, owners who do not update the value are making implicit or explicit bets that a trigger event will happen to the other shareholder(s) before it happens to them. In other words, there is bet that the other guy(s) will die first. And one of them is correct!

We think the point is clear, but a couple of real-life examples should drive it home.

Poster-Child Examples of Fixed Price Agreements

Bet and Lost. A friend of mine told me the true story of his family's experience. His father was an initial, minority shareholder and employee of a business during the early 1960s. At the outset of the enterprise, the shareholders implemented a buy-sell agreement with a fixed price. The father's shares were valued at his investment value of $250 thousand.

Fast forward to 1974. The business grew and was successful. My friend, who is quite knowledgeable about business valuation, said that his father's interest would have been worth more than $1.0 million by 1974 – the year his father died.

Neither the corporation nor the other shareholders offered to update the price in the buy-sell agreement to purchase the shares from the father's estate, so the shares were purchased for $250 thousand. My friend noted that receiving $250 thousand in 1974, and not $1.0 million, made a significant difference in his mother's independence for the remaining 25 years of her life. In addition, it caused a great deal of bitterness towards his father's former partners.

My friend's father probably did not think in terms of making a bet on his company's buy-sell agreement, but the fact that it was not updated did indeed create a betting situation. He bet and, we don't mean this in any personal way, his family lost.

Bet and Did Not Lose. We have chosen our words carefully with this subtitle. You have heard the story about the cobbler's children having no shoes. This next example is illustrative of that expression. Sometimes, there is no better way to illustrate a point than with one's own mistakes.

Mercer Capital has had, throughout its history, several ownership structures. It began as a proprietorship which was followed by three shareholders, followed by an extended period of two shareholders, followed by its current form of ownership – one shareholder and an employee stock ownership plan.

There were times during this period when the company did not have a buy-sell agreement. At times, there was a fixed price agreement. Hindsight has brought a great deal of perspective. If anything, the focus on growing the business deflected attention from the buy-sell agreement. If, knowing better, we allowed this situation to perpetuate for so long; you have to believe that there are other situations that cry out for attention.

Conclusion

In our opinion, fixed price buy-sell agreements should be avoided like a contagious disease in most situations. However, if you have one, you must have the discipline to update the price periodically.

TAKE AWAY THOUGHT

If you have a fixed price buy-sell agreement, first, determine whether the price is current or not. If it is not, update it immediately! And read on. Better alternatives are available to you.

CHAPTER 7

Formula Buy-Sell Agreements

Companies (and their shareholders) with formula agreements may believe that these agreements are superior to fixed price agreements, but, as we will see, formula agreements have their own issues. They fix a *single formula* today for transactions that will occur at future dates. We examine formula agreements through four key aspects of buy-sell agreements. Formula agreements:

1. **Require agreement** *at a point in time* between shareholders of a corporation and/or the corporation. With a formula agreement, the shareholders simply (or not so simply) agree on a formula to determine price, which is memorialized in the agreement.

2. **Relate to transactions** that may or will occur *at future points in time* between the shareholders, or between the shareholders and the corporation.

3. **Define the conditions** that will cause the buy-sell provisions to be triggered. These are the business conditions that will trigger the operation of the buy-sell agreement, and the obligation of the company (or the shareholders) to repurchase the shares.

4. **Determine the price** (per share or per unit or per member interest) at which the identified future transactions will occur. Formula agreements state a formula, which is typically applied to the then-current balance sheet or income statement metrics, to determine value. Some agreements call for the averaging of two or more separate calculations. Therefore, the series of calculations is the "formula" for those agreements. The formula can be changed over time by agreement of the parties, however, until such a change is made, the initial formula is determinative of value.

Advantages

As with other types of buy-sell agreements, formula agreements have certain advantages, including:

1. **(Initially) Easy to understand.** Once the formula is selected, the specific calculations necessary to determine the buy-sell price are known. Some typical formulas include multiples of net income, pre-tax income, operating income, and earnings before interest, taxes, depreciation and amortization (EBITDA). These formulas refer to what is called the *capitalization of earnings*. Book value (or a multiple of book value) is sometimes used as well.

2. **Easy to negotiate.** When a formula agreement is installed, there is generally a common belief among the shareholders about the then-current value of the business. The value is effectively converted into the formula.

3. **Inexpensive.** Formula agreements require less legal documentation and typically less involvement of other professionals.

Disadvantages

Formula buy-sell agreements also have certain disadvantages. The primary disadvantage is that no formula selected at a given time can provide reasonable and realistic valuations over time.[3] This is true because of the myriad changes that occur within individual companies, local or regional economies, the national economy, and within industries.

One summary representation of business value, i.e., a generalized formula, can be expressed as:

Value = Earnings x Multiple

---

3 We have suggested that formulas, agreed upon at a point in time, are not reliable mechanisms for determining value at future trigger dates under the operation of the agreements. For more information, visit www.merceronvalue.com.

To develop a formula for a buy-sell agreement, "all one has to do" is to decide on the appropriate measure of earnings, and then, the appropriate multiple to be applied to that earnings measure (i.e., with which to *capitalize* the earnings). As we have said in many speeches, if valuation were that simple, appraisers would not be necessary. As Ken Patton, Mercer Capital's president, is fond of saying: "Whenever someone tells you that 'all you have to do is *it*,' [whatever *it* is], you know for sure that there is more to *it* than *it*!" And so it is with formula valuation.

Possible Formulas and Future Earnings Patterns

The purpose of the analysis and tables that follow is not to try to illustrate any particular formula. Rather, it is included to illustrate the complexity which underlies the use of formulas. As is quickly seen, the use of formulas is not simple.

The analysis in Figures 2 and 3 considers different formulas based on earnings, and different earnings multiples, all of which could be, at a point in time, reasonably reflective of value for a given enterprise. In addition, three different earnings scenarios are considered; 1) sustained growth; 2) variable earnings, with expected earnings down; and 3) variable earnings, with expected earnings up. Assume we are discussing pre-tax earnings.

Examples of the three earnings scenarios noted above are illustrated in Figure 2, along with 18 possible weights to be assigned to combinations of historical or expected earnings.

	Prior Year 4	Prior Year 3	Prior Year 2	Prior Year 1	Most Recent Year	Expected Next Year
Sustained Growth	**600**	**700**	**800**	**900**	**1,000**	**1,100**
Variable-Down	*600*	*400*	*300*	*600*	*1,100*	*750*
Variable-Up	*600*	*400*	*300*	*600*	*1,100*	*1,400*
Weights						
1					1	1
2				1	1	1
3					1	1
4				1	1	
5			1	1	1	
6		1	1	1	1	
7	1	1	1	1	1	
8					2	1
9				3	2	1
10			4	3	2	1
11		1	2	3	4	5
12	1	2	3	4	5	
13			1	2	3	4
14		1	2	3	4	
15				1	2	3
16			1	2	4	
17					1	2
18				1	2	

FIGURE 2

If you use an earnings capitalization formula, chances are it will be something like one of the above weighting schemes applied to some measure of earnings.

Possible Multiples

If you use a formula method, you have to select a multiple. Multiples change over time in most industries based on industry conditions, interest rates, the economy, the stock market, and company-specific factors.

You be the judge. Assume for the moment that the appropriate earnings multiple is in the range of 4x to 6x the selected measure of earnings. Figure 3 illustrates the range of possible conclusions of value based on the 18 different weighting scenarios and the range of multiples from 4x to 6x earnings for steadily growing earnings (the "sustained growth" example in Figure 2).

	Prior Year 4	Prior Year 3	Prior Year 2	Prior Year 1	Most Recent Year	Expected Next Year	Weighted Avg. Earnings	Values at Multiples 4.0	5.0	6.0
Sustained Growth	600	700	800	900	1,000	1,100				
Weights										
1					1	1	1,050	4,200	5,250	6,300
2				1	1	1	1,000	4,000	5,000	6,000
3					1	1	1,050	4,200	5,250	6,300
4				1	1		950	3,800	4,750	5,700
5			1	1	1		900	3,600	4,500	5,400
6		1	1	1	1		675	2,700	3,375	4,050
7	1	1	1	1	1		660	2,640	3,300	3,960
8					2	1	1,033	4,133	5,167	6,200
9				3	2	1	967	3,867	4,833	5,800
10			4	3	2	1	900	3,600	4,500	5,400
11		1	2	3	4	5	920	3,680	4,600	5,520
12	1	2	3	4	5		773	3,094	3,867	4,641
13			1	2	3	4	1,000	4,000	5,000	6,000
14		1	2	3	4		830	3,320	4,150	4,980
15				1	2	3	1,033	4,133	5,167	6,200
16			1	2	4		943	3,771	4,714	5,657
17					1	2	1,067	4,267	5,333	6,400
18				1	2		967	3,867	4,833	5,800
						Minimums	660	2,640	3,300	3,960
						Maximums	1,067	4,267	5,333	6,400

FIGURE 3

We make the following observations from Figure 3:

- **Multiple.** The range of 4x to 6x for the selected measure of earnings (we use the EBITDA multiple here) indicates a 50% swing from low to high. Multiples change over time, so the selection of any single multiple for a formula today can be wrong, relative to the market, by as much as 50% based solely on that selection.

- **Weighting.** The range of calculated values for any given multiple indicates a 62% swing from minimum to maximum.

- **Combination.** The combination of variations in multiples and weightings indicates a swing of 142% from the lowest value ($2.6 million) to the highest ($6.4 million).

Keep in mind, Figure 3 shows the range of weighted earnings and multiples based on steadily rising earnings. The range of value conclusions is even greater if expected earnings are variable.

If you have but one chance to select the appropriate valuation mechanism at a future date from the figures above, which would you pick? Might there not be a better way to decide the pricing mechanism for your buy-sell agreement?

Other Caveats re Formula Agreements

It is one thing to think you understand a formula. It is quite another to write it down so that those who are called upon to calculate its intended value will understand exactly what the parties meant when the formula agreement was signed. As an example, review the following formula that might be found in a buy-sell agreement:

a. The corporation's earnings before interest, taxes, depreciation and amortization (EBITDA) for the trailing twelve months ending the month-end prior to the event giving rise to the required transaction ("the Determination Date") times a multiple of 5.0. The product of the calculated EBITDA and 5.0 will represent the market value of the total capital of the business (MVTC).

b. From the MVTC of the business, the interest-bearing debt (IBD) outstanding on the balance sheet as of the month-end immediately prior to the event giving rise to the required transaction will be subtracted, with the difference representing the market value of the equity of the business (MVE).

c. The MVE of the business will be divided by the number of shares outstanding as of the Determination Date (Shares Outstanding, or SO), with the result being MVE per share.

d. MVE per share will be multiplied by the number of shares subject to the required transaction (Shares to be Purchased, or SP), with the result being the amount due to the selling shareholder (the Due Amount, or DA) from the corporation under the terms of Section 7.3 below.

e. The Due Amount will therefore be calculated by the following formula:

$$DA = (((EBITDA \times 5.0) - IBD) / SO) \times SP$$

Now assume the following as of the Determination Date:

1. EBITDA, as calculated by the corporation's outside accountant is $10.0 million for the trailing twelve months ending closest to the Determination Date.

2. Interest-bearing debt (IBD) totals $5.0 million as of the month-end prior to the Determination Date.

3. Shares Outstanding, or SO, as of the Determination Date are 1,000,000 shares.

4. The Shares to be Purchased, or SP, equals 10% of the Shares Outstanding, or 100,000 shares.

The corporation's outside accountant calculates the Due Amount as follows:

DA = ((($10,000,000 x 5.0) - $5,000,000) / 1,000,000) x 100,000

= (($50,000,000 - $5,000,000) / 1,000,000) x 100,000

= $45 per share x 100,000 shares

= $4,500,000

While the algebra may seem frightening to the math-impaired, it is actually fairly straightforward. Therein lies the attractiveness of formula buy-sell agreements. They are conceptually easy to understand and, supposedly, not difficult to implement.

Should the Selling Shareholder be happy with the resulting calculation? Let's dig a bit further. What if we learned that EBITDA, but for a one-time charge to write down stale inventory, would have been $12 million rather than $10 million? If an adjustment were made for this non-recurring item, which would be fairly routine in most appraisals, the resulting value would have been $5.5 million.

What if the corporation had $5 million of excess cash on its balance sheet (with earnings of $10 million)? The Due Amount would have been $5 million.

Under these circumstances, the Selling Shareholder would likely be quite upset if he were offered only $4.5 million for his shares. However, given the language of the agreement, he might have no right to his pro rata share of excess assets accumulated (i.e., not distributed) during his tenure as a shareholder.

Situations like the above, where the application of formula pricing yields a conclusion obviously different from actual economic value will create the potential for litigation, unhappiness, anger, loss of friendships, and many other unfavorable results.

Needless to say, we do not recommend the use of formulas in corporate buy-sell agreements.

BOOK VALUE AS THE "FORMULA"

For additional perspective, we offer the following comments on the use of book value in buy-sell agreements from Richard M. Wise, FASA, MCBA, FCBV, FCA, a prominent Canadian business appraiser.[4]

> "'Book value' (which would generally be at historical cost) may be totally inappropriate in determining price in a buy-sell agreement and unfair as a basis for the acquisition of the *terminating* shareholder's shares. Either the continuing shareholder(s) or the terminating shareholder will be unfairly treated if the buy-sell price is book value (except perhaps in portfolio investment-type situations).
>
> ... Stated differently, book value is the net amount of assets as shown by the books, or the amount that the shareholders will receive immediately following a no-loss liquidation.
>
> If the buy-sell clause employs the term 'book value,' payment to the withdrawing or deceased shareholder at such a price may be substantially below a fair and reasonable amount because, of course, increases in the values of fixed and certain other assets and the existence of valuable intangibles, including intellectual property,

4 Wise, Richard M., "Valuation Aspects of Shareholders' Buy-Sell Agreements," *Business Valuation Review*, March 2005, Volume 24, No. 1, pp. 6-12.

generally will not be recognized in the calculation of book value. This is because tangible assets are generally recorded at original or historical cost, and intangibles, unless they are either purchased or there has been a business combination, will not even be reflected on the face of the balance sheet. Nor are contingent assets and liabilities reflected on the balance sheet; they may be commented upon in the notes accompanying the financial statements.

'Book value' has several other important shortcomings when it is used for purposes of setting the buy-sell price. Consider the result in each of the following unrelated hypothetical situations:

- A business has substantial earnings power, and goodwill is not reflected on the balance sheet. Moreover, the terminating shareholder was instrumental in creating and maintaining the goodwill.
- A business is construction-related (a construction company, a firm of architects, etc.) and has long-term construction contracts. The firm recognizes its profits using the completed-contract-method of accounting rather than the percentage-of-completion method. Over 90% of the work has been completed but, adhering to the firm's consistent accounting policies, revenue recognition will not occur until after the shareholder departs.
- Future income taxes payable are reflected on the company's balance sheet. For valuation purposes, depending upon how such tax credits arise, should they be considered a liability or a part of shareholders' equity in computing book value per share?
- The company has large unused loss carryforwards (which have substantial value), but the related losses for accounting purposes have a negative effect on the calculation of the book value of the company's issued shares.
- There are various *potential* liabilities (distinct from *contingent* liabilities) such as letters of credit available but not yet presented to or paid by the bank, environmental considerations, etc.
- During the intervening period there was an issuance of common stock from treasury at a price in excess of book value; retirement of preferred stock at a price below the book value of the preferred; conversion of funded debt into common stock; issuance of stock dividends; a stock split; or a reverse stock split.
- At the time of the signing of the agreement, the circumstances were different from those prevailing when the triggering event occurs.
- Accounting policies such as the capitalization of certain repairs or the treatment of depreciation, etc. have not been consistent from year to year since the signing of the buy-sell agreement.

- There have been errors in the preparation of the current year's or the previous year's financial statements.
- The company is on a cash basis of accounting rather than on an accrual basis.
- There are pending lawsuits or substantial claims by or against the company (referred to in the notes to the financial statements), and it is impossible to determine their potential outcome. In addition, the company has just been reassessed for the previous taxation year for a substantial amount, and believes that the reassessment is ill-founded and will file an objection.
- The company has consistently excluded overhead from its inventory. Had such normal overhead been included, regained earnings would have been increased (net of income taxes on such overhead).
- There are inventory and other hidden reserves.
- The company's balance sheet reflects purchased goodwill which has lost value since acquisition and has not yet been written down pursuant to the annual impairment test under GAAP.
- Transactions between the company and non-arm's length parties have taken place at other than fair market value.
- There are "special purchasers" in the marketplace.
- The specified event is death, and life insurance proceeds will be payable to the company as beneficiary and owner of the policy.
- The company is the guarantor of bank loans to a third party.
- There are product warranties outstanding which have not been booked (but only noted) on the financial statements.
- There is long-term debt owing to arm's-length creditors, but bearing interest at rates substantially below current market rates on similar obligations."

Mr. Wise concludes: "In summary, although 'book value' may be the simplest term to understand – and to calculate – it will often yield unfair results."

ACTION STEPS

Having noted the supposed ease of the formula calculations, formulas written by attorneys are seldom so clearly presented in the context of buy-sell agreements. There seems to be a tendency to put formulas (like the example above) in ponderous paragraphs and to omit the algebraic presentation of the actual formulas.

1. It is a good idea to be sure you know how your formula works and that the parties affected by the formula agree to how it is used.
2. It is an even better idea to calculate the formula value periodically so you will know what the buy-sell price would be if a trigger event occurred.
3. The changes you see in the price over time may cause you to reevaluate the use of the formula in your buy-sell agreement.

CHAPTER 8

Shotgun Agreements

Shotgun agreements are occasionally found in some older buy-sell agreements, although we seldom see them recommended for agreements today. These agreements:

1. **Require agreement** *at a point in time*, usually between shareholders of a corporation, or else between corporate joint venture partners.

2. **Relate to transactions** that may or will occur *at future points in time* between the shareholders, or between the shareholders and corporate joint venture partners, or between corporate joint venture partners.

3. **Define the conditions** that will cause the buy-sell provisions to be triggered. These are the business conditions that will trigger the operation of the buy-sell agreement, and the obligation to purchase shares pursuant to the agreement.

4. **Determine the price** (per share or per unit or per member interest) at which the identified future transactions will occur. The shotgun process will determine the price at which future transactions will occur, but no one knows until an offer is made what that price will be. One version of the agreement might require that:

    a. *One party* is called upon to offer a price at which he will buy or sell.

    b. The *other party* then has the right to buy or sell at that price.

    c. In either event, the "shotgun" aspect of the agreement requires that there be a transaction, but the initial offeror does not know whether he or she will be a seller or a buyer at the time the offer is made.

d. The concept is quite simple. The initial offering side (which will that be?) virtually has to name a reasonable price, since it is a price at which that side must be willing to sell or to buy. However, there are implicit assumptions with these agreements that both sides have sufficient financial capacity to engage in the transaction and are sufficiently knowledgeable about the business in order to make an informed offer or to evaluate the offer made.

Advantages

As with formula and fixed price agreements, shotgun agreements appear simple. Advantages include:

1. **Easy to understand.** Once the shotgun mechanism is decided upon, the parties know that it may be invoked at a point in the future upon the occurrence of a trigger event.

2. **Easy to negotiate.** The logic of shotguns can seem compelling. All we have to do today is to agree that one party will have to name a price at which they will be willing to sell or to buy, and the other party has to similarly agree that they will buy or sell.

3. **Inexpensive.** The agreement requires less legal documentation and no appraisers to determine the price.

4. **Pressure for reasonable price.** As we have already noted, there is pressure on the initial offering party to establish a reasonable price.

Disadvantages

There are some disadvantages to shotgun buy-sell agreements.

1. **Implicit assumptions may not hold.** The parties seldom have equal financial capacities and may have different knowledge about the business. For example, a non-operating shareholder may be at a distinct disadvantage in terms of making an offer to buy. Assume there are two operating partners, each owning 50%. Certainly a shotgun agreement is fair, or is it? Assume further that one partner dies. The surviving spouse is not active in management and might be at a distinct disadvantage.

2. **Minority shareholders may be at a disadvantage.** It is easier for a 90% shareholder to acquire a 10% interest than vice-versa. A smaller shareholder, unable to swing the big deal, may have to offer a relatively low price in order to ensure his capability to either buy or sell, thereby increasing the odds that the other side will buy.

3. **Uncertainty as to final outcome.** Relative to fixed price and formula agreements, there is great uncertainty as to what will happen when a shotgun agreement is triggered. Sellers usually don't want to become buyers, or vice versa.

CHAPTER 9

Rights of First Refusal

Rights of first refusal (ROFRs) are sometimes considered to be a form of buy-sell agreement. A right of first refusal is an agreement designed, for the most part, to restrict ownership of shares by limiting their marketability. The typical right of first refusal states the conditions under which shares of a corporation can be sold. Rights of first refusal tend to work along these lines:

1. If a shareholder desires to sell his or her shares to a third party and the third party provides a concrete offer, the corporation retains a right of first refusal to purchase the shares at the same price and on the same terms offered to the existing shareholder by the third party. The corporation generally has a period of time, from 30 to 60 days or more, during which to match the third party offer and purchase the subject shares.

2. If the corporation does not match the offer within the specified period, many agreements allow what could be called a "right of second refusal" to the other shareholders of the corporation. The other shareholders then have a period of time, from 30 to 60 days or more, during which to match the third party offer and purchase the subject shares.

3. In some cases, the corporation may have a last look opportunity to purchase the shares if the other shareholders do not. The corporation is granted some additional time, perhaps 30 to 60 days or so, to make this final decision.

4. If all of the prior rights are refused, *then and only then,* is the original shareholder allowed to sell his or her shares to the third party.

Rights of first refusal are not the same as buy-sell agreements. They may seem to operate like a buy-sell agreement, in that they provide procedures related to possible future stock transactions. But ROFRs do not assure that transactions will occur.

Rights of first refusal restrict the marketability of shares during the period of time shareholders own stock in a corporation. They restrict marketability because they discourage third parties from engaging in the time, effort, and expense of due diligence regarding investments. Rights of first refusal often add months to the time that a transaction could occur, and they create great uncertainty for potential third party buyers as well as for selling shareholders.

Rights of first refusal are designed to do several things from the viewpoint of a corporation and remaining shareholders:

- First, they discourage third parties from making offers to buy shares from individual shareholders.

- They also give the corporation control over the inclusion of third parties as new shareholders.

- If a third party offer is low relative to intrinsic value as perceived by the corporation and the other shareholders, the third party will know (or likely believe) that there is a high likelihood that the offer will be matched by either the corporation or the other shareholders, so there is little opportunity to purchase shares at a bargain price.

- If a third party offer is at the level of perceived intrinsic value, the corporation and/or the shareholders are likely to purchase the shares if there is any likelihood that they do not want to be in business with the third party.

- Additionally, if the third party offer is in excess of perceived intrinsic value and the corporation does allow the third party as a shareholder, the third party almost certainly knows that he or she is paying more than either the corporation or any of its shareholders believed the shares to be worth.

- Finally, most ROFRs require that any successful third party purchaser agree to become subject to the same (restrictive) agreement.

Agreements including ROFRs are often written so that shareholders can sell shares to each other (often requiring that such transactions do not impact control of the entity), or transfer shares within their families. These provisions provide flexibility for shareholders who are "on the team," so to speak.

The bottom line about rights of first refusal is that they restrict marketability. Buy-sell agreements provide for marketability under specified terms and conditions upon the occurrence of specified trigger events.

Many corporations have a buy-sell agreement which incorporates a right of first refusal. The buy-sell portion of the agreement provides for liquidity for shareholders under the conditions established in the agreement. The right of first refusal then determines the ability of shareholders to transfer their shares up to the point of a trigger event.

SECTION THREE

Process Buy-Sell Agreements

CHAPTER 10

Introduction to Process Buy-Sell Agreements

Process agreements, as discussed in this book, are buy-sell agreements involving the use of one or more business appraisers in processes specified for determining value. Mercer Capital professionals have been involved in many valuation processes for determining price (valuations) for buy-sell agreements. In fact, a primary impetus for writing this book has been our experiences with problem processes.

If appraisers are to determine price, they need a definition of the assignment. Five elements must be defined in order for the appraiser(s) to provide the type of valuation sought pursuant to the agreement.[5] A sixth element is so important from a business perspective that we include it as an additional defining element.

1. Standard of Value	4. Qualifications of Appraisers
2. Level of Value	5. Appraisal Standards
3. The "as of" Date	6. Funding Mechanisms

5 Arguably, there are more elements necessary to fully define a particular valuation assignment. We limit this list to five, however, because if the qualifications of appraisers and appraisal standards to be followed are specified, compliance with applicable standards will assure complete specification.

Let's begin with the first five defining elements.

1. **Standard of value**. The standard of value is the identification of the type of value being used in a specific engagement. The proper identification of the standard of value is the cornerstone of every valuation. The parties to the agreement may select that standard of value. Will value be based on "fair market value" or "fair value" or some other standard? These words can result in dramatically different interpretations from a valuation perspective. Some agreements simply specify "the value" of the company or interest, which is not adequate to define the standard of value. The likelihood of a successful appraisal process diminishes greatly if the standard of value is not clearly specified.

2. **Level of value.** Will the value be based on a *pro rata share of the value of the business* or will it be based on the *value of an interest in the business*? The differences bring minority interest and marketability discounts into play which may cause wide differences in the conclusion of value. Two appraisers could agree on the total value of a business, but if one applies a minority interest or a marketability discount, their conclusions may be significantly different. This is not surprising because their conclusions represent two different levels of value. One appraiser will have valued the business, while the other will have valued an interest in the business. The desired level of value needs to be crystal clear in your agreement.

3. **The "as of" date for the valuation.** Every appraisal is grounded at a point in time. That time, referred to as the "valuation date" or "effective date" or the "as of" date, provides the perspective, whether current or historical, from which the appraisal is prepared. Unfortunately, some buy-sell agreements are not clear about the date as of which the valuation(s) should be determined by appraisers. This can be extremely important, particularly in corporate partnerships and joint ventures when events (QFRDD) establish the valuation date. Because value changes over time, it is essential that the "as of" date be specified.

4. **Qualifications of appraisers.** Some buy-sell agreements provide a list of firms that the parties agree are mutually acceptable. In other cases, the specific, individual qualifications of appraisers are spelled out (e.g., credentials from a major credentialing organization, experience in appraisal, experience with the industry, etc.). Unfortunately, many agreements are

silent on this issue. Absent clear specification of the appraiser qualifications, there is no assurance that appraisers considered for buy-sell valuations will be qualified to provide the required services.

5. **Appraisal standards to be followed.** Some buy-sell agreements go so far as to name the specific business appraisal standards that must be followed by the appraisers. For example, some agreements state that the appraiser(s) must follow the *Uniform Standards of Professional Appraisal Practice*, the *Business Valuation Standards* of the American Society of Appraisers, or other standards, as well. These and other valuation standards will be footnoted and discussed in Section Four. Qualified business appraisers will understand the importance of specifying appraisal standards and be familiar with and able to follow relevant standards.

The sixth defining element relates to the funding of buy-sell agreements.

6. **The funding mechanisms.** The funding mechanism is thought of separately from valuation. However, there may be interrelationships between the valuation and the funding mechanism that should be considered in your buy-sell agreement. As we will see in Chapter 21, funding mechanisms such as life insurance and sinking funds can have a direct impact on value. This aspect aside, the funding mechanism does determine in substantial measure whether the valuation, however developed, can be implemented in future transactions. An agreement is no better than the ability of the parties and/or the company to fund any required purchases at the agreed upon price. An agreement that is silent can be like having no agreement at all.

What's so hard about specifying these defining elements? Getting specific often makes people think about things they don't want to think about. But think about them they must. If you think it is difficult to address these issues with your partner(s) in the *here and now*, just think how difficult it will be when one of you is in the *hereafter*.

Know this: if these defining elements are unclear in your (or your clients') buy-sell agreement(s), following a trigger event they may be the only thing you will be able to think about until the situation is resolved. Absent a clear agreement, this can take lots of money, lots of time, and create lots of hard feelings. In addition, dealing with these issues under adverse circumstances will absolutely distract you from running your business.

In Section Four of this book, we'll explore each of these defining elements in greater detail.

TAKE AWAY THOUGHT

The assignment definition is critical to the successful outcome of an appraisal process. A failure to define any one of the critical elements introduced in this chapter could doom the process to an unacceptable outcome.

Remember this about buy-sell agreements: someone will buy and someone will sell. You just don't know who that will be when you sign the agreement. Your agreement needs to work for you and your family whether you are the buyer or seller. It also needs to work for your partner(s) and their families (or their shareholders) whether they are the buyers or sellers. And it needs to work for the corporation. Your buy-sell agreement won't meet all these needs by chance alone. You have to make it work. Take action if necessary or appropriate.

CHAPTER 11

Process Buy-Sell Agreements

Process buy-sell agreements, or agreements where a *valuation process* is used to establish value, share certain commonalities. Process agreements:

1. **Require agreement** *at a point in time* between shareholders of a corporation and/or the corporation. With a process agreement, the shareholders and the corporation reach agreement about the process that will determine the price (valuation) for future transactions, rather than stating a particular price or formula.

2. **Relate to transactions** that may or will occur *at future points in time* between the shareholders, or between the shareholders and the corporation.

3. **Define the conditions** that will cause the buy-sell provisions to be triggered. These are the business conditions that will trigger the operation of the buy-sell agreement and the obligation to purchase shares pursuant to the agreement.

4. **Determine the price** (per share or per unit or per member interest) at which the identified future transactions will occur. The process, usually involving one or more appraisers, determines the price for future transactions.

We identify three groups of process agreements:

- Multiple appraiser agreements
- Single appraiser process agreements
- Hybrid agreements

In each process agreement group, we present different variations: four variations of the multiple appraiser process agreement and three variations of the single appraiser agreement. Each variation is discussed in this chapter. Subsequent chapters detail the advantages and disadvantages of each.

We have created a third group, "hybrid agreements," and briefly describe "the single appraiser agreement with multiple appraiser options" in this chapter and more fully in Chapter 14.

Multiple Appraiser Agreements

Multiple appraiser agreements call for the selection of two or more appraisers to engage in a process that will develop one, two, or three appraisals whose conclusions form the basis for the prices. There are a number of variations that can be employed in multiple appraiser process agreements. We focus on four here and use non-technical, descriptive terms to differentiate between various types of processes.

Two and a Tie-Breaker

Two appraisers are retained initially to provide appraisals, and a third appraiser is selected if needed to resolve disparate valuation conclusions.

1. The buying party typically retains one appraiser and the selling party another appraiser.

2. Both appraisers then provide valuation opinions according to the time schedule specified in the agreement or agreed to by the parties.

3. If the conclusions are within some percentage range (10% or 15%, or you pick the percentage) of each other, the buy-sell price is determined by the average of the two conclusions.

4. If the conclusions are more than the selected percentage apart, the two appraisers are generally required to select a third appraiser who also provides a valuation conclusion.

5. Typically, this third conclusion is averaged with the nearest of the first two, and that average becomes the price.

6. Occasionally, if all three appraisal conclusions are sufficiently close together (you pick the percentage), the price for the agreement is the average of all three conclusions.

7. Sometimes, the lower of the first two appraisals becomes a lower bound with the higher becoming the upper bound, regardless of the third appraiser's conclusion. For example, if the third appraiser's conclusion exceeded the upper bound, the higher of the first two appraisals would become the value.

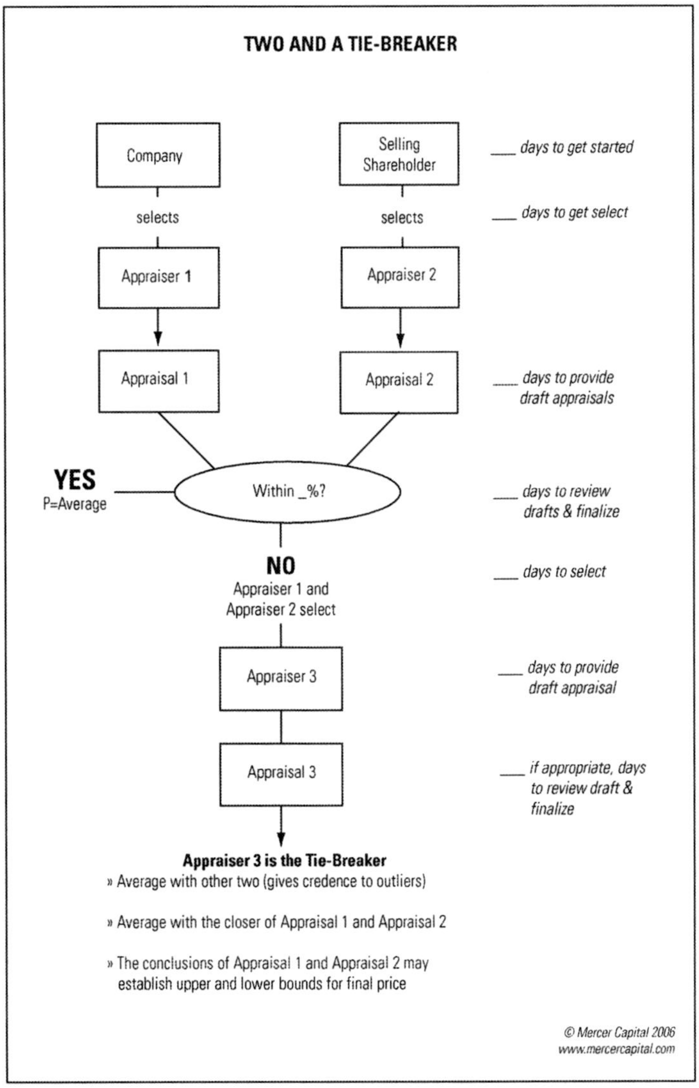

Two and a Determiner

Two appraisers are hired initially, and their sole function is to mutually select a third appraiser who provides the sole and determinative appraisal.

1. With this variation, the buying party retains one appraiser and the selling party another. These appraisers do not provide valuation opinions.
2. Rather, they select a mutually agreeable third independent appraiser.
3. The third appraiser provides the sole valuation opinion which determines the price. This process foreshadows the single appraiser processes discussed further on in this chapter.

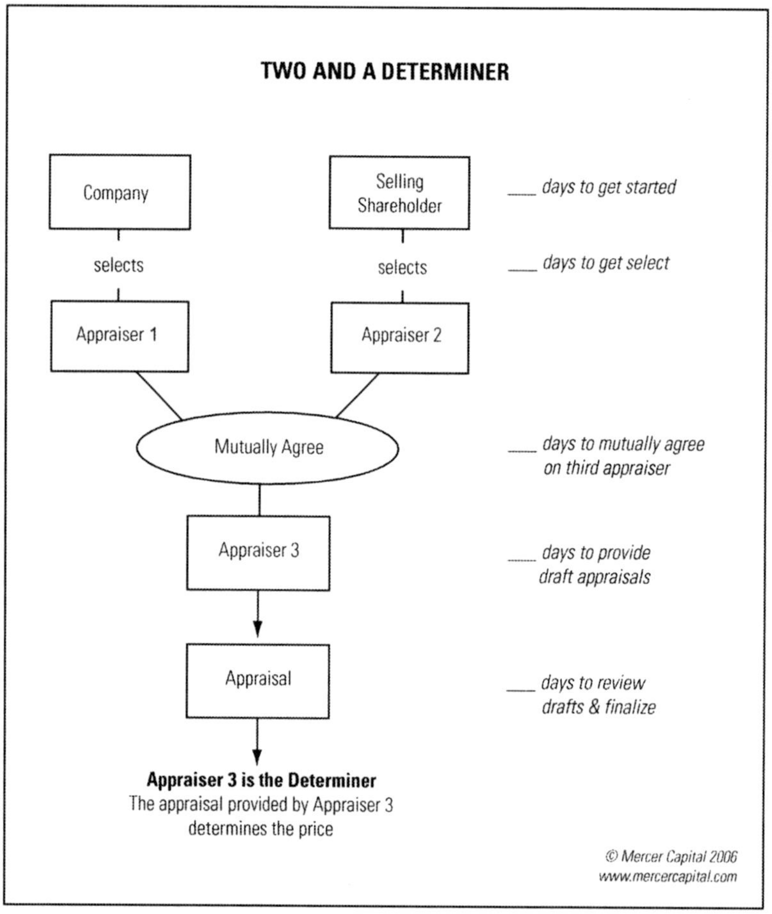

Two and a Back-Breaker

Two appraisers are selected to provide appraisals, and the third appraiser picks the "better" appraisal.

1. The buying party retains one appraiser and the selling party selects another. Both provide valuation conclusions.

2. If the appraisal conclusions are within a pre-determined percentage of each other, the price per the agreement is determined by the average of the two.

3. If the conclusions are sufficiently apart, the two original appraisers must then select a third independent appraiser.

4. The third appraiser must then select which of the first two appraisals he or she believes to be the more correct or reasonable valuation, and this selection becomes the price per the buy-sell agreement.

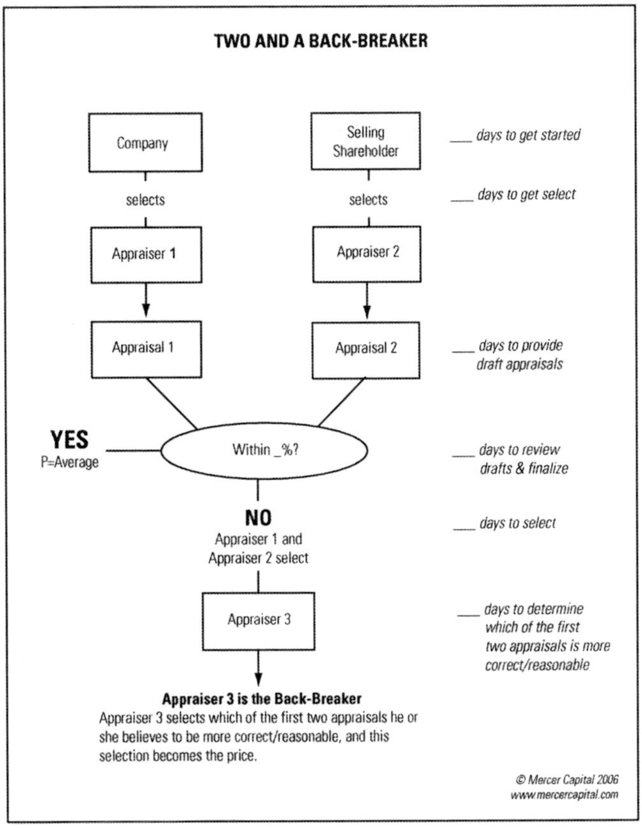

Two and Let's Talk

There are several possibilities to this category, all of which are designed to facilitate resolution with the first two appraisers. Two appraisers are selected and they provide valuation conclusions. If their conclusions are within the specified range (10% or 15% or you pick), the price is determined as the average of the two conclusions. If not, the two appraisers are required to work together to reach a mutually acceptable conclusion. Two ways this process could work include:

1. *Negotiation.* If the two appraisers can resolve their differences in direct negotiation and agree on a conclusion, their agreed-upon value becomes the price for the agreement. If they are not successful, the agreement may call for the selection of a third appraiser, whose role would be that of the tie-breaker or the back-breaker as outlined previously.

2. *Mediation.* If the two appraisers can resolve their differences and agree on a conclusion, their agreed-upon value becomes the price for the agreement. If they are not successful, the agreement may call for a third appraiser to be selected who will mediate the differences between the first two appraisers. If the mediation is successful in reaching agreement, this conclusion becomes the price for the agreement. If the mediation is not successful, the mediator may become the third appraiser. The agreement could also call for the first two appraisers, or the first two and the mediator, to agree on another appraiser to become the third appraiser. In either event, the third appraiser's role would be that of the tie-breaker or the back-breaker as outlined previously.

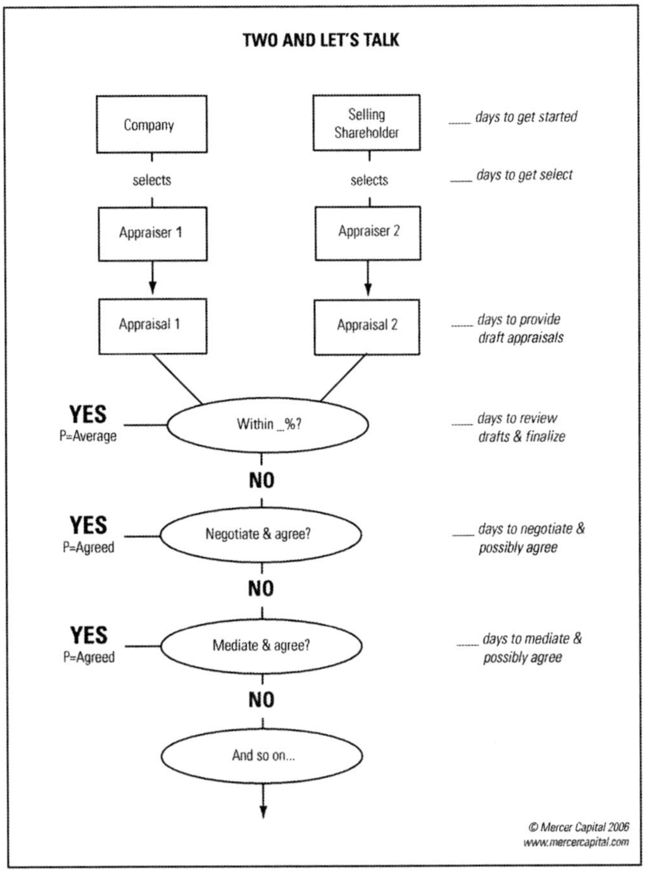

Multiple Appraiser Process Conclusion

All of the general forms of multiple appraiser agreements either call for, or potentially call for, the selection of a third appraiser. What is the role of the third appraiser? The role of the third appraiser is to bring resolution to the valuation process, whether as tie-breaker, sole appraiser, sole determiner, mediator or otherwise.

In many processes, the proverbial ox is already in the ditch when the third appraiser is named – there are two appraisals with conclusions more than __% (you pick) apart. Whether the differences relate to differing understandings or interpretations of the assignment definition or valuation assumptions and judgments, the third appraiser is expected to get the ox out of the ditch. The third appraiser's valuation is the tool to reconcile such differences.

What if, however, the differences are irreconcilable? One way of addressing these issues with multiple appraiser agreements is to consider employing single appraiser agreements.

Single Appraiser Agreements

Single appraiser agreements call for the selection of one appraiser who provides an appraisal for purposes of the agreement – the conclusion of which becomes the price. We use descriptive terms to differentiate between potential processes. A discussion of the advantages and disadvantages of each variation is found in Chapter 13.

Select and Value at Trigger Event

The agreement calls for the single appraiser to be selected by the parties at the time of a trigger event. The selected appraiser then provides the valuation based on his interpretation of the language in the buy-sell agreement. The single appraiser's valuation conclusion then sets the price for purposes of the buy-sell agreement.

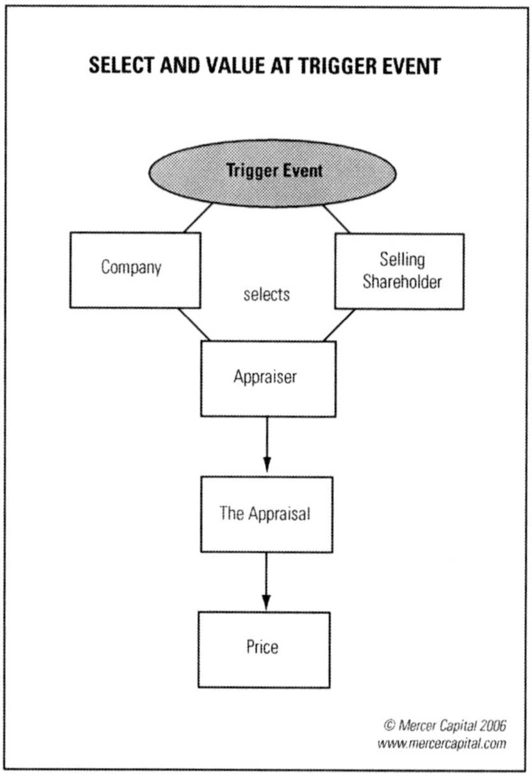

Select Now and Value at Trigger Event

At the time the agreement is created (or an older agreement is revised), the parties discuss potential appraisers (appraisal firms), perhaps interview one or more firms, and select a mutually agreeable appraiser/firm. This appraiser provides the valuation called for at the time of a trigger event.

The *Select Now and Value at Trigger Event* form of agreement eliminates the future uncertainty of selecting an appraiser, which is an improvement over *Single Appraiser – Select and Value at Trigger Event* agreements.

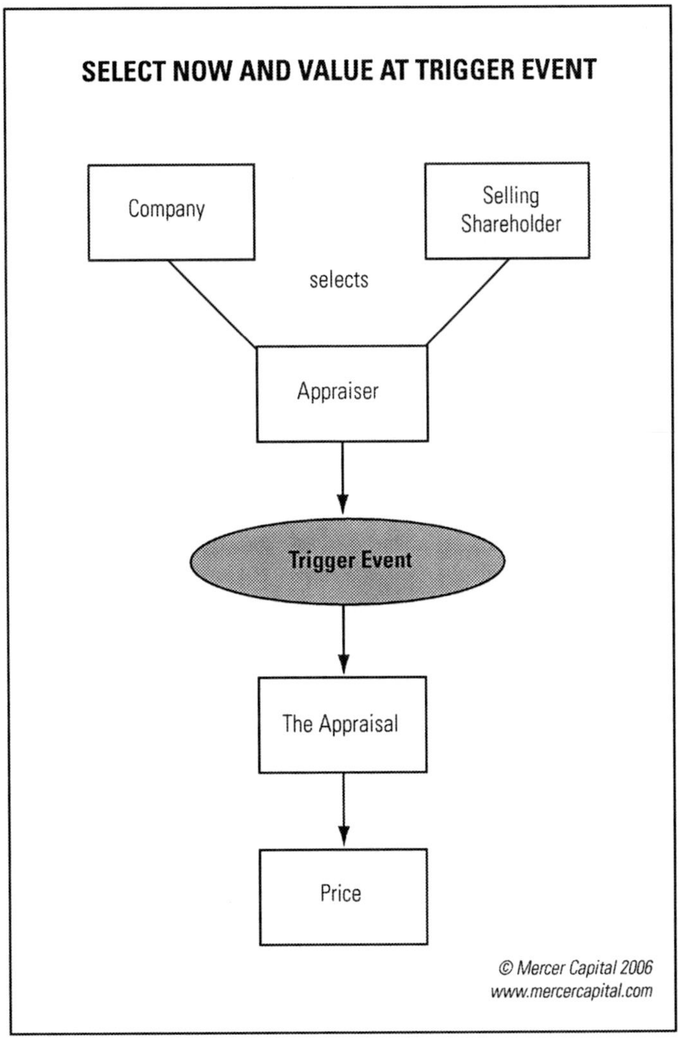

Select Now, Value Now

With the *Select Now, Value Now* process, the valuation process is invoked at the time the buy-sell agreement is signed. A baseline price is established and all parties are aware of the price and the process. The appraiser may provide periodic reappraisals. An additional appraisal may be required at the time of a trigger event, depending upon how long it has been since the last appraisal.

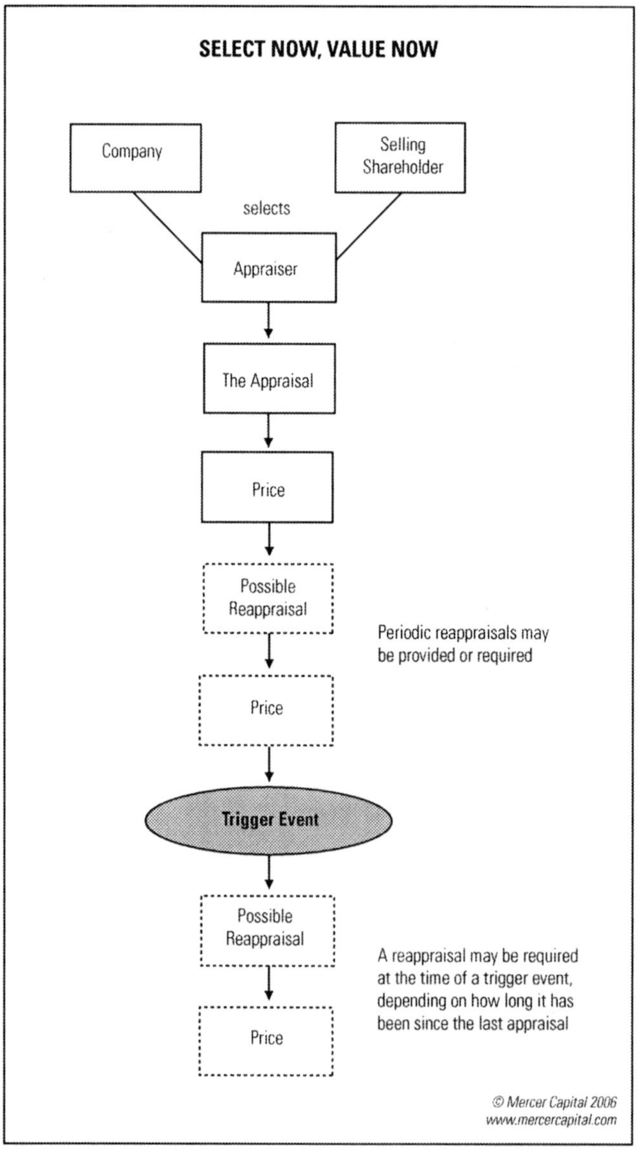

Hybrid Agreement (Single Appraiser Agreement with Multiple Appraiser Options)

We have not yet seen hybrid agreements in operation like the one we are introducing in this book. We introduce this type of agreement to address some of the disadvantages of multiple appraiser agreements together with potential concerns that parties could have with single appraiser agreements. In the "single appraiser agreement with multiple appraiser options":

1. A single appraiser is retained and values the company initially, and then periodically, and at trigger events when appropriate. Parties have the option of accepting the valuation conclusion and the process is over.

2. Parties have the option of hiring two additional appraisers to review the first appraiser's report and to offer suggestions to him or her. These suggestions can be considered without prejudice by the first appraiser in finalizing his report.

3. Parties could, in the alternative, retain two additional appraisers to provide valuations. The final valuation would be some predetermined combination of two, or possibly all three, conclusions.

We discuss the advantages and disadvantages of multiple appraiser and single appraiser processes in the next chapters. Then we present the "single appraiser agreement with multiple appraiser options" in more detail in Chapter 14.

HOW CLOSE SHOULD APPRAISALS BE BEFORE REQUIRING A THIRD APPRAISER?

Many process buy-sell agreements establish the threshold for requiring a third appraiser if the difference between the conclusions of the first two appraisers is greater than 10%. The issue of selecting a "closeness" threshold raises at least two important questions. However, even this selection can be confusing. Which appraiser's value is to be the base from which the 10% threshold is determined?

1. *Why 10%?* A surprising number of buy-sell agreements use 10% as the difference between appraisals within which agreement is assumed by averaging. Just how close should one reasonably expect two appraisals to be? Mercer Capital recently provided a second fairness opinion for a private company sale transaction. The company was placed into an auction process and some twenty potential qualified buyers were contacted. More than a dozen signed confidentiality agreements and received the offering memorandum. Four qualified, strategic buyers made bids and the highest bid was more than 35% greater than the lowest. Upon analysis, the lowest bid was clearly within the range of pricing for similar companies in the recent timeframe. Differences in bids in real world transactions are often of this magnitude or even greater. In light of these facts, a difference of 15% or even 20% as the agreement threshold could be reasonable.

2. *Which 10% is it?* Assume that the stated threshold differential in an agreement is 10%, plus or minus. Appraiser #1 reaches a conclusion of $100 per share. Appraiser #2 reaches a conclusion of $90 per share. At first glance, it looks as if the concluded value per share would be $95, or the average of the two valuation conclusions. However, remember that ambiguity in the agreement can encourage gamesmanship.

   If the upper conclusion ($100 per share) is the base, the range will be $90 per share to $110 per share. If the lower conclusion ($90 per share) is the base, the range will be $81 per share to $99 per share.

   If the party retaining Appraiser #1 believes that a third appraiser would reach a conclusion of $100 per share or greater, there is an incentive to argue for the $90 per share base. Why? Because that would mean that the relevant range is $81 to $99 per share and the 10% threshold is, therefore, not met ($100 per share is outside the range). Thus, it would be necessary to retain a third appraiser.

> If the party retaining Appraiser #2 believes that a third appraiser would reach a conclusion of $90 per share or lower, there is, again, incentive to argue for the $90 per share conclusion. That would be the only way to achieve a conclusion lower than $95 per share. One or both parties could have an incentive to argue that agreement has not been reached.

In our opinion, a 10% threshold is probably too small for the operation of a process buy-sell agreement. The expense and angst of a third appraiser probably exceeds the precision added, particularly if the two original appraisals are within 15% to 20%, or so, of each other.

TIME FOR APPRAISERS TO DELIVER APPRAISALS

Many buy-sell agreements require that appraisers deliver their final reports within 30 days of being retained. This timeframe is not realistic in most circumstances. A 60 day period is much more reasonable, and is more in keeping with normal delivery practices of most appraisal firms. Even then, an appraiser's ability to deliver a timely report will be dependent on the swift receipt of the information required for the appraisal and scheduling appropriate visits with management and tours of appropriate facilities.

CHAPTER 12

Multiple Appraiser Agreements

The interests of shareholders (or former shareholders) and corporations (and remaining shareholders) often diverge when buy-sell agreements are triggered.

In the real world, motivations, whether actual or perceived, are embedded in many process agreements. These motivations are clear for buyers and sellers whose interests are obviously different. The motivations for the appraisers are less clear. Appraisers are supposed to be independent of the parties. Nevertheless, based on our experience, it is rare for the appraiser retained to represent a seller to reach a valuation conclusion that is lower than that reached by the appraiser for the buyer. This does not at all imply that both appraisers are biased. Consider the following possibilities:

- Valuation reflects both art and science and is the result of the exercise of judgment. It seems that many buy-sell agreements call for two appraisal conclusions to be within 10% of each other for the two to be averaged. Given the potential for differences in judgments, a range of 10% may be too small.[6] In other words, the process may create the appearance of bias by creating the expectation that two appraisers will reach conclusions so close to each other.[7]

---

6 See "How Close Should Appraisals Be Before Requiring a Third Appraiser?" in Chapter 11.

7 Appraisers try to estimate the kind of value specified in buy-sell agreements. Consider the real world of actual transactions. In a typical auction process for a company, the range from the low bid to the high bid may be 50% to 100% or more, based on the varying interests and motivations of the group of buyers.

- The buy-sell agreement may be unclear as to the engagement definition. In such cases, two independent appraisers who interpret the agreement differently from a valuation perspective may reach conclusions that are widely disparate.

Legal counsel for each side desires to protect the interests of their clients. As such, in the context of buy-sell agreements, the thinking may occur as follows:

> "If my client is the seller, we need to be able to select 'our' appraiser, because the company will select its appraiser. Since I am concerned that the company will try to influence its appraiser on the downside, I want to be able to try to influence our appraiser on the upside. Since we are selling and they are buying, this is only natural."

For purposes of this discussion, if the two appraisals are not sufficiently close together, they can be viewed as advocating the positions of the seller and buyer, respectively. All the parties and their legal counsel may begin to think:

> "What is needed now is a 'truly' independent appraiser to finalize the process."

Many process agreements call for the two appraisers to select a third appraiser who is mutually acceptable to them because:

> "Surely, 'our' appraiser and 'their' appraiser, working together, can select a truly independent appraiser to break the log jam since neither side has been successful in influencing the outcome of the process. But, now that we have a third appraiser, what should his or her role be?"

The role of the third appraiser will be determined by the agreement reached by the parties. Consider the following:

- Chances are, it is not a good idea for the third appraiser's conclusion to be averaged with the other two since the first two conclusions create a broader specified range than the range giving rise to the third appraisal. Averaging could provide too much influence to an outlier conclusion.

- Often, the third appraiser's conclusion will be averaged with that of the conclusion closest to his own. Since the first two appraisers often know this on the front end, they should be motivated to provide independent conclusions, since no one desires to have the outlier (ignored) conclusion. (See "Two and a Tie-Breaker in Chapter 11.)

- On the other hand, wouldn't the process be more independent if the third appraiser had to select, in his opinion, the more reasonable of the first two conclusions? Surely, that would tend to influence the first two appraisers to reach more similar conclusions. It would be embarrassing to have provided the conclusion that was not accepted. (See "Two and a Back-Breaker" in Chapter 11.)

- Still further, the first two appraisers would be under pressure if the third appraiser were to provide the defining conclusion. As discussed previously, some processes provide for the selection of the first two appraisers whose sole function is to mutually agree on the third appraiser, whose conclusion will be binding. Then all the pressure falls on the third appraiser. (See "Two and a Determiner" in Chapter 11.)

We speak here from personal experience. Professionals at Mercer Capital have been the first, second, and third appraisers in numerous buy-sell agreement processes. Clients sometimes do attempt to influence the appraisers, either in blatant or subtle fashion. This is to be expected and is not nefarious. Clients are naturally influenced by their desire for a conclusion favorable to them.[8] The purpose of process buy-sell agreements, however, regardless of their limitations, is to reach *reasonable* conclusions.

Advantages

Multiple appraiser buy-sell agreements have advantages.

1. They provide a defined structure or process for determining the price at which future transactions will occur.

2. All parties to the agreements know, at least generally, what the process will entail.

8 I have said many times to young appraisers, "Don't be surprised if a client tells you or hints at the appraisal result they desire." In most cases, our clients are parties with particular interests in appraisal outcomes. They cannot help that. What is important in these situations is our response, which must be to provide our independent conclusions of value – ones we can support and defend.

3. Multiple appraiser agreements are fairly common and generally understood by attorneys. Many believe that process agreements are better than fixed price or formula agreements, particularly for substantial companies.

4. Parties to such agreements may think that they are protected by the process since they will get to select "their" appraiser. This is an illusory benefit.

Disadvantages

There are several disadvantages to multiple appraiser buy-sell agreements:

1. *The price is not determined now.* The actual value, or price, is left to be addressed at a future time, i.e., upon the occurrence of a trigger event. No one knows, until the end of an appraisal process, what the outcome will be.

2. *There is potential for dissatisfaction with the process, the result, or both, for all parties.* Multiple appraiser process agreements are designed with the best of intentions, but as we have seen, they have a number of potential flaws. At best, they are time-consuming and expensive. At worst, they are fraught with potential for discord, disruption, and devastating emotional issues for one or all parties.

3. *There is danger of advocacy with multiple appraiser agreements.* Even if there is no advocacy on the part of the appraisers, the *presumption of advocacy* may taint the process from the viewpoint of one or more participants.

4. *There is considerable uncertainty regarding the process.* All parties to a multiple appraiser agreement experience uncertainty about how the process will work, even if they have seen another such process in the past. In our experience, the process, as it actually operates, is different in virtually every case, even with similar agreements. This is true because the parties, including the seller, company management and its directorate, and the appraisers are all different.

5. *There is considerable uncertainty as to the final price.* The price is not determined until the end of the process. As a result, there is great and ongoing uncertainty regarding the price at which such future transactions will occur. First, before a trigger event occurs, no one has any idea what the price would be in the event that one did occur. Second, following a trigger event, there can be great uncertainty regarding the ultimate price for many, many months.

6. *Process problems are not identified until the process is invoked.* We noted in Chapter 10 that five defining elements are necessary to determine the price (value) at which shares are purchased pursuant to process agreements. Problems with agreements, such as a failure to identify the standard of value or the level of value, or the failure to define the qualifications of appraisers eligible to provide opinions or the appraisal standards they are to follow, are deferred until the occurrence of a trigger event. At this time, the interests of the parties are financially adverse and problems tend to be magnified. Based on our experience, the failure of multiple appraiser agreements to "pre-test" the process can be the most significant disadvantage on this list.

7. *Multiple appraiser agreements can be expensive.* The cost of appraisals prepared in contentious, potentially litigious situations tends to be considerably higher than for appraisals conducted in the normal course of business.

8. *Multiple appraiser agreements are time-consuming.* The typical appraisal process takes at least 60 to 90 days after appraisers are retained. The search for qualified appraisers can itself take considerable time. If a third appraiser is required, there will be additional time for his or her selection as well as for the preparation of the third appraisal. It is not unusual for multiple appraiser processes to drag on for six months to a year or more – perhaps much more.

9. *Multiple appraiser agreements are distracting for management.* The appraisal process for a private company is intrusive. Appraisers require that substantial information be developed. They also visit with management, both in person and on the telephone, as part of the appraisal procedures. We worked with the CEO of a sizeable private company to determine the price for the purchase of a 50% interest of his family business. The selling shareholder hired another, very qualified business appraiser and we both provided appraisals, with the intention of negotiating a settlement rather than invoking the burdensome, formal procedures of the buy-sell agreement. Our appraisals were about 10% apart and the parties agreed to average them. During the nearly three months that this "less burdensome" process was underway, the CEO (and his CFO and his COO) could scarcely think about anything else.

10. *Multiple appraiser agreements are potentially devastating for shareholders.* If the seller is the estate of a former shareholder, there is not only uncertainty regarding the value of the stock, but family members are involved in a valuation dispute (yes, that's pretty much what it is) with the friends and associates of their deceased loved one. Combine these issues with the fact that some agreements require that selling shareholders pay for their share (side) of the appraisal process and there is even more cause for distress.[9]

We summarize the disadvantages of multiple appraiser process agreements in Figure 5 for comparison with other options as the discussion progresses.

Disadvantages	Multiple Appraisers
1. Price *not* determined now	x
2. Potential for dissatisfaction with the process for all parties	x
3. Danger of advocacy	x
4. Uncertainty over what will happen when a trigger event occurs	x
5. Uncertainty over final price if the process is invoked	x
6. Problems or issues with definition of value, qualifications of appraisers, or any other aspects of the operation of the agreements are deferred until a trigger event – when the interests of the parties are adverse	x
7. Expensive	x
8. Time-consuming	x
9. Distracting for management	x
10. Potentially devastating for affected shareholders and their families	x

FIGURE 5

Concluding Observations

Based on our experience, multiple appraiser process agreements seem to be the norm for substantial private companies and in joint venture agreements among corporate venture partners. The standard forms or templates found for process agreements at

9 See Chapter 15 for a discussion of "Who Bears the Costs of the Appraisal Process?".

many law firms include variations of multiple appraiser processes similar to those described previously.

As business appraisers, we participate in multiple appraiser buy-sell agreement processes with some frequency. Because of the reputation of our senior professionals and our firm, we are called into valuation processes around the country. Speaking personally, I have been the appraiser working on behalf of selling shareholders and companies, and I have been the third appraiser selected by the other two on other occasions. As the third appraiser, I have been required to provide opinions where the process called for the averaging of my conclusion with the other two as well as averaging with the conclusion nearest mine. I have also been asked to pick the better appraisal, in my opinion, given the definition of value in agreements. I have also been the third appraiser who provided the only appraisal. Others at Mercer Capital have also performed similar roles.

This experience is mentioned to emphasize that the disadvantages of multiple appraiser appraisal processes outlined here are quite real. We have seen or experienced first hand every disadvantage in the list above. We hope to provide alternatives with more advantages and fewer disadvantages based on our collective experience at Mercer Capital.

CHAPTER 13

Single Appraiser Agreements

Single appraiser agreements come in two general forms. The first calls for the appraiser to be mutually selected by the parties at the time of a trigger event. The second form calls for selection of the appraiser in advance of any trigger event, perhaps at the inception of the agreement.

Agreements calling for appraiser selection at the time of trigger events often need a resolution process, sometimes arbitration, in the event that the parties cannot agree on the single appraiser. When the appraiser is selected in advance, there is obviously no need for such a dispute resolution process. The parties continue talking until agreement is reached.

We have identified three variations of the single appraiser process agreement:

1. Single Appraiser – Select and Value at Trigger Event
2. Single Appraiser – Select Now and Value at Trigger Event
3. Single Appraiser – Select Now, Value Now

Single Appraiser – Select and Value at Trigger Event

In *Single Appraiser – Select and Value at Trigger Event* agreements, the selection of the single appraiser is called for at the time of a trigger event. The selected appraiser then provides the valuation based on his interpretation of the language in the buy-sell agreement. The single appraiser's valuation conclusion then sets the price for purposes of the buy-sell agreement.

The advantages of a single appraiser process are similar to those of the multiple appraiser processes previously outlined.

- It provides a defined structure or process for determining the price at which future transactions will occur.
- All parties to the agreement know in advance, at least generally, what the process will be.
- The cost of the process, if not known precisely in advance, is reasonably definable.
- The general process is fairly commonly known and understood by attorneys. The single appraiser process is simpler than multiple appraiser processes since only one appraiser must be selected.
- Parties to single appraiser agreements should believe they are protected by the process since they will have a voice in the selection of the appraiser. All sides have a role to ensure that an independent appraiser is selected, i.e., one who will provide a balanced analysis and a "fair" valuation, taking into account the interests of both sides during the appraisal process.[10]

There are, however, disadvantages specifically to the *Single Appraiser – Select and Value at Trigger Event* process as shown in Figure 6.

Disadvantages	**Multiple Appraisers**	**Single Appraiser – Select & Value at Trigger Event**
1. Price *not* determined now	x	x
2. Potential for dissatisfaction with the process for all parties	x	x
3. Danger of advocacy	x	x
4. Uncertainty over what will happen when a trigger event occurs	x	x
5. Uncertainty over final price if the process is invoked	x	x
6. Problems or issues with definition of value, qualifications of appraisers, or any other aspects of the operation of the agreements are deferred until a trigger event – when the interests of the parties are adverse	x	x
7. Expensive	x	
8. Time-consuming	x	
9. Distracting for management	x	
10. Potentially devastating for affected shareholders and their families	x	

FIGURE 6

10 The company (its CEO or CFO) may be the primary driver in the process of selecting the appraiser. It is, therefore, important that the party(ies) subject to the agreement have an active role in the selection process (probably veto power). In other words, both sides must agree or there will almost definitely be a perception of bias.

1. *The price is not determined now.* The actual value, or price, is left to be determined upon the occurrence of a trigger event.

2. *There is potential for dissatisfaction with the ultimate result for all parties.* If one has no idea what the price for a transaction will be before it is determined by someone else, chances are that the appraiser's price will be exactly what one thought it should be only by chance. Hopefully, with a qualified, independent appraiser, both parties will be satisfied and consider that the process and the price are mutually fair.

3. *There can be danger of the perception of advocacy with single appraiser agreements.* The selected appraiser can be viewed by one side as more friendly to the other. Selling shareholders are more likely to have this perception because the appraiser is normally formally retained and paid by the corporation, and it can be thought that the selected appraiser would tend to favor the corporation in hopes of developing future business.

4. *There is some uncertainty regarding the process.* Generally, none of the parties to a single appraiser (select later) process have done business with the appraiser who is ultimately selected. As a result, none of the parties may be familiar with the appraiser and his or her work product.

5. *There is considerable uncertainty as to the final price.* Because there was no initial appraisal, there is great and ongoing uncertainty regarding the price at which future transactions will occur. First, prior to a trigger event, no one has any idea what the price would be in the event that one did occur. Second, following a trigger event, there is great uncertainty regarding the ultimate price for the duration of the single appraiser's engagement.

6. *Process problems are not identified until the process is invoked.* Once again, we cannot overemphasize the importance of this disadvantage. As with multiple appraiser agreements, problems such as a failure to properly define the engagement, failure to define the qualifications of appraisers eligible to provide opinions, or the appraisal standards they are to follow, are deferred until the occurrence of a trigger event. Given the nature of the process, the appraiser who identifies problems with the definition of value, for example, may have to make a decision that is viewed by one or both parties as adverse to their respective interests.

On balance, the *Single Appraiser – Select and Value at Trigger Event* process eliminates a number of the disadvantages of multiple appraiser agreements, but still leaves room for perceptions of bias and has considerable uncertainty for both parties.

Single Appraiser – Select Now and Value at Trigger Event

The second single appraiser process is the *Single Appraiser – Select Now and Value at Trigger Event*. The appraiser is named in the agreement and will be called upon to provide the required appraisals at the time of future trigger events. At the time the agreement is created (or an older agreement is revised), the parties discuss potential appraisers (appraisal firms), perhaps interview one or more firms, and select a mutually agreeable appraiser/firm.

The *Single Appraiser – Select Now and Value at Trigger Event* form of agreement eliminates the future uncertainty of selecting an appraiser, which is an improvement over *Single Appraiser – Select and Value at Trigger Event* agreements, but the other uncertainties and disadvantages remain. However, concerns over the degree of perceived appraiser advocacy should be minimized since the parties have time to agree on the selected appraiser absent the pressure of a trigger event.

Single Appraiser – Select Now, Value Now

The third single appraiser process is *Single Appraiser – Select Now, Value Now*. The appraiser is not only named in the agreement, but he or she is engaged to provide an initial appraisal for purposes of the agreement. We at Mercer Capital have long recommended that parties creating buy-sell agreements with a named appraiser have the appraiser perform a baseline appraisal pursuant to the terms of the agreement. This option provides several distinct advantages relative to other process agreements, including:

- The structure and process, in addition to being defined in the agreement, will be known to all parties to the agreement in advance.
- The selected appraiser will be viewed as independent with respect to the process; otherwise, he or she would not have been named. At the very least, the suspicion of bias is minimized.
- The appraiser's valuation approaches and methodologies are seen first hand by the parties.

- The appraiser's valuation conclusion is known at the outset of the agreement by all parties and becomes the agreement's price until the next appraisal, or until a trigger event between recurring appraisals occurs.
- The process is observed at the outset; therefore, all parties know what will happen when a trigger event occurs.
- The appraiser must interpret the valuation terms of the agreement in conducting the initial appraisal. Any lack of clarity in the valuation-defining terms will be fleshed out and can be corrected to the parties' mutual satisfaction.
- Having provided an initial valuation opinion, the appraiser must maintain independence with respect to the process and render future valuations consistent with the instructions in the agreement.
- Because the appraisal process is exercised at least once, or on a recurring basis, it should go smoothly when employed at trigger events and be less time-consuming and less expensive than other alternatives.

One further element can improve the *Single Appraiser – Selection Now, Value Now* option even more – regular reappraisals. In our opinion, larger companies should have an annual revaluation for their agreements. By larger, we mean those for which the cost of the appraisal process is insignificant relative to the certainty provided by maintaining the pricing provisions on a current basis. Smaller companies should have reappraisals every two years, or at least, every three years. [11]

Additional benefits from annual or periodic reappraisal for buy-sell agreements include:

- The parties will tend to gain confidence in the process. The selected appraisal firm should provide valuations that are consistent with prior opinions, taking into account relevant changes in the company, the industry, the economy, and other relevant factors. Subsequent appraisals should be reconciled with prior appraisals so that all parties understand why value has changed.

---

11 If the buy-sell agreement calls for an enterprise level of value (marketable minority or financial control), the appraiser can provide a supplemental appraisal at the nonmarketable minority level for gift and estate tax purposes. This supplemental appraisal would have to consider the impact of the buy-sell agreement on the value of nonmarketable minority interests.

- The parties will know the most current value for the buy-sell agreement. This can be beneficial for a company's planning purposes, for example, facilitating the maintenance of adequate life insurance on the appropriate shareholders. The periodic appraisal will also be helpful for the planning purposes of shareholders.

- Importantly, because the appraisals are recurring in nature, the appraisal firm's knowledge of a company's business and industry will grow over time, which should further enhance the confidence all parties have in the process and conclusion of value.

In all cases, if the most current appraisal is more than ___ months (you pick) old, then the agreements should provide for a reappraisal upon the occurrence of a trigger event.

Let's examine the remaining disadvantages (#2 to #6 in Figure 7) and see how the *Single Appraiser – Select Now, Value Now* process addresses these remaining disadvantages. Recall that disadvantage #1 regarding establishing the price is currently resolved by this process.

Disadvantages	Multiple Appraisers	Single Appraiser – Select & Value at Trigger Event	Single Appraiser – Select Now & Value at Trigger Event	Single Appraiser – Select Now, Value Now
1. Price *not* determined now	x	x	x	
2. Potential for dissatisfaction with the process for all parties	x	x	x	Minimized
3. Danger of advocacy	x	x	Minimized	Minimized
4. Uncertainty over what will happen when a trigger event occurs	x	x	x	Minimized
5. Uncertainty over final price if the process is invoked	x	x	x	Minimized
6. Problems or issues with definition of value, qualifications of appraisers, or any other aspects of the operation of the agreements are deferred until a trigger event – when the interests of the parties are adverse	x	x	x	Minimized
7. Expensive	x			
8. Time-consuming	x			
9. Distracting for management	x			
10. Potentially devastating for affected shareholders and their families	x			

FIGURE 7

2. *There is potential for dissatisfaction with the ultimate result for all parties.* There will always be potential for dissatisfaction. Buyers naturally want lower prices and sellers want higher prices. However, if the process works

as it should, all parties are much more likely to believe that the prices created by the buy-sell process are *reasonable.*

3. *There can be danger of the perception of advocacy with single appraiser agreements.* At the outset, it is possible that one or more parties might believe that the selected single appraiser could be biased. Such perceptions would likely be mitigated over time as the appraiser provides subsequent appraisals and as all parties become more comfortable with the process.

4. *There is some uncertainty regarding the process.* With a single appraiser who is selected in advance providing recurring reappraisals, there should be little, if any, uncertainty about the process that will be invoked when trigger events occur. The process is seen on a recurring basis by all parties.

5. *There is considerable uncertainty as to the final price.* Given that there is a baseline appraisal and the potential for reappraisals over time, much of the uncertainty regarding the price at a trigger event should be eliminated. The price should be reasonably consistent with changes in the company's earnings, industry multiples, and other factors familiar to the parties, assuming that the selected appraiser continues to provide appraisals on a consistent basis.

6. *Process problems are not identified until the process is invoked.* Clearly, any issues with the process would be identified and fixed at the outset or along the way. The process should be clear and well-understood.

In summary, the *Single Appraiser – Select Now, Value Now* process eliminates one of the six remaining disadvantages applicable to multiple appraiser and other single appraiser processes. This process also minimizes the adverse impact of the remaining five disadvantages. This form of single appraiser process is, based on my experience over nearly thirty years, the most reasonable valuation process for many privately owned businesses.

THE BENEFITS OF RECURRING PRIVATE COMPANY APPRAISAL

As of this writing, Mercer Capital provides annual, or regularly recurring appraisals, for more than 80 companies. The majority of these appraisals are conducted on behalf of trustees of Employee Stock Ownership Plans (ESOPs). However, a growing number of companies are choosing to have annual appraisals for reasons other than ESOPs, including buy-sell agreements, granting of options, estate tax planning for their shareholders, making a market in their (private) shares, tracking their growth in value in a disciplined fashion, and others.

We have clients, generally quite large private companies, who have annual or quarterly valuations, either for purposes of an ESOP or for shareholder and corporate planning purposes. These companies and their employees and shareholders have collectively bought or sold billions of dollars of stock at the same appraised values.

A growing number of companies are using recurring, independent appraisals to facilitate transactions in their shares. In so doing, they provide a means of facilitating liquidity for their shareholders on a planned basis and for recycling ownership within relevant groups, or, in some instances, by bringing on new investors. In so doing, they are able to prolong their independence as private companies by minimizing shareholder pressure for sale.

The *Single Appraiser – Select Now, Value Now* process for your buy-sell agreement can also provide many of the benefits noted above for recurring private company appraisals.

CHAPTER 14

A Hybrid Agreement (Single Appraiser Agreement with Multiple Appraiser Options)

It is important to address one more issue that could subconsciously be nagging some readers. Let's ask it directly:

Just how much faith can we put in a single appraiser?

Perhaps you are thinking a single appraiser process with recurring appraisals is fine so long as there's no trigger event, because real money is not yet on the line. But when there is a trigger event, particularly involving a substantial shareholder, the stakes can be quite high for both the company and the selling shareholder. After reading thus far, several questions may have come to your mind:

- Can a process be designed to provide greater comfort to both sides in a buy-sell agreement?
- What happens if, with the single appraiser process, either the company or the selling shareholder is dissatisfied, or even mildly dissatisfied, with the result?
- Can the lingering suspicions of bias or distrust that create the desire for multiple appraiser agreements in the first place be addressed?
- Can the comfort offered by me having "my appraiser" and you having "your appraiser," at least potentially, be provided?

- Can a single appraiser process that provides the potential for multiple appraisers to be involved be designed?
- Is there a process where the balancing influence of the "third appraiser" in a multiple appraiser process could be brought to bear?

We believe that the answer to all these questions is "yes" through a process we call a *Hybrid Agreement* or, more specifically, a *Single Appraiser with Multiple Appraiser Options* process. The question is, of course, how?

Hire the Third Appraiser First

The beginning point of the *Hybrid* or *Single Appraiser with Multiple Appraiser Options* process is the discussion addressing remaining uncertainties of the *Single Appraiser – Select Now, Value Now* process. The outline is straightforward:

1. Upon the creation of the buy-sell agreement, the parties agree upon and select an appraiser/firm.

2. The appraiser/firm provides a benchmark appraisal, which is the initial price for the buy-sell agreement. Assume that all issues regarding the engagement definition and the process are worked out during this initial appraisal and that any appropriate changes to the buy-sell agreement indicated by the process are made.

3. Assume further that the appraiser/firm will provide recurring appraisals, either annually or biennially over time.

4. Now, assume that a trigger event occurs far enough removed in time from the last appraisal that a reappraisal for the buy-sell agreement is required.

5. Further assume that the required appraisal will be provided by the named appraiser/firm.

6. At this point, let's call the single appraiser/firm the "third appraiser," because when selected in this manner, his appraisal can serve many of the same reconciling functions as the third appraiser in the multiple appraiser agreements discussed in Chapters 11 and 12.

Everyone is Satisfied with the Appraisal

The appraisal is rendered by the single, "third appraiser." If both the company and/or the affected shareholder(s) believe that the price set pursuant to the agreement by the single appraiser/firm is reasonable, there is no need for any further action. The buyer can purchase the subject shares at the determined price and on the terms provided in the agreement. The new price is established as the price for the agreement until the next annual or recurring appraisal is made.

The *Single Appraiser – Select Now, Value Now* process has worked as hoped for and according to everyone's expectations. There is no dispute, no disagreement, and no discord. Everyone is happy, or at least, satisfied.

Not Everyone is Satisfied with the Appraisal

The appraisal is rendered by the single, "third appraiser" but unfortunately, not everyone is satisfied. What *objective* provisions can be made to provide comfort to the selling shareholder or the buyer (the company or other shareholders) that the appraisal is reasonable and should stand as the price per the agreement? We say *objective* provisions, because it would not be reasonable to dispute the valuation with no objective basis.

The buy-sell agreement at this point could provide for the option of multiple appraisers in the event that there was a change of more than ___ % (plus or minus, you pick the percent) from the prior appraisal provided pursuant to the agreement, or, if based on the last appraisal, the change in appraised price exceeds $____ (you pick). This provision would not suggest that a change in value of the chosen magnitude indicates a potential problem. The appraisal should provide a reconciliation of the former and new values showing the reasons for the change. Nevertheless, the agreement could provide for the opportunity for one or both sides to initiate a further process.

We now introduce two options for the utilization of multiple appraisers. In the first, the process is completed with two additional appraisers providing appraisal reviews for consideration by the original "third appraiser." In the second option, the two additional appraisers provide valuation opinions, and all three conclusions are considered or not, per the terms of the agreement, in arriving at the final price. We would view these two options as mutually exclusive. The parties would agree at the outset as to which option would be used, if necessary.

Option 1: Appraisal Review

If Option 1 is invoked, one or both sides could retain qualified independent business appraisers to review the report presented by the "third appraiser," who in this example was obviously hired first.

These appraisers should have to meet the qualifications specified in the agreement. Their roles could be to determine whether the original appraisal was prepared in conformity with appropriate business valuation standards, and whether it had any mistakes or errors of fact or judgment that might impact value. The reviews could be compliant with Standards Rule 3 of the *Uniform Standards of Professional Appraisal Practice (USPAP)*, or they could be less formal, with the intent to be discussion documents for the "third appraiser's" consideration.[12]

Upon discussion with the review appraisers, the "third appraiser" could have the option to make any corrections or changes he or she believed appropriate following the review(s), if any. Such changes or corrections could be made without prejudice. In other words, he or she would be free to make changes suggested by one or both of the review appraisers and to adjust the conclusion accordingly.

At this point, the original appraisal, or the original appraisal as modified, would be the determining opinion for the price in the buy-sell agreement.

Clearly, the "third appraiser" will know of the potential for future independent review of his or her work during the preparation of the original appraisal as well as during the preparation of all subsequent reappraisals. The potential for such review upon the occurrence of a trigger event would serve as additional, implicit pressure for balance in the appraisal process, i.e., pressure to ensure that appropriate weight is given to all relevant factors.

The process would allow for the "third appraiser" to correct any mistakes found in his or her report. Further, it would enable the "third appraiser" to consider input from two independent appraisers and to determine whether, as result of their input, the conclusion should be modified.

---

12 *Uniform Standards of Professional Appraisal Practice* (Washington, D.C., The Appraisal Foundation, 2006). Standards Rule 3 of *USPAP*, "Appraisal Review, Development and Reporting," provides an outline for a formal appraisal review process to assure compliance with USPAP. See also Appendix C.

Both sides would know that they had the opportunity to retain review appraisers who, collectively, could possibly influence the "third appraiser" to modify the opinion. The cost of retaining the services of review appraisers would likely be lower than that of hiring appraisers to provide full valuations.

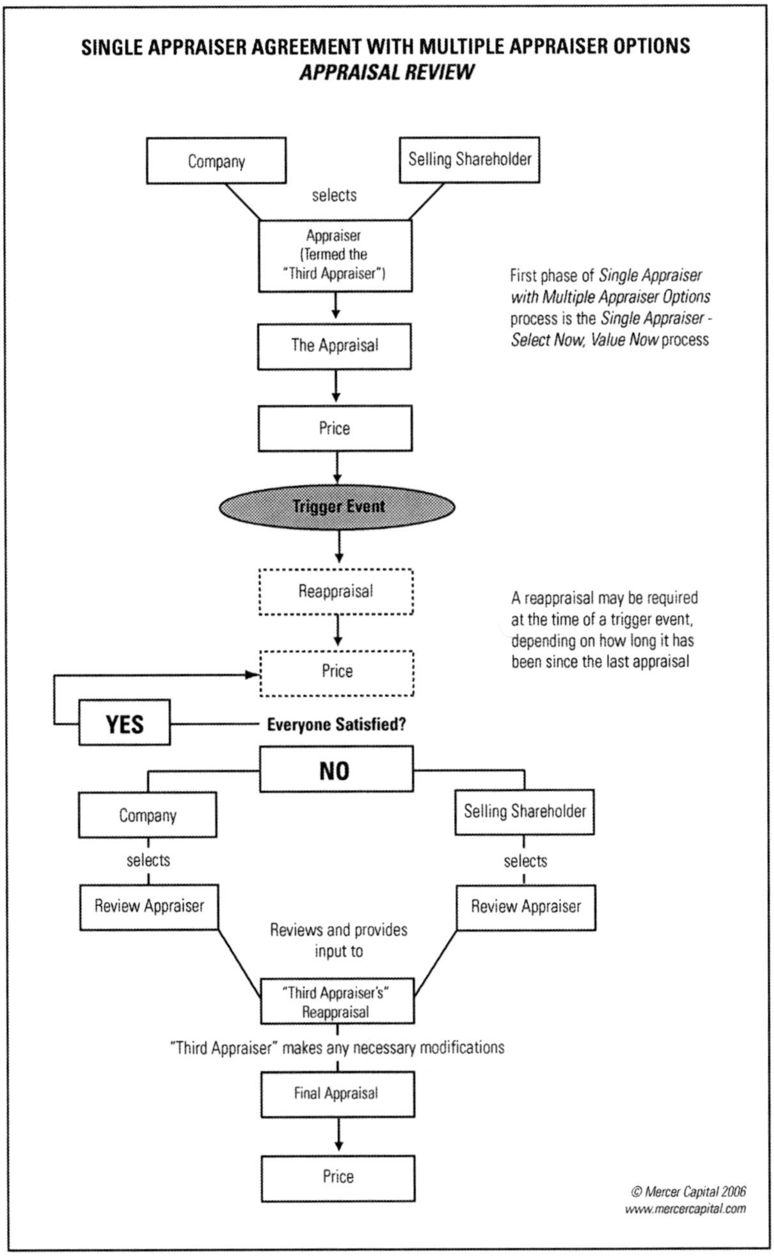

Option 2: Additional Appraisals

If Option 2 is invoked, the selling shareholder would select a qualified, independent appraiser, as would the company and each would provide appraisals.[13] Because of the prior appraisal(s) and the language in the buy-sell agreement, the engagement definition should be clear to both new appraisers, therefore, eliminating two of the greatest potential sources of disagreement over value.

In the typical multiple appraiser process, the first two appraisals, and often, the first two appraisers, are available to the third appraiser. Their conclusions are known before any opinion must be rendered. In the typical three-appraiser process, the third appraiser is supposed to bring independence and balance to the valuation process.

In this *Single Appraiser with Multiple Appraiser Options* process, the original appraisal (and prior appraisals, if any, that have been provided) would be given to both new appraisers, and both would be allowed to talk with the "third appraiser" in the process of developing their opinions. Their opinions would be rendered within 60-90 (or you pick) days of their being retained, allowing ample time for normal valuation procedures as well as communication with the original appraiser.

With this process, the final valuation might be determined as follows:

1. If the two new appraisals are within plus or minus ____% (you pick) of the original appraisal, the final price would be the average of all three appraisal conclusions. All three appraisals were relatively close together, and they are all considered in the final price.

2. If one of the new appraisals is within ___% (you pick) of the original appraisal and the other is not, the final price would be the average of the original conclusion and the one closest to it. This would tend to discourage advocacy on the part of any of the two additional appraisers, since the outlier appraisal would be ignored.

3. If neither appraisal is within ____% (you pick) of the original appraisal, and both are above the original appraisal, the conclusion would be the average of the two new appraisals.

---

13 Most frequently, the buyer is the company but may also be another shareholder(s).

4. If neither appraisal is within ____% (you pick) of the original appraisal, and both are below the original appraisal, the conclusion would be the average of the two new appraisals.

5. If neither appraisal is within ____% (you pick) of the original appraisal, and one is above and one below it, the conclusion:

   a. *Could be the average of all three appraisals.* This should tend to create pressure on all appraisers to provide balance in their opinions, since disparate conclusions would be averaged, tending to force the conclusion towards that of the original appraiser.

   b. *Could be the original appraisal conclusion.* This would suggest that outliers would have no influence in the process.

6. Other provisions to reach a final price could be agreed upon by the partners and specified in the agreement.

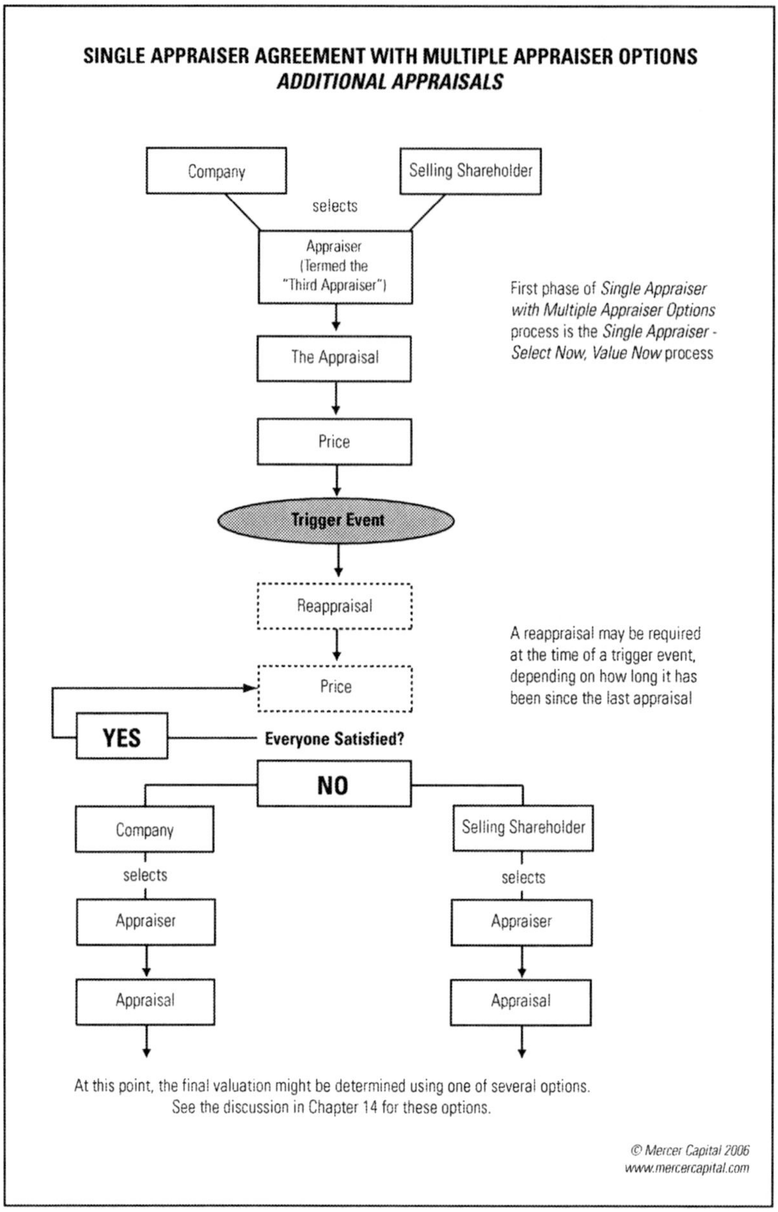

This second appraisal option to resolve disagreements over value is likely more expensive than hiring review appraisers. However, it may be necessary in some circumstances.

Final Comparison of Processes

In terms of advantages, the *Hybrid* or *Single Appraiser with Multiple Appraiser Options* process provides all the advantages of the *Single Appraiser – Select Now, Value Now* process. In addition, this form of agreement has the advantage of having a built-in disagreement resolution process. We can now compare the disadvantages of the various forms of agreements.

Disadvantages	Multiple Appraisers	Single Appraiser – Select & Value at Trigger Event	Single Appraiser – Select Now & Value at Trigger Event	Single Appraiser – Select Now, Value Now	Hybrid (Single Appraiser with Multiple Appraiser Options)
1. Price *not* determined now	x	x	x		Maybe
2. Potential for dissatisfaction with the process for all parties	x	x	x	Minimized	Minimized Further
3. Danger of advocacy	x	x	Minimized	Minimized	Minimized Further
4. Uncertainty over what will happen when a trigger event occurs	x	x	x	Minimized	Minimized Further
5. Uncertainty over final price if the process is invoked	x	x	x	Minimized	Minimized Further
6. Problems or issues with definition of value, qualifications of appraisers, or any other aspects of the operation of the agreements are deferred until a trigger event – when the interests of the parties are adverse	x	x	x	Minimized	Minimized Further
7. Expensive	x				Potentially
8. Time-consuming	x				Potentially
9. Distracting for management	x				Potentially
10. Potentially devastating for affected shareholders and their families	x				Minimized

FIGURE 8

Figure 8 provides an interesting, cumulative perspective regarding process buy-sell agreements. It focuses on the *disadvantages* of each type of process.

Process buy-sell agreements were developed to address the problems with fixed price and formula agreements. However, the typical multiple appraiser process, in addition to having advantages over more limited agreements, carries with it a number of disadvantages, at least relative to other process alternatives (Items 1-10 in Figure 8).

In our opinion, single appraiser processes eliminate certain of the disadvantages of multiple appraiser processes (Items 7-10). They are certainly less expensive, less time-consuming, and less distracting for management and shareholders. In the *Single Appraiser – Select Now, Value Now* option, the remaining disadvantages of multiple appraiser processes are either addressed (Item 1, the value becomes known) or minimized (Items 2-6).

The *Hybrid* or *Single Appraiser with Multiple Appraiser Options* process further minimizes the remaining disadvantages of process agreements (Items 2-6), but at a potential cost. If the multiple appraiser portions of the option are invoked, the process will certainly become more expensive and time-consuming (Items 7-8), and potentially distracting for management (Item 9). While the multiple appraiser process could be distracting for affected shareholders, it is less likely to be devastating, either emotionally or financially, because of the known factors in the process.

Regarding item 1 (the price is not determined now), the *Hybrid* process provides the potential for resolution with a single appraiser. To the extent that annual reappraisals are obtained, all parties have an evolving benchmark of value. If the process goes on to involve three appraisers, the price for the buy-sell agreement will not be known until the conclusion of the process.

CHAPTER 15

Other Items of Importance in Process Buy-Sell Agreements

Several other issues related to valuation should appropriately be addressed in your buy-sell agreements. The following discussion is by no means exhaustive, but includes items that are helpful in minimizing problems or uncertainties with the operation of process buy-sell agreements. While some of these items may seem obvious when identified, they are quite often overlooked or are unclear in buy-sell agreements.

Financial Statements

It is enormously helpful to specify the financial statements to be used by the appraiser(s).[14] In the absence of specification, the parties must agree on the financial statements to be used, or else the appraiser(s) must decide. Significant differences in valuation conclusions can result from the selection of financial statements of different dates and quality. This confusion should be avoided.

Possible alternatives for specifying financial statements include:

1. *Most Recent Audit,* or the audited financial statements for the most recent fiscal year relative to the valuation date. Note that there is room for

---

14 We are assuming for purposes of this discussion of financial statements that the valuation date, or the "as of" date, has been clearly defined in the buy-sell agreement. For a complete discussion of the "as of" date, see Chapter 18.

confusion here. Assume that the fiscal year is the calendar year. Suppose that the trigger date for a valuation process is January 15, 2007. The most recent audit was issued as of December 31, 2005 on April 27, 2006. If the buy-sell agreement calls for the use of the most recent audit available on the trigger date, the financial data may be more than one year old as in this example.

The agreement might specify that if a trigger event occurs between the end of a fiscal year and the issuance of the audit for that year, the appraisers would rely on the audit when it becomes available. That audit would then be used for the rest of the fiscal year.

In the alternative, if the trigger date was December 15, 2006, the most recent audit would be the 2005 audit issued in April 2006, but internal financial statements for the full year 2006 would be available within weeks, and the audit for 2006 would be available in three or four months, perhaps within the timeframe that appraisals would be prepared.

Suffice it to say that disagreements over which audit (i.e., which fiscal year) to use as the base for financial analysis could cause material differences in the concluded results. Note that the confusion could result whether the buy-sell agreement required the use of either the most recent audit or the most recent fiscal year statements.

2. *Trailing 12-Months at the Most Recent Quarter-End (Month-End) to the Trigger Date.* In the absence of specific guidance, many appraisers, if not most, would utilize financial statements for the most recent twelve months as of the quarter-end (or month-end) immediately prior to the trigger date. Use of the trailing 12 months would automatically include the most recent fiscal year (and audit, if available), and would also include any routine year-end adjustments for that year-end.

   We generally recommend the use of the trailing 12-month financial statements for the most recent quarter-end preceding the valuation date (or month end, depending on the completeness and quality of the monthly financial statements).

Process Timetables

Many buy-sell agreements provide for unrealistic timetables, and therefore, begin with process problems from the outset. The typical buy-sell process contains a number of phases where time is required:

1. *Time to Get Process Started.* It takes time to kick off a valuation process. If the trigger event is the death of a shareholder, no one will be focused on the buy-sell agreement until the passage of a reasonable time. On the other hand, if the trigger event is a retirement or termination, the parties may be ready to initiate the buy-sell agreement process immediately.

2. *Time to Select Appraiser(s).*

    a. Most process agreements call for the parties to retain an appraiser. If a company or a shareholder is beginning from scratch to select an appraiser(s), it can easily take 30 to 60 days or more to identify firms, review qualifications, interview appraisers, and select an appraiser(s).

        i. Some agreements allow only 30 days for this process, which may be unrealistic for one party or the other.

        ii. Some agreements are silent regarding the selection process, thereby providing no pressure for the appraisal process to get started (or concluded).

    b. Many process agreements call for two appraisals at the outset. If they are within a designated percentage of each other, no further appraisals are required. If not, however, the two initial appraisers must agree on a third appraiser. This process takes time – often considerable time. Some agreements provide timetables for this process and others do not. In some agreements, the sole role of the first two appraisers is to select the third appraiser. The same time issues relate to this selection. Allow at least 30 to 60 days for this process. (The obvious way to avoid this time lag in getting appraisals started is to select the appraiser at the initiation of the buy-sell agreement using one of the single appraiser processes previously discussed.)

3. *Time to Prepare Appraisal(s).*

   a. Once selected, the appraiser(s) must prepare their appraisal(s). Experience has taught that the appraisal process normally takes from 60 to 90 days. Mercer Capital engagement letters typically state that we will use our best efforts to provide a draft valuation report for review within 30 days of an on-site visit with management. We hit that target the great majority of the time, and most often miss it because of client-related issues. Note that the entire process would still take 60 days or more, depending on how quickly the client responds to the information request, schedules the visit, and how long the client takes to review the draft. It takes many companies 30 to 60 days to provide the basic information that we require prior to the on-site visit because the activities of running their businesses preclude prompt action.

   b. If a third appraiser is retained, this appraiser will require time for his or her process. If this is the only appraisal being provided, the process normally takes from 60 to 90 days. If there have been two appraisals already, the third appraiser may be helped by the fact that the company has already developed most of the information that will be required. On the other hand, being the third appraiser can be a fairly dicey situation. In addition to preparing one's own appraisal as the third appraiser, it is also necessary to review the appraisals of the other two firms. Allow at least 30 to as many as 90 days or more for this process.

4. *Time to Review Draft Appraisals.* The procedures of many appraisal firms call for the preparation of draft reports to be reviewed by management, and in the case of some buy-sell agreements, by all sides. This review process will generally take from 15 to 30 days or more, particularly in contentious situations.

5. *Time to Arrange Financing or to Close.* Once the appraisal process has been concluded, it normally takes some time to bring the process to closure. The company may be allowed 30 days, or some amount of time to close the transaction.

We can summarize the process timelines to get a picture of how the various types of process agreements might look in operation. You may be surprised at how the various processes actually lay out, regardless of what the written timetables suggest. The timelines in Figure 9 are estimated based on actual experiences with the operation of buy-sell agreements. Three kinds of process agreements are listed to provide a realistic overview.

BUY-SELL AGREEMENT TIMELINES

Process Activities (in days)	Multiple Appraisers		Single Appraiser - Select Now, Value Now		Hybrid (Single Appraiser with Multiple Appraiser Option)	
	Low	***High***	***Low***	***High***	***Low***	***High***
Trigger Event Occurs	0	0	0	0	0	0
Time to React	1	30	1	30	1	30
Pick Appraiser(s)	30	60	0	0	0	0
Provide Appraisal(s)	60	90	30	60	30	60
Review Appraisal(s)	15	30	15	30	15	30
Earliest Time to Resolution	**106**	**210**	**46**	**120**	**46**	**120**
Select Other Appraiser(s)	30	60			30	60
Reviews by Appraisers						
Prepare Additional Appraisal(s)	30	60			30	60
Review Appraisals/Reviews	15	30			15	30
Agree on Conclusions	15	30			15	30
Finalize Transaction	0	30			0	30
Additional Time for Process	**90**	**210**	**0**	**0**	**90**	**210**
Potential Time to Resolution	**196**	**420**	**46**	**120**	**136**	**330**

FIGURE 9

The existence of defined timetables in agreements serves to keep the parties focused on the timeline; however, they are seldom binding.

Figure 9 illustrates three examples, *Multiple Appraiser* processes, the *Single Appraiser – Select Now, Value Now* option, and the *Single Appraiser with Multiple Appraiser Options.*

- *Multiple Appraiser* processes can be accomplished in the broad range of 100 to 200 days or so *if the initial process involving two appraisers is conclusive.* If it is necessary to select and retain a third appraiser, it is likely that considerable additional time will pass before resolution occurs. It is not surprising for a multiple appraiser process involving three appraisers to take six months to a year or more to complete.

- *The Single Appraiser – Select Now, Value Now* option is potentially the most rapid option for process buy-sell agreements. If a trigger event occurs after the initial appraisal, the valuation process will be known by all parties, and the appraiser will be familiar with the company. This option should be able to be accomplished within six weeks or so, on the short end, and four months on the longer end.

- The *Hybrid* or *Single Appraiser with Multiple Appraiser Options* can take as long as the typical multiple appraiser option; however, the *probability* of it being accomplished in much shorter time is significant. If the parties agree on the concluded value of the "third appraiser," this option is akin to the *Single Appraiser – Select Now, Value Now* option and can be accomplished accordingly.

Note that the estimates here assume that there is no litigation and that the parties are generally cooperating to move the process along.

The bottom line is that it is good to agree on realistic timelines in your buy-sell agreements. It is then easier to ask the various appraisers and other parties to stick to them. The operation of process buy-sell agreements can take a long time. This means that the process may be a considerable distraction to management, particularly when significant transactions are involved. It should be obvious, but the prolonged operation of a buy-sell agreement can not only be distracting, but frustrating and confusing to the family of a deceased shareholder, or to a terminated employee.

Who Bears the Costs of the Appraisal Process?

Appraisal processes involving between one and three appraisers can become expensive. This is particularly true when large companies and/or large dollar-value interests are involved.

So who pays the costs of the appraisal(s)? Some agreements state that the company will pay for its appraiser and the shareholder will pay for his or her appraiser. We very seldom inject opinion into the operation of agreements; however, the company is often in a position of economic advantage relative to a shareholder (or a deceased shareholder's family). Therefore, we suggest consideration of a clause providing that the company pay the appraisal costs of selling shareholder(s). Consider that:

- The company pays for its expenses in pre-tax dollars.
- The company typically experiences an economic benefit from the operation of the agreement. More particularly, the other shareholders experience a net benefit (pro rata increases in their percentages of ownership) from the share repurchase program. There is no corresponding benefit for the selling shareholder.
- It is likely that the company is better able to afford a more experienced appraiser than is an individual shareholder, creating a potential disadvantage at the outset.
- The shareholder is being asked to pay to realize the value of his or her shares according to the agreement. The agreement calls for a certain price. The shareholder receives that price, determined by the process, less the expenses of the operation of the process. Therefore, if the shareholder pays appraisal costs, the operation of the agreement does not actually provide the specified price.

It could be argued that this position is too generous to the selling shareholder. After all, if and when the remaining shareholders sell the company, they will incur transaction costs. These costs are the "friction" or transaction costs of changing ownership, including legal and accounting fees, investment banking or brokerage fees, and even appraisal fees. In recognition of the reality of friction costs, the parties could agree that the concluded price for buy-sell agreement purposes will be the appraised price less a transactions cost allowance of __%. The transaction cost allowance would likely be in the range of 2% to 5% or so of transaction value, depending on the size of the business.

If the company agrees to pay appraisal costs of selling shareholder(s) (with or without consideration of a transaction cost allowance), shareholders might be concerned that the selected appraiser would have an allegiance to the company since the company is the financially responsible party. Never mind that all selected appraisers are supposed to be independent. This concern can be addressed by having the appraisal firm's engagement letter be with the selling shareholder(s) rather than the company. The company could then be a party to the engagement letter to accept financial responsibility only for fees and, perhaps, indemnification. From the company's viewpoint, it may be necessary to specify a maximum amount for its responsibility for the shareholder's appraisal expenses.

This issue is moot, of course, if the buy-sell agreement calls for the *Single Appraiser – Select Now, Value Now* option. The company will pay for the initial appraisal and subsequent appraisals.

Who Benefits (or Loses) from Unavoidable (or Avoidable) Delays?

The purpose of buy-sell agreements is to facilitate the sale (and corresponding purchase) of shares following defined trigger events. They do not necessarily contemplate the economic interests of the various parties during the process of their operation.

Buy-sell agreements specify certain trigger events. These events may determine the "as of" date for the required appraisals. Suppose, for example, that the death of a shareholder triggers the operation of a buy-sell agreement. The date of death is the valuation date, or the "as of" date. Further suppose that the operation of the agreement, including time spent dealing with litigation regarding its operation, takes two years to complete. Several questions illustrate potential issues that may need to be addressed in an agreement:

- Should the company pay interest from the valuation date to the date of the finalization of the transaction? A shareholder who does not receive payment on or near the valuation date clearly incurs an opportunity cost. No funds are available to earn interest or for other reinvestment. Arguably, the shareholder still bears some of the risks of an equity holder during this period with no provision for interim returns.

- What happens if the company's performance was stellar during the year or two between the trigger event and the final settlement? Should the valuation date be moved forward?

- What happens if the company's performance declined over the same period?

- Who owns the shares following a trigger event? Is the ownership interest converted into a right to receive the buy-sell price as soon as that price is determined for the "as of" date? Or does the shareholder retain ownership of shares until purchased? This is clearly a legal question.

- Can the shareholder vote the shares if there is a shareholder's meeting prior to their being purchased?

- Is the shareholder entitled to receive distributions or dividends until the shares are repurchased? Is the company obligated to maintain its distribution policy (if applicable) during the interim period between the "as of" date and finalization of the process?

- If the company is an S corporation or other tax pass-through entity, does the agreement ensure that the shareholder will receive sufficient distributions to pay shareholder-level taxes on corporate earnings for the entire period of ownership?

These questions are best addressed before an agreement's processes are initiated. When agreements are silent, one or both parties can lose.

SECTION FOUR

Six Defining Elements of Buy-Sell Agreements

CHAPTER 16

Defining Element #1: The Standard of Value

We use the term "words on the page" a number of times in this and the following chapters. Appraisers retained pursuant to the operation of buy-sell agreements are normally bound to prepare their valuations in accordance with the kind of value described or defined within the agreements. In other words, the "words on the page" will determine the kind of value to be developed in the appraisal. Collectively, these criteria become the assignment definition.

The first defining element is the standard of value which must be specified in the engagement.

1. Standard of Value	4. Qualifications of Appraisers
2. Level of Value	5. Appraisal Standards
3. The "as of" Date	6. Funding Mechanisms

The word "value" has many meanings. Value, like beauty, may lie in the eye of the beholder. That there is some confusion about what is meant by value is confirmed by legal scholar James C. Bonbright, who stated:

> As long as common law and statute law persist in using the "value" as a legal jack-of-all-trades, judges are forced, willy-nilly, to reject the precedent of economists and instead to follow the precedent of

> Humpty Dumpty (from *Through a Looking Glass*): "When I use a word, it means what I choose it to mean – neither more nor less."[15]

If the words on the pages are not clear regarding the standard of value, appraisers may be placed in the position of Humpty Dumpty, and have to decide what the words on the page mean. When agreements are silent or unclear as to the standard of value, the appraiser(s) may have to make decisions they would prefer not to make, or the parties, whose interests have already diverged, will have to decide on the standard of value to provide instructions to the appraiser(s).

Neither situation is ideal. At this point, we briefly review the most common standards of value and then discuss how to avoid confusion on this point when preparing buy-sell agreements.

Fair Market Value

The most common standard of value is that of "fair market value." This standard of value applies to virtually all federal and estate tax valuations matters, including charitable gifts, estate tax issues, ad valorem taxes, and other tax-related issues. Fair market value is also the applicable standard of value in many bankruptcy cases involving valuation issues.

Fair market value has been defined in many court cases. It is also defined in Internal Revenue Service Revenue Ruling 59-60 as:

> ....the price at which a property would change hands between a willing buyer and a willing seller when the former is not under any compulsion to buy and the latter is not under any compulsion to sell, both parties having reasonable knowledge of relevant facts. Court decisions frequently state in addition that the hypothetical buyer and seller are assumed to be able, as well as willing, to trade and to be well-informed about the property and concerning the market for such property.[16]

---

15 Bonbright, *Valuation of Property* (1937), as quoted in George D. McCarthy and Robert E. Healy, *Valuing a Company: Practices and Procedures* (New York: Ronald Press, 1971), p. 3.

16 Revenue Ruling 59-60, Internal Revenue Bulletin 1959-1 CB 237, IRC Sec. 2031.

Fair market value is an arms' length standard that assumes willing and informed buyers and sellers, neither acting under any compulsion, as well as buyers and sellers with the financial capacity to engage in transactions. Under the standard of fair market value, both the buyers and sellers are *hypothetical*, and the transactions contemplated by the standard are also *hypothetical*. In other words, appraisal conclusions are based on hypothetical transactions involving hypothetical parties. Fair market value also assumes that the contemplated hypothetical transactions are transacted in terms of cash ("money's worth").

Revenue Ruling 59-60 suggests that "all available financial data, as well as all relevant factors affecting fair market value, should be considered."[17] Eight specific factors are listed in RR 59-60 as fundamental and the subject of required analysis in fair market value determinations. We call these factors the Basic Eight factors of valuation:

1. The nature of the business and the history of the enterprise from its inception.
2. The economic outlook in general and the condition and outlook of the specific industry in particular.
3. The book value of the stock and the financial condition of the business.
4. The earning capacity of the company.
5. The dividend-paying capacity.
6. Whether or not the enterprise has goodwill or other intangible value.
7. Sales of the stock and the size of the block to be valued.
8. The market price of stocks of corporations engaged in the same or a similar line of business having their stocks traded in a free and open market, either on an exchange or over-the-counter.

In any consideration of the Basic Eight factors, there is considerable room for the exercise of judgment. Just prior to enumerating these factors for analysis, Revenue Ruling 59-60 states the following:

---

17 Ibid.

> A determination of fair market value, being a question of fact, will depend upon the circumstances of each case. No formula can be devised that will be generally applicable to the multitude of different valuation issues arising in estate and gift tax cases. Often, an appraiser will find wide differences of opinion as to the fair market value of a particular stock. In resolving such differences, he should maintain a reasonable attitude in recognition of the fact that valuation is not an exact science. A sound valuation will be based upon all the relevant facts, but *the elements of common sense, informed judgment and reasonableness* must enter into the process of weighing those facts and weighing their significance.[18] [*emphasis added*]

The emphasized elements – common sense, informed judgment and reasonableness – are critical in fair market value determinations.

Fair market value is the standard of value specified in many buy-sell agreements. It is, therefore, important that business owners, attorneys, and other advisors have a working knowledge of this standard.

An important question to ask is: the fair market value of what? The statutory and case law history of fair market value place significant attention on the business interest being valued. It tends to link the concept of value to the attributes of the specific business interest.

Fair market value is a standard of value that can be applicable to any level of value, ranging from the fair market value of an entire enterprise to the fair market value of a small, minority interest. In the context of buy-sell agreements, it is necessary to specify the "what," or, the particular kind of value the parties to an agreement desire. We will address this question "the fair market value of what?" as we talk about the other defining elements of a buy-sell agreement from a valuation perspective.

Fair Value (Statutory or Accounting?)

"Fair value" is the applicable standard of value in nearly all states in matters pertaining to rights of shareholders under their dissenters' rights statutes. Generally speaking, when corporations engage in sales, mergers, or other transactions

---

18 Ibid.

involving substantial recapitalizations, minority shareholders are provided with the right to dissent to the transactions.

Shareholders who perfect their rights to dissent, typically by following procedures outlined in a state's statutes, are entitled to the *fair value* of their shares. In other words, they can dissent to the transaction and the corporation is required to purchase their shares at their fair values. What then is fair value?

Fair value is typically described statutorily in a general sense. The Uniform Business Corporation Act (UBCA) defines fair value as follows:

> "Fair value, with respect to dissenter's shares, means the value of the shares immediately before the effectuation of the corporate action to which the dissenter objects, excluding any appreciation or depreciation in anticipation of the corporate action unless exclusion would be inequitable."

This definition of fair value provides no valuation guidance for appraisers about *how* value is to be determined. When fair value is so-defined in a state's statutes, it must be interpreted judicially. Some states, like Delaware, have relatively well-developed case law defining fair value. Other states do not.

It is Mercer Capital's policy that the interpretation of cases is a legal matter, and we look to legal counsel to provide their interpretation as to the kind of value that the courts have described in relevant cases. These legal interpretations must be condensed into actionable terms from a valuation perspective. As we will see in the next chapter on *levels of value*, there are at least four levels at which a state's courts could define fair value:

1. Strategic control value
2. Financial control value
3. Marketable minority value
4. Nonmarketable minority value

We mention these levels of value in advance of their more detailed treatment in the next chapter to make the point that the legal term, fair value, is subject to a number of interpretations, each of which could impact the value to be determined by an appraiser in an appraisal proceeding.

The term fair value is also associated with financial statement reporting.[19] Current accounting rules call for certain assets, including businesses that are purchased, to be carried on a corporation's books at their fair values. So in the absence of guidance in an agreement specifying the meaning of fair value, it is possible that an appraiser could look to guidance in the accounting literature for assistance. Suffice it to say that there is no room in your buy-sell agreement for confusion over the meaning of fair value.

Inadequate Value Descriptions

Other standards of value sometimes appear in buy-sell agreements. If the standard of value is not clearly defined, the result is ambiguity and uncertainty. Appraisers may disagree in their interpretations, or may have to request interpretations from parties whose interests are now adverse. Consider the following "standards" of value:

- *Provide a valuation on a going-concern basis.* This description suggests that the appraisal be provided assuming that the subject enterprise will continue as a going concern. However, there is ambiguity as to the particular level of value that should be applicable and appraisers could legitimately exercise different judgments in interpreting its meaning.

- *Investment value.* Investment value is typically described as value from the perspective of a particular buyer. But which buyer? Appraisers will not know unless there is more complete specification of the kind of value desired by the parties. Differing interpretations can lead to disparate valuation conclusions between appraisers.

- *The value.* Agreements calling for "the value" of the shares or, for example, "the current value" of the shares, are not helpful. Such language is non-specific and subject to wide-ranging interpretations. Recall the quote from Humpty Dumpty at the beginning of this chapter.

---

19 See *Statement of Financial Accounting No. 157*, "Fair Value Measurements" which is formally effective for financial statements issued for fiscal years beginning after November 15, 2007 and for the interim periods within those fiscal years. FAS 157 does not apply under accounting pronouncements that address share-based payment transactions such as FAS 123.

Conclusion

The standard of value must be clearly stated. If the definition or terms used to describe the particular kind of value that the parties to a buy-sell agreement have agreed to is ambiguous, the probability for problems, disagreements, and potentially, litigation rises to unacceptable levels.

RECOMMENDED STANDARD OF VALUE

Fair market value is a "willing buyer, willing seller" concept that has appeal in the arena of buy-sell agreements. It describes a valuation process where neither hypothetical party is under compulsion to sell or to buy (in spite of the fact that a buy-sell agreement may force both buying and selling). It assumes that both parties are knowledgeable about the subject of the valuation. It further assumes bargaining parity between the parties, as well as reasonably equivalent financial capacities to engage in a transaction. Finally, "fair market value" is the best known, most understood, and most widely employed standard of value.

In the absence of a compelling reason to use another standard of value, we generally recommend fair market value as the standard of value for buy-sell agreements. It is well-known, well-defined and familiar to all business appraisers. However, business owners should consult counsel to ensure that the proper standard of value is chosen.

TWO ACCEPTABLE DEFINITIONS OF FAIR MARKET VALUE

To avoid any possibility of confusion, consider quoting one of the definitions below in your buy-sell agreement (or cite it).

Fair Market Value is defined in Section 2.02 of Revenue Ruling 59-60

Section 20.2031-1(b) of the Estate Tax Regulations (section 81.10 of the Estate Tax Regulations 105) and section 25.2512-1 of the Gift Tax Regulations 108) define fair market value, in effect, as the price at which the property would change hands between a willing buyer and a willing seller when the former is not under any compulsion to buy and the latter is not under any compulsion to sell, both parties having reasonable knowledge of relevant facts. Court decisions frequently state in addition that the hypothetical buyer and seller are assumed to be able, as well as willing, to trade and to be well informed about the property and concerning the market for such property.

Fair Market Value is defined in the *Business Valuation Standards* of the American Society of Appraisers (see Appendix D)

The price, expressed in terms of cash equivalents, at which property would change hands between a hypothetical willing and able buyer and a hypothetical willing and able seller, acting at arm's length in an open and unrestricted market, when neither is under compulsion to buy or sell and when both have reasonable knowledge of the relevant facts. [NOTE: In Canada, the term "price" should be replaced with the term "highest price."]

CHAPTER 17

Defining Element #2: The Level of Value

The term "level of value" is not a defined term in the glossary of the *Business Valuation Standards* of the American Society of Appraisers.[20] So what are the levels of value and why are they important? These are two of the most important questions facing drafters of buy-sell agreements.

1. Standard of Value	4. Qualifications of Appraisers
2. Level of Value	5. Appraisal Standards
3. The "as of" Date	6. Funding Mechanisms

Defining the Levels of Value

There is no such thing as "the value" of a closely held business. That is an implicit assumption in the field of business appraisal. Confusion over an appraiser's basis of value, either by appraisers or by users of appraisal reports, can lead to the placing of inappropriately high or low values on a subject equity interest. Therefore, it is essential that both business appraisers and the parties using appraisals be aware of the correct basis of value and that appropriate methodologies be applied in deriving the conclusion of value for any interest being appraised.

20 The complete glossary is reprinted with permission in Appendix D.

The levels of value chart is an economic or financial model used by many appraisers to describe the complexities of behavior of individuals and businesses in the process of buying and selling businesses and business interests. It attempts to cut through the detailed maze of facts that give rise to individual transactions involving particular business interests and to describe, generally, the valuation relationships that seem to emerge from observing thousands upon thousands of individual transactions.

It is understandable for a client to confuse the various levels of value. Business owners tend to think of value in terms of an "enterprise" basis or perhaps a "sale" basis. Valuation professionals look more at terminology like "controlling interest" basis or "minority interest" basis.

Figure 10 presents the levels of value chart and then each level of value is defined with a more technical definition of each found in the Addendum to this chapter.[21]

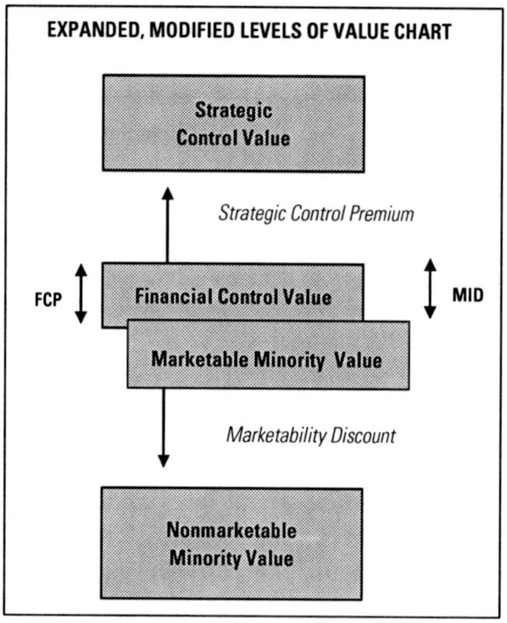

FIGURE 10

21 For more information on the development of this levels of value chart, see the Addendum to this chapter as well as Chapter 3 of the *Integrated Theory of Business Valuation* (Z. Christopher Mercer, ASA, CFA: Peabody Publishing, LP 2004).

- *Strategic control value* refers to the value of the enterprise as a whole incorporating the strategic intent that may motivate particular buyers and the expected business and financial synergies that may result from an acquisition. Higher expected cash flows relative to financial buyers enable strategic purchasers to pay a premium, often called a strategic control premium, relative to financial control value. A strategic buyer may also increase the price it will pay based on the use of its own, presumably lower, cost of capital.

- *Financial control value* refers to the value of the enterprise, excluding any synergies that may accrue to a strategic buyer. This level of value is viewed from the perspective of a financial buyer, who may expect to benefit from improving the enterprise's cash flow but not through any synergies that may be available to a strategic buyer.

  As more fully developed in the Addendum to this chapter, it is generally believed that the marketable minority level of value and the financial control level of value are, if not synonymous, then essentially so. One way of describing the financial control value is that buyers are willing to pay for the expected cash flows of enterprises, and will pay no more than the marketable minority value unless they believe they can run a company better *and* the competitive bidding situation requires that they share a portion of potential improvements with the seller.

  - *FCP* is the *financial control premium.* The financial control premium is shown, conceptually, to be nil, or at least very small in Figure 10.

  - *MID* is the *minority interest discount.* The minority interest discount is also shown to be conceptually nil or very small. This is consistent with the discount being the conceptual inverse of the control premium, which is itself nil or very small.

Recently, with the large influx of capital into private equity groups and hedge funds, competitive pressure for deals has caused some financial buyers to compete with strategic buyers. To do so, they must lower their expected rates of return, since strategic or synergistic cash flow benefits are not available to them.

- *Marketable minority value* refers to the value of a minority interest, lacking control, but enjoying the benefit of liquidity as if it were freely tradable in an active market. This level of value is also described as the "as-if-freely-traded" level of value.

- *Nonmarketable minority value* refers to the value of a minority interest, lacking both control and market liquidity. Value at this level is determined based on the expected future enterprise cash flows that are available to minority shareholders, discounted to the present at an appropriate discount rate over the expected holding period of the investment. The nonmarketable minority level of value is derived indirectly by applying a marketability discount directly to marketable minority indications of value, or directly, by determining the present value of expected cash flows to minority interests.

Early Levels of Value Charts

The first levels of value chart appeared in the valuation literature around 1990 and has since evolved. We present this evolution for the benefit of those with existing buy-sell agreements that may have been drafted using one of these earlier levels of value charts. If your agreement was drafted prior to 1990, know that the general concepts embodied in the chart were known by appraisers (and courts) prior to that time.

The early chart showed three conceptual levels. The chart is so important to an understanding of valuation concepts that analysts at Mercer Capital have included it in virtually every valuation report since about 1992 (see Figure 11).

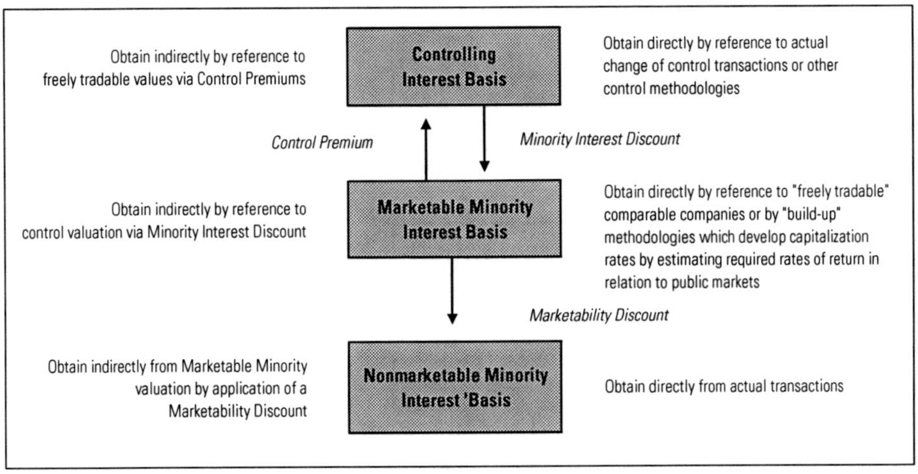

FIGURE 11

Prior to the early 1990s, we like most appraisers, assumed the existence of the conceptual adjustments to value known as the *control premium*, the *minority interest discount*, and the *marketability discount.*

Our thinking evolved during the 1990s. By the mid-1990s, there was recognition that the change-of-control studies relied upon to reach the top level in the three-level chart were for the most part strategic transactions. Therefore, appraisers began to present four distinct levels of value instead of three (see Figure 12).

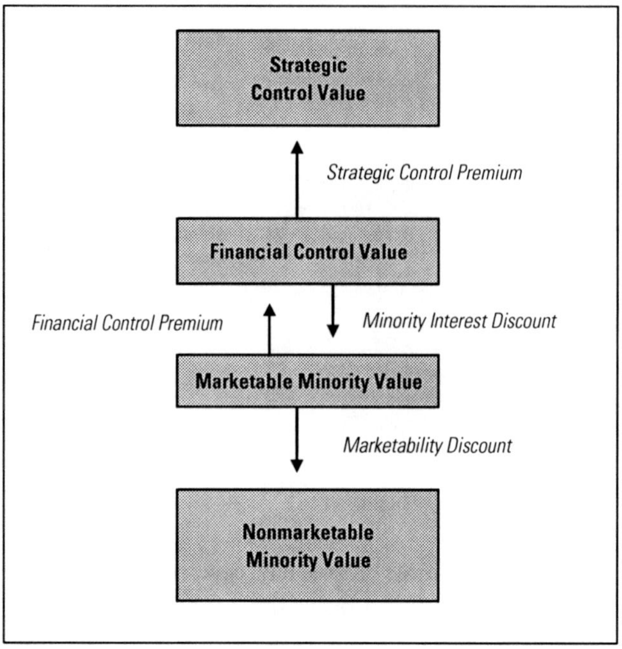

FIGURE 12

In Chapter 3 of *The Integrated Theory of Business Valuation*, we presented the "expanded, modified" levels of value chart (Figure 10). The financial control value has been placed near or on top of the marketable minority value and the former control value has been renamed strategic control value.[22]

22 See the Addendum to this chapter for citations.

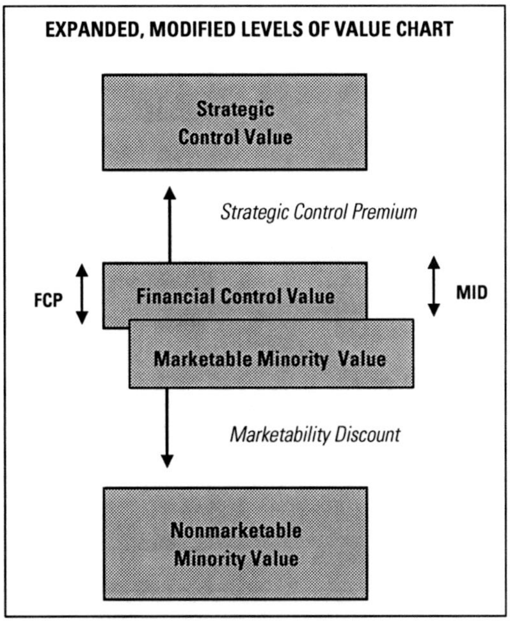

Practical Thoughts on the Levels of Value

Let's look at the levels of value and the desired kind of value in buy-sell agreements in a more practical light. We have noted the interests of the parties to a buy-sell agreement diverge at a trigger event. Rational buyers desire to purchase at the lowest possible price. Rational sellers desire to maximize the proceeds of a sale.

Please note that we are *not* making a recommendation regarding the appropriate level of value for your buy-sell agreement, or for any buy-sell agreement for that matter. However, we are making a critical point. If you are a direct party to a buy-sell agreement, you need to come to agreement with the other parties as to the appropriate level of value to define the valuation for *purposes of your agreement.* If you advise business owners, you need to insist that they reach such agreement.

In Figure 13, we see the impact of diverging interests in the conceptual levels of value chart.

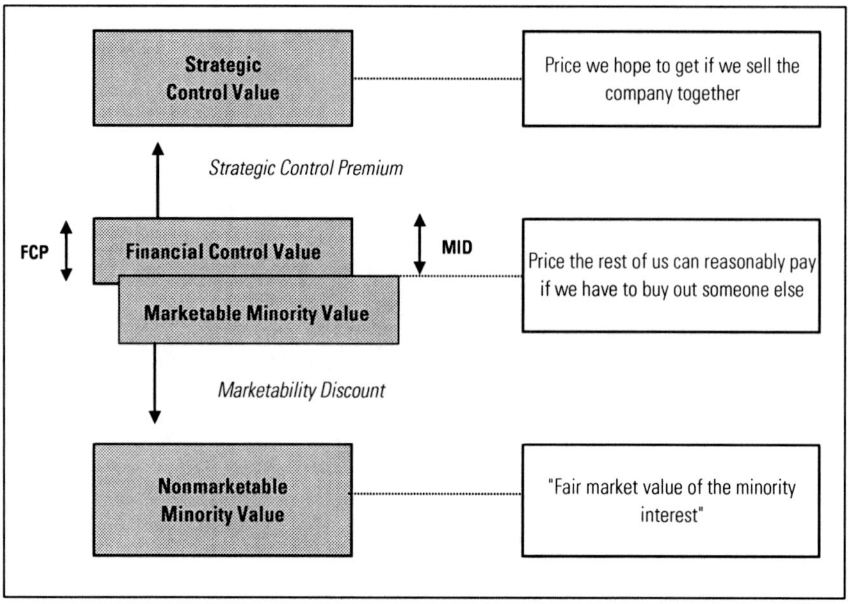

FIGURE 13

In the levels of value chart in Figure 13, the optimal price will vary depending on one's perspective as either a buyer or a seller.

1. The *strategic control value* (top of the chart) can be described as the price we would hope to obtain if we sell the company together. If you are a seller, you would clearly like to achieve this kind of value. If I am a buyer, I definitely do not want to pay a strategic control value, because the remaining shareholders may never obtain that value in an ultimate sale. Poorly worded language describing valuation in buy-sell agreements can allow for the possibility of such an interpretation.

2. The *nonmarketable minority value* (bottom of the chart) can be described as the price I'd like to pay if I am the buyer. However, if you are the seller, such pricing as an illiquid minority interest would be disadvantageous. Poorly worded language describing valuation in buy-sell agreements can allow for the possibility of such an interpretation.

3. The *marketable minority and/or financial control value*s (middle of the chart) can be described as the price the rest of us can reasonably pay if we have to buy you out (or that I could reasonably pay if I have to buy you out).

Many business persons and shareholders will agree, at least in casual conversation that, in most cases, an illiquid, minority interest value may not be equitable as a buy-sell price for departing shareholders. Those same persons will generally agree that asking the remaining shareholders to pay a strategic control value to departing shareholders also may not be equitable. This logic leads to the conclusion that, at least in many cases, the best price could be the marketable minority or financial control pricing.

An Example

Now, you may ask, how can there be any confusion about the appropriate level of value in a buy-sell agreement? Isn't everyone familiar with these valuation concepts? The answer is "no." Where there is a lack of understanding about valuation concepts, confusion will reign. Not everyone is familiar with the valuation concepts we have discussed thus far. We will see in Chapter 22 how such confusion can occur when we examine several examples of the valuation language in actual buy-sell agreements.

Recall the old expression: "A picture is worth a thousand words." Here's a word picture and then in a visual picture.

The word picture. Assume there is a buy-sell agreement where the parties failed to specify the appropriate level of value. The agreement was triggered and the company was required to acquire a shareholder's shares per its terms. Unfortunately, the agreement had vague and confusing language regarding the level of value.

The company retained a well-qualified business appraiser, as did the shareholder. Under the terms of the agreement, each was required to provide a valuation.

- The company's appraiser interpreted the level of value as the *nonmarketable minority* level of value, citing specific language in the agreement to support her conclusion. In developing her opinion, she concluded that the financial control/marketable minority level of value was $100 per share. A marketability discount of 40% was applied and the interest was valued at $60 per share.

- The shareholder's appraiser interpreted the level of value as the *strategic control* level of value, citing specific language in the agreement in support of his conclusion. He also concluded that the financial control/marketable minority level of value was $100 per share. A control premium of 40% was applied and the interest was valued at $140 per share.

The visual picture. The conclusions of value at each level of value are shown in Figure 14. Note that there is exact agreement on value at the financial control/marketable minority level. Further note the dramatic difference in concluded values after reaching their respective final values - $60 per share versus $140 per share.

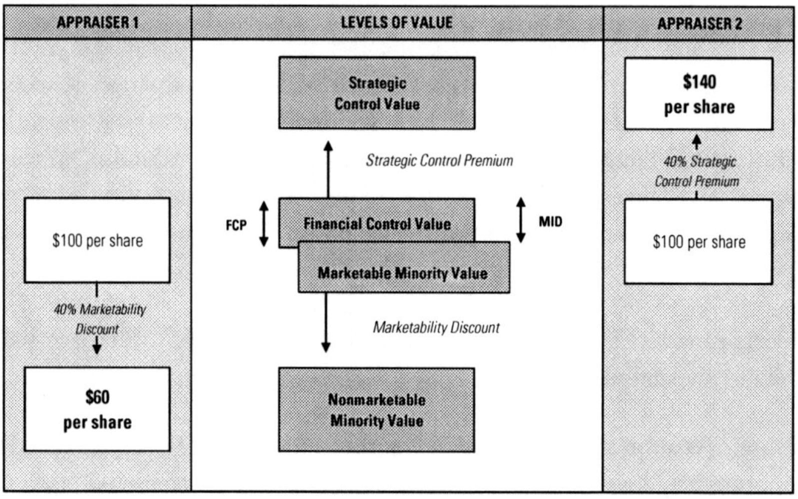

FIGURE 14

The parties now have two appraisals. They are quite similar in many respects, but widely different in their conclusions of value. The visual picture raises several questions for consideration:

- How could this have happened?
- How will the mandatory third appraiser reconcile the (irreconcilable) differences in concluded values?
- Could this happen to you? or to your client(s)?

The fact that this sort of thing *does* happen is one of the reasons we are writing this book. We hope you find that it helps you, or helps you help your clients avoid making the same mistakes. Situations like this can and do happen and they are never pretty in their resolution, nor are the parties generally satisfied with the ultimate results.

Suggestions for Specifying the Desired Level of Value

We make no recommendation regarding which level of value is appropriate for purposes of your agreement. However, we do suggest the following:

- Reach agreement on which level of value is desired for your agreement.
- Specify that level of value in your agreement by specific reference to a levels of value chart.

THE LEVELS OF VALUE

The most certain way to describe the desired level of value for a buy-sell agreement is to agree on the level while the agreement is being finalized. We recommend referencing a levels of value chart in a book by name and page number so that there is no question whatsoever as to the specific level of value for purposes of the agreement.

Here is such a chart for ease of reference.

The Levels of Value

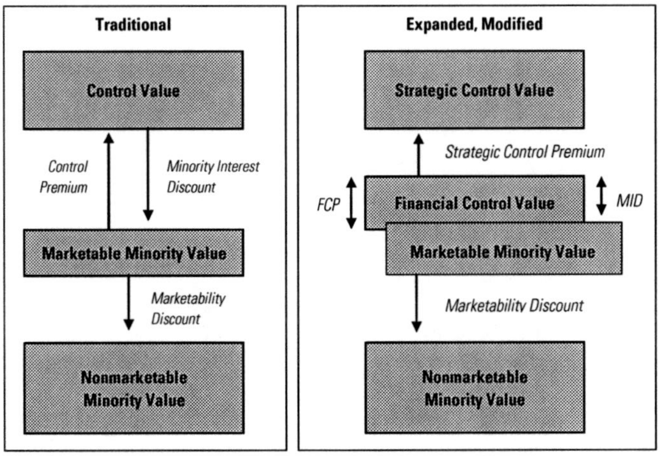

Our suggestion is that you (or your clients) agree on a specific level of value from the chart on the right (the "expanded, modified" levels of value chart). It is important to make the selection to ensure that appraisers know exactly which kind of value is intended, and which are not. A copy of the chart can be placed as an exhibit to the agreement.

There are a number of advantages to pre-selecting the desired level of value for your buy-sell agreement, including:

1. In selecting the desired level of value at the time of the agreement, the parties will reach agreement on this important issue before the occurrence of a trigger event, at which time their interests will diverge. This agreement will eliminate future uncertainty and provide comfort with the collective understanding of the buy-sell agreement's valuation mechanism.

2. Experienced business appraisers are familiar with the four levels of value shown in the chart on the right. If you select, say, the marketable minority level, most appraisers will be clear as to the kind of value you have chosen and the particular valuation methods that are appropriate to develop it. If you specify financial control value, appraisers will know that it approximates marketable minority value and is *not* strategic control value.

3. Reference to this book should further clarify the meaning of the level you have agreed upon and eliminate questions over the issue in the event of a trigger event. We suggest that you reference the entire chapter, including the Addendum.

ADDENDUM TO CHAPTER 17

The Levels of Value and the Integrated Theory of Business Valuation

The following discussion is placed in this Addendum to supplement the discussion in Chapter 17 because it departs from the non-technical nature of the rest of the book. The Addendum is important because it discusses, in "appraiser-speak," what is meant by each level of value.

The levels of value chart first appeared in the valuation literature some time around 1990 and showed three conceptual levels.[23] However, the general concepts embodied in the chart were known by appraisers (and courts) prior to that time. Most discussions regarding levels of value in the valuation literature are somewhat general in nature with little coverage of the factors giving rise to value differences at each level. It is, therefore, appropriate to provide a somewhat detailed discussion of the topic in this book.

In this Addendum, we will examine the chart in the context of the "Integrated Theory of Business Valuation," which was introduced in this author's recent book,

---

23 Eric W. Nath, "Control Premiums and Minority Interest Discounts in Private Companies," *Business Valuation Review*, Vol. 9, No. 2 (1990). Z. Christopher Mercer, "Do Public Company (Minority) Transactions Yield Controlling Interest or Minority Interest Pricing Data?," *Business Valuation Review* Vol. 9, No. 4 (1990). See also James H. Zukin, *Financial Valuation: Businesses and Business Interests* (New York: Maxwell MacMillan/Rosenfeld Launer, 1990), p. 2-3. While the concepts of the levels of value had been around for some time prior to 1990, to the best of our knowledge, the levels of value chart was not published until the Mercer article as well as in the Zukin text appeared in 1990.

Valuing Enterprise and Shareholder Cash Flows: The Integrated Theory of Business Valuation.[24]

The Integrated Theory is a vehicle to describe the financial characteristics of each level of value and to define each conceptual adjustment (see below) in financial terms. The end result is that it is possible to describe exactly the kind of value that you want for your buy-sell valuation in terms that appraisers everywhere will recognize and understand.

The original levels of value chart had three distinct levels, with conceptual adjustments leading from one level to the next. Prior to the early 1990s, we like most appraisers, assumed the existence of the conceptual adjustments to value known as the *control premium*, the *minority interest discount*, and the *marketability discount*. We relied on market evidence provided from control premium studies to help ascertain the magnitude of control premiums (and minority interest discounts).[25] We also relied on certain benchmark studies, the so-called pre-IPO Studies and the restricted stock studies as the basis for estimating the magnitude of marketability discounts. Such reliance contributed to a failure to understand the basis for the premiums and discounts being estimated.

Our thinking evolved during the 1990s. By the mid-1990s, there was a recognition that the change-of-control studies relied upon to reach the top level in the three-level chart were, for the most part *strategic transactions*. Therefore, appraisers began to present four distinct levels of value instead of three.[26]

---

24 This discussion borrows heavily and quotes frequently from Chapter 3 of *The Integrated Theory of Business Valuation*, Supra 21.

25 *Mergerstat Review* is published annually in book form by FactSet Mergerstat, LLC.

26 Shannon Pratt's *Valuing a Business, 3rd Edition* shows a three-level chart on page 301. The 4th Edition of *Valuing a Business* shows a four-level chart on page 347 and sources it to: Jay E. Fishman, Shannon P. Pratt, J. Clifford Griffith, and D. Keith Wilson, *Guide to Business Valuations*, 10th. Ed. (Forth Worth, TX: Practitioners Publishing Company, 2000).

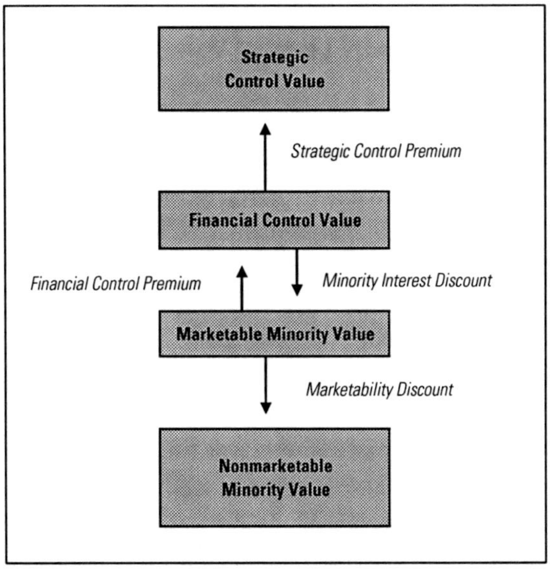

In 2004, Chapter 3 of *The Integrated Theory of Business Valuation* was drafted with the purpose of integrating the Gordon Model, as a basic statement of how the markets value companies, and the conceptual framework of the levels of value.[27]

The Integrated Theory of Business Valuation:

- Explains each level of value in the context of the Gordon Model.

- Uses the components of the Gordon Model to define the conceptual adjustments between the levels of value, e.g., the control premium (and its inverse, the minority interest discount) and the marketability (financial) discount.

- Explains why the resulting integrated valuation model is illustrative of pricing behavior in the marketplace for public securities (the marketable minority level), and the markets for entire companies (the controlling interest level(s) of value), and the markets for illiquid, minority interests of private enterprises (the nonmarketable minority level of value).

---

27 The Gordon Model is discussed at length in Chapter 1 of *The Integrated Theory of Business Valuation,* Supra 21.

The (Benchmark) Marketable Minority Level of Value

Let's begin at the beginning. The valuation of private companies and their securities is based, either directly or indirectly, on comparisons with alternative investments, typically investments in shares of publicly traded companies. Financial and valuation theory is based on such comparisons. Chapter 3 of *The Integrated Theory* begins:

> In this chapter, we introduce the Integrated Theory of Business Valuation, or the Integrated Theory. Simply stated, the Integrated Theory of Business Valuation allows business appraisers to account for all the cash flows of an enterprise, whether at the level of the enterprise or by examining the portions of enterprise cash flows attributable to specific interests of those enterprises. It does this by harmonizing the Gordon Model (and implicitly, the discounted cash flow model) with the levels of value concept with which we are all familiar.
>
> More specifically, the Integrated Theory of Business Valuation employs the Gordon Model and explains each level of value in the context of financial and valuation theory as well as why value might differ from level to level. In addition, the Integrated Theory defines the conceptual adjustments relating the various levels of value to each other (control premiums and minority interest discounts and marketability discounts) in terms of the discounted cash flow analysis summarized by the Gordon Model. Importantly, however, the Integrated Theory also describes the conditions necessary for the relevant valuation premiums and discounts to exist.[28]

Chapter 3 of *The Integrated Theory* addresses each of the levels of value in words before showing them in conceptual form in charts. Because of its critical importance in defining any valuation, we quote from the initial discussion of the level of value known as the marketable minority level of value:

> It is generally accepted that the Gordon Model provides a shorthand representation of the value of public securities at the marketable minority interest level of value. For privately owned enterprises, it is

---

28 *The Integrated Theory of Business Valuation,* Supra 21, p. 81.

> indicative of the same level, i.e., the "as-if-freely-traded" level. In developing the Integrated Theory, we discuss the Gordon Model in the context of the levels of value to understand how they relate to each other. To do so, we introduce a symbolic notation to designate which elements of the model relate to each level of value. Equation 3-2 introduces the conceptual math of the benchmark level of value – the marketable minority value.
>
> $$V_{mm} = \frac{CF_{e(mm)}}{R_{mm} - G_{mm}} \quad \text{or} \quad \frac{CF}{R - G}$$
>
> **EQUATION 3-2**
>
> The marketable minority level of value was just described as the "benchmark level of value." It is so described because it is the level *to which* control premiums are added to achieve controlling interest indications of value. It is also the level *from which* marketability discounts are subtracted to reach the nonmarketable minority level of value. As we will see, the Integrated Theory affirms that the marketable minority level of value is the appropriate benchmark from which to compare the other levels.[29]

So we have a basic definition of a benchmark level of value, the marketable minority level of value. That is the middle level of value in the three-level chart above (and the second from the bottom in the four-level chart). It is worth repeating. The conceptual, marketable minority level of value is the level of value *from which* marketability discounts are taken to arrive at the nonmarketable minority interest level of value, or the lowest level in the chart above. It is also the level *to which* appropriate control premiums (as we will see, financial or strategic) are added to arrive at the controlling interest levels of value, or the top-most levels in the charts above.

Suffice it to say at this point that the levels of value suggest a range of values, from the strategic controlling interest level of value of the enterprise as a whole, to the nonmarketable minority interest level of value applicable to illiquid, minority interests in the enterprise.

---

29 *The Integrated Theory of Business Valuation*, Supra 21, p. 86.

Not surprisingly then, differences in assumptions regarding the appropriate level of value are, in our experience, the sources of some of the largest differences in valuation opinions by appraisers involved in the operation of process buy-sell agreements. These differences almost inevitably result from either absence of or unclear specification regarding the level of value applicable in particular agreements.

Expanded, Modified Levels of Value Chart

The Integrated Theory suggests an alternative levels of value chart after developing each of the conceptual adjustments (control premiums, minority interest discounts, and marketability discounts) in theoretical terms. This chart is shown below as it appears in Chapter 3.[30] The expanded, modified, levels of value chart is shown adjacent to the traditional chart.

The Levels of Value

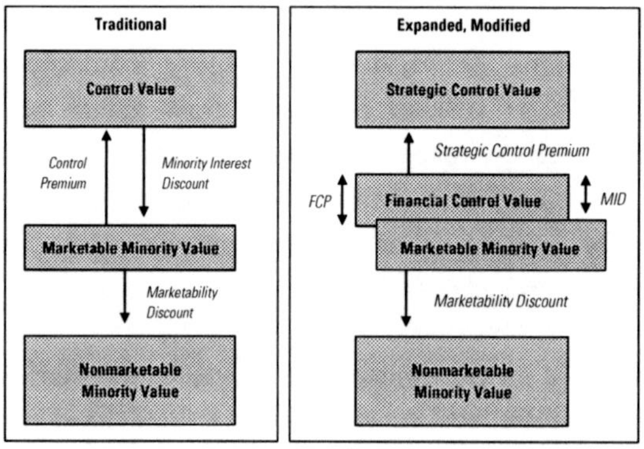

- *Marketable minority value.* We refer to this level of value as the "benchmark" level. The marketability minority value is the benchmark to which control premiums are added to derive controlling interest indications of value and from which marketability discounts are subtracted to reach the nonmarketable minority level of value. This level of value is also described as the "as-if-freely-traded" level of value. It is the proxy, in private company valuation, for value as if there were an active market for the shares of a business. This level is not new, and correlates to the marketable minority level of value in the three-level chart introduced at the beginning of the chapter ("the traditional" levels of value). This level of value is developed based on comparisons with publicly traded guideline companies, or through

30 *The Integrated Theory of Business Valuation*, Supra 21, p. 110.

the capitalization of earnings using a market-derived discount rate (perhaps the Adjusted Capital Asset Pricing Model, or another derivation of the Capital Asset Pricing Model). Typically, appraisers *normalize* the earnings of businesses, adjusting for non-recurring items, excess owner compensation, and related items to place them on a "public-equivalent" basis, in the process of developing marketable minority indications of value.

- *Financial control value.* It is generally believed that the marketable minority level of value and the financial control level of value are, if not synonymous, then essentially so. This level of value describes what a financial buyer is able (or willing) to pay for control of a business. Financial buyers acquire companies based on their ability to extract reasonable (to them) rates of return, often on a leveraged basis. One way of describing the financial control value is that buyers are willing to pay for the expected cash flows of enterprises, and will pay no more than the marketable minority value unless they believe they can run a company better *and* the competitive bidding situation requires that they share a portion of potential improvements with the seller. Appraisers would make *(financial) control adjustments* to the earnings stream only to the extent that typical financial control buyers would include expected earnings improvements in their earnings expectations and would share those benefits with sellers.

    - *FCP is the financial control premium.* The financial control premium is shown, conceptually, to be nil, or at least very small in the chart above for the reasons outlined above.

    - *MID is the minority interest discount.* The minority interest discount is also shown to be conceptually nil or very small. This is consistent with the discount being the conceptual inverse of the control premium, which is itself nil or very small.

- *Strategic control value.* This second control level is the highest conceptual level on the chart. This level is referred to as the strategic control level, or, alternatively, the synergistic control level. Strategic buyers can (and do) pay more for companies than financial buyers because they expect to realize synergies or other strategic benefits from acquisitions, perhaps through the elimination of duplicate expenses or achieving cross-selling revenue opportunities, that increase expected future cash flows. Strategic buyers would include *(strategic or synergistic) control adjustments* to the earnings stream only to the extent that their typical competitive buyers would include expected earnings improvements in their earnings expectations and would share those benefits with sellers. The "control premiums" found in *Mergerstat Review* and other studies that examine public company acquisitions reflect, for the most part, *strategic control premiums*. Because of this, it is generally considered inappropriate to utilize these control premiums to estimate the minority interest discount. The conceptual chart makes the logic of this position clear.

- *Nonmarketable minority value.* The bottom level on the chart is the nonmarketable minority level of value. Value at this level is determined based on the expected future enterprise cash flows that are available to minority shareholders, discounted to the present at an appropriate discount rate over the expected holding period of the investment. The nonmarketable minority level of value is derived indirectly by applying a marketability discount directly to marketable minority indications of value, or directly, by determining the present value of expected cash flows to minority interests.

  - *Marketability discount.* Historically, business appraisers have developed marketability discounts by making comparisons with average discounts from studies of restricted stock (of public companies) transactions, or studies of valuations in pre-IPO transactions. Increasingly, appraisers are using the direct approach to valuing minority interests (and determining marketability discounts) using the Quantitative Marketability Discount Model (QMDM) or similar discounted cash flow methods focusing on cash flows to minority interests.[31]

We can observe from the two charts above:

- There are no changes in the conceptual relationships between the marketable minority and the nonmarketable minority interest levels of value.
- Financial control value has been placed near or on top of the marketable minority value, as explained in the above references to Chapter 3 of *The Integrated Theory*. The former control value has been renamed strategic control value.

31 *The Integrated Theory of Business Valuation,* Supra 21.

- The control premium from the traditional chart is disaggregated into two premiums, the FCP (or financial control premium which, visually and conceptually, would be zero to very small) and the strategic control premium (SCP).
- The minority interest discount on the traditional chart appears to be comprised of the MID (minority interest discount) on the expanded chart, plus a portion of the old minority interest discount that is labeled with a question mark.

We can make a number of observations about the concept of financial control value in relationship to the marketable minority value:[32]

- Value at the marketable minority level of value presumes that enterprise cash flows are *normalized.* Normalization is the process of adjusting enterprise cash flows for non-recurring items and discretionary items such as above-market owner compensation or other related expenses. For a public company, if cash flows were not "normal," market pressures would force such a process to occur, and/or takeovers would occur.[33] Because valuation theory is based on comparisons with public markets, we normalize private company cash flows in the process of valuing at the enterprise levels (marketable minority, financial control and strategic control).[34]
- Unless the financial control buyer will price an expectation for greater cash flows (level or expected growth) than the normalized earnings of an enterprise, there is no conceptual reason for there to be a distinction in value between the financial control and marketable minority levels.[35]
- The financial control premium is *not* a payment to reflect the value of the so-called prerogatives of control. Those prerogatives are vested with

---

32 Chapter 3 of the *Integrated Theory* develops these concepts in much more depth. The entire chapter is incorporated into this Addendum by reference. Supra 21.

33 This statement is the essence of the "Nath hypothesis," the name attributed to the observations in Eric Nath's important 1990 article in *Business Valuation Review.* Supra 23.

34 Some appraisers have argued that when valuing minority interests, which lack the power to cause normalizing adjustments (often incorrectly referred to as "control adjustments"), private company earnings should not be normalized. Chapter 6 of *The Integrated Theory* addresses the concept of normalizing adjustments at length. *Normalizing adjustments* are necessary to reach the marketable minority or financial control levels of value. *Control adjustments* are those that might be made by strategic or synergistic buyers that increase cash flows *from their perspectives.* Supra 21.

35 This was first recognized in the 1990 article by Eric Nath, which shocked the appraisal profession, including this author. Supra 23.

managements and directorates of public entities, and are presumed vested for purposes of deriving private company values at the marketable (as-if-freely-traded) minority level of value.

- The minority interest discount is *not* a discount to reflect the absence of the so-called prerogatives of control. Lack of control on the part of minority shareholders is presumed in the pricing of public securities and at the marketability minority level.
- Application of strategic acquisition premiums may overstate value in the context of fair market value.
- Use of strategic acquisition control premium data to infer minority interest discounts from financial control values will tend to overstate the magnitude of minority interest discounts.
- The need to understand the conceptual nature of the marketability discount and the causes of often-observed large differences between marketable minority values and the values of illiquid securities of private (or public) enterprises is critical.

The Levels of Value and Buy-Sell Agreements

It should be clear on a *theoretical basis* that the specification of the desired level of value is important when defining the kind of value desired in a process buy-sell agreement. Clarity is essential because the "words on the page" in your buy-sell agreement will likely be the only instructions that your appraiser(s) will receive regarding the kind of value that you intend(ed). Different interpretations of those "words on the page" by different appraisers can lead to widely disparate valuation conclusions and problems and/or dissatisfaction with the operation of process buy-sell agreements.

CHAPTER 18

Defining Element #3: The "As Of" Date of the Appraisal

This chapter addresses the concept of the "as of" or the "effective date" or the "valuation date." The issue of the "as of" date is far more important than the brevity of this chapter might otherwise indicate.

1. Standard of Value	4. Qualifications of Appraisers
2. Level of Value	5. Appraisal Standards
3. The "as of" Date	6. Funding Mechanisms

The "as of" date is called for in the *Business Valuation Standards* of the American Society of Appraisers.[36] Three terms are used interchangeably in these standards to peg the date as of which a valuation will be rendered: effective date, valuation date, and appraisal date. We, nevertheless, use the term "as of" date to focus attention on "the specific point in time as of which the valuation's opinion of value applies."[37]

The "as of" date is the date as of which available information pertaining to a valuation should be considered by appraisers. The effective date grounds the

36 *ASA Business Valuation Standards* (Herndon, Virginia, American Society of Appraisers, 2005). Available on the web at http://www.bvappraisers.org/glossary. See Appendix D.

37 Ibid. Definitions: Valuation Date. See Appendix D.

appraiser not only in the background and financial condition of a subject company, but its local, regional, or national economy, its industry, and other relevant aspects.

We know from the definition of fair market value that both parties to a transaction are assumed to have reasonable knowledge about an investment and the relevant facts pertaining to it. *This knowledge is grounded in the "as of" date.*

Real life transactions are based on facts and circumstances known up to the minute of their closings, and consider reasonable outlooks for the future. Reasonably, or fully informed, does not mean having a crystal ball that eliminates uncertainties by forecasting the future with precision.

Appraisers engaging in *after-the-fact* valuations should not abuse the standard of reasonable knowledge based on facts that clarified themselves shortly or long after an historical valuation date. Attorneys representing the side in a dispute benefiting by knowledge of post-valuation date events may *want* to believe that the certainty of those events was reasonably knowable at the valuation date. And parties to a buy-sell agreement may *want* to believe similarly, depending on their perspective with respect to a contemplated transaction. Independent appraisers do not have this luxury.

In some instances, the fact that an event *might* occur in the future is known at the time of the valuation date. What is not generally known is *when* or with *what probability* the event might occur. Appraisers must assess those probabilities and incorporate the risks or potential benefits appropriately in their appraisals – the way that reasonably informed hypothetical willing investors might, based on information available as of a valuation date.

An Example of a Non-Specified "As Of" Date

How, you might ask, could the "as of" date not be clearly defined in the buy-sell agreement? Well, unless the words on the page state specifically that the valuation date is the date of the trigger event or some other date, there is often ample room for confusion. Consider the following case.

Two companies entered into a joint venture. The partners owned the joint venture 50% each. A large private company contributed the initial operations for the venture. A much larger public company contributed an equivalent amount of growth capital. A detailed joint venture agreement formalized the arrangement, and the partnership operated profitably and grew substantially for more than a decade.

As it turns out, this particular agreement provided a put option which provided for one joint venture partner the option to buy out the other's 50% interest in the event that the other's parent company was sold (i.e., changed control).

Several issues arose:

- "Change of control" was not defined in the agreement, so when one party engaged in a "merger of equals" (or so they thought), there was a question as to whether a change of control, at least for purposes of the agreement, had occurred. There was an arbitration on this issue which took considerable time, the conclusion of which was that a change of control had indeed occurred.

- The "as of" date was not specified. If the valuation process had occurred smoothly and quickly, it might not have mattered. The appraiser would have used available information and valued this company.

    - With the passage of time (going on two years), changes in the company and the industry were favorable to value. So what date should the appraiser use in his appraisal? The seller argued that the date should be as of a current date where pricing is often determined as close to the closing date as possible. After all, the partnership continued to operate and each party bore all the risks of ownership during this period. The buyer argued that the as of date should be the date that they gave notice of their intent to purchase pursuant to the agreement.

    - Neither the qualifications of the appraiser nor the applicable appraisal standards were specified.[38] Fortunately, the parties were able to agree upon a well-qualified, credentialed appraiser (not Mercer Capital). The appraiser, to his credit, refused to do anything until there was an agreement regarding the "as of" date.

    - The sole issue of the appropriate "as of" date was the subject of a second arbitration. We were involved (on behalf of the seller) in this arbitration, as were several other appraisers. For a multitude of reasons, we concluded that the appropriate "as of" date was a date as close to the closing as possible. The arbitration panel agreed.

---

38 See Chapters 19 and 20 for a complete discussion of appraiser qualifications and appraisal standards.

- The appraisal process was finally concluded. The buyer did not exercise its option, and the joint venture continues to operate.

Interestingly, we do not know if the parties have renegotiated the provisions in their joint venture agreement which defined the buy-sell arrangement. However, it is probably safe to say that neither party desires to go through that same process again.

Conclusion

It is critical that the "as of" date be specified. As we saw in Chapter 15, it may also be important to determine what happens in the event of delays in the appraisal process. Otherwise, one or both parties may be at risk to changes in the company or its industry over time.

THE "AS OF" DATE

The parties should decide the "as of" date for appraisals upon the occurrence of a trigger event. In so doing, they should understand that the selection of this date will include all information known or reasonably knowable as of that date, and should exclude all information, positive or negative, that develops or becomes known after that date.

Potential "as of" dates for discussion include:

1. The exact date of the trigger event (whether quitting, firing, dying, retiring, divorcing, or other).
2. Date determined by availability of financial statements:
   a. The date of the monthly financial statements immediately preceding the trigger event.
   b. The date of the quarterly financial statements immediately preceding the trigger event.
   c. The date of the monthly financial statements for the month during which the trigger event occurs.
   d. The date of the quarterly financial statements for the quarter during which the trigger event occurs.
   e. The date of the most recent annual audit (watch out for this one – see Chapter 15).
3. Date determined by the appraisal process:
   a. The date the appraiser(s) are selected and hired.
   b. The date that the appraisal report(s) is (are) submitted. Note that any third appraiser would have to use this same date.
4. Other, as agreed upon by the parties.

The important thing is that the parties select an "as of" date that is clearly established and defined. This selection will eliminate uncertainty and misunderstandings when trigger events occur.

CHAPTER 19

Defining Element #4: Appraiser Qualifications

Buy-sell agreements are often silent regarding the qualifications of the appraiser(s). This is particularly true of agreements signed in the 1980s and 1990s, many of which have not yet been tested by trigger events.

1. Standard of Value	**4. Qualifications of Appraisers**
2. Level of Value	5. Appraisal Standards
3. The "as of" Date	6. Funding Mechanisms

Several aspects of appraiser qualifications should be considered. As stated earlier, we believe it can be beneficial for the parties to go through an appraisal selection process at the outset of agreements. The logical requirements become fairly apparent as parties begin to consider individual appraisers and appraisal firms. Danger, in the form of future angst and uncertainty, arises for the operation of agreements when qualifications are not specified.

Qualifications of Appraisal Firms

When selecting an appraisal firm it is desirable that the firm (or, at least, its legitimate successor) will be around when future trigger events occur. It may be a good idea to describe the qualifications of appraisal firms in the context of their size and longevity, as well as the scope of their business.

Qualifications of Appraisers

Appraisal firms do not render appraisal reports – appraisers do. Therefore, it is also important to consider the qualifications of the individual appraisers. Evaluation of the qualifications of business appraisers can include consideration of a number of distinguishing factors, including:

- *Education.* Business appraisers typically have college degrees in fields like finance, economics, accounting, and mathematics, among others. Many appraisers also have advanced degrees.

- *Valuation training.* The various appraisal societies, including the American Society of Appraisers (ASA), the Institute of Business Appraisers (IBA), the National Association of Certified Valuation Analysts (NACVA), the American Institute of Certified Public Accountants (AICPA), and the Canadian Institute of Chartered Business Valuators (CICBV) provide business valuation courses as part of their ongoing education and credentialing processes. To date, there are very few business valuation courses taught in colleges and universities across America. Most of the basic concepts of valuation are taught as part of corporate finance classes.

- *Appraisal experience.* You may want to specify the level of experience necessary to qualify an appraiser for your buy-sell agreement. However, all experience is not equal. While two appraisers may have the same number of years of experience, one may have had ten years of continuing growth as a professional, while the other may have had the same year of experience repeated ten times. Appraisers with mid-sized and larger firms are likely to have good experience because of the nature of their businesses. There are also many qualified, experienced appraisers in smaller firms and practices. You will not be able to make a judgment without some personal investigation.

- *Industry experience.* Sometimes, specific industry experience is noted as a requirement. This is a potentially dangerous qualification since industry experience is not equivalent to valuation experience and training. Many companies are in narrow industry niches which are simply too small to have appraisers who have focused on them. (See Appendix A: *The "Valuation Professional" vs. The "Industry Expert."*)

- *Continuing education.* There are numerous sources for ongoing study. The appraisal societies and other groups provide CPE credit in a variety of local, regional and national seminars and conventions. Some firms, like Mercer Capital, provide specific valuation training for their professionals on a regular basis. For example, an analyst who attends the approximately 40 training sessions per year held at Mercer Capital would earn up to 40 or more hours of related continuing education. The various societies require continuing education ranging from 12 hours per year (IBA) to 40 hours per year (AICPA).

- *Publications.* Individual appraisers may demonstrate their knowledge, training, and experience by writing about business and valuation issues. Some appraisers have written books. There are a number of recognized business appraisal publications, some of which require peer review and approval prior to publication.[39]

- *Credentialing.* A number of professional designations are offered by the professional appraisal associations. Details about the various credentials can be found on the websites of the respective associations.
    - American Institute of Certified Public Accountants (AICPA). http://bvfls.aicpa.org
    - American Society of Appraisers (ASA). www.appraisers.org
    - Canadian Institute of Chartered Business Valuators (CICBV). www.cicbv.ca
    - CFA Institute. www.cfainstitute.org
    - Institute of Business Appraisers (IBA). www.go-iba.org
    - National Association of Certified Valuation Analysts (NACVA). www.nacva.com

---

39 *The Business Valuation Review* published by the American Society of Appraisers
Business Appraisal Practice published by The Institute of Business Appraisers
The Value Examiner published by The National Association of Certified Valuation Analysts
Valuation Strategies published by RIA Group
Business Valuation Update published by Business Valuation Resources
The CPA Expert published by the AICPA
Financial Valuation and Litigation Expert published by Valuation Products & Services, LC
CCH's Business Valuation Alert published by CCH
The Business Valuation Digest published by the Canadian Institute of Chartered Business Valuators

See Appendix B prepared by Business Valuation Resources which summarizes the professional accreditation criteria of the major organizations offering business appraisal credentials.

- *Expert testimony experience.* Hopefully, there will be no need for expert testimony regarding your buy-sell agreement. However, acceptance as an expert by courts as an expert witness in adversarial proceedings does represent another aspect of independent review of qualifications.

- *Required compliance with professional standards.* Individuals who are accredited by the above organizations are required to follow codes of ethics and professional standards promulgated by their respective organizations. Members of the American of Society of Appraisers must also follow the *Uniform Standards of Professional Appraisal Practice* promulgated by The Appraisal Foundation. Other appraisers can comply with these standards voluntarily. We will address these important issues in the next chapter.

- *Speaking.* Individual appraisers may also demonstrate their knowledge, training, and experience by speaking to professional and business organizations. As with publishing, speaking is a form of educating one's peers and fellow professionals in related fields.

There are a variety of professional designations in the business valuation field. A number of well-respected and well-published appraisers have earned and maintain two or more professional designations.

SELECTING APPRAISERS

Option 1. We believe that an excellent way to avoid uncertainty regarding the future selection of appraisers is to select the appraiser prior to the signing of the buy-sell agreement. This chapter serves as a guide for the process and helps focus the parties on the important aspects of appraiser qualifications and experience. A further aspect of this recommendation is that the selected appraiser can provide an initial appraisal under the agreed upon standard of value at the agreed upon level of value. Further, the firm employing the selected appraiser may have other qualified appraisers who can carry out necessary future assignments in the event the named appraiser is not available.

Option 2. Using this chapter as a guide, the parties could decide on the specific, minimum qualifications for any future appraiser selection under the buy-sell agreement. While this may seem unnecessary, it is far better to have the discussions now. If each side will obtain an appraiser, it is critical that they have similar experience levels and operate under the same business valuation standards. Note that if you select accreditation by the American Society of Appraisers as one qualification, you are assured that their appraisers' reports must comply with the *ASA Business Valuation Standards* and the *Uniform Standards of Professional Appraisal Practice* promulgated by The Appraisal Foundation.

CHAPTER 20

Defining Element #5: Appraisal Standards

Professions are defined by the existence of requirements for entrance into them, as well as by professional standards which govern the minimum requirements of operation and conduct.

1. Standard of Value	4. Qualifications of Appraisers
2. Level of Value	**5. Appraisal Standards**
3. The "as of" Date	6. Funding Mechanisms

Business appraisers who are credentialed by the organizations named in the previous chapter are required to operate their appraisal practices in accordance with standards of professional practice and codes of ethics.

There are several sets of business appraisal standards, including:

- *Uniform Standards of Professional Appraisal Practice (USPAP).*[40] Promulgated by the Appraisal Standards Board of The Appraisal Foundation, USPAP, as the standards are known, was developed originally in 1986-87. USPAP has been adopted by major appraisal organizations in North America, and "represents the generally accepted and recognized standards of appraisal

40 *Uniform Standards of Professional Appraisal Practice,* Supra 12. See also Appendix C.

practice in the United States."[41] The Preamble and Standards Rules 3, 9 and 10 of USPAP are reproduced with permission in Appendix C for convenient reference.

- *ASA Business Valuation Standards.*[42] The Business Valuation Committee of the American Society of Appraisers develops and maintains these standards. Development began in about 1990 and the first standards were published in 1992. They have been regularly expanded and updated since that time, with the most recent revisions being published in November 2005.[43] The *ASA Business Valuation Standards* are reproduced with permission in Appendix D for convenient reference.
    - *Principles of Appraisal Practice and Code of Ethics.*[44] This document is published by the American Society of Appraisers and is applicable to all members of the Society, including members in the business valuation discipline.
- *NACVA Professional Standards.*[45] The National Association of Certified Valuation Analysts publishes these professional standards applicable to its members.
- *Institute of Business Appraisers Business Valuation Standards* and *Rules of Professional Conduct.*[46] The Institute of Business Appraisers advances standards and rules of professional conduct for its members.
- *AICPA Proposed Business Valuation Standards.*[47]

---

41 Ibid.

42 *ASA Business Valuation Standards,* supra 36. See also Appendix D.

43 The author served on the Standards Sub-Committee of the Business Valuation Committee of the American Society of Appraisers from 1990 until 2003.

44 *Principles of Appraisal Practice and Code of Ethics,* American Society of Appraisers, www.appraisers.org.

45 *NAVCA Professional Standards,* National Association of Certified Valuation Analysts, www.nacva.com.

46 *The Institute of Business Appraisers Business Valuation Standards and Rules of Professional Conduct,* Institute of Business Appraisers, www.go-iba.org.

47 As of the printing of this book, the AICPA had yet to finalize its business valuation standards. http://bvfls.aicpa.org.

The set(s) of appraisal standards to be followed in valuations for buy-sell agreements is a defining element from a valuation perspective. We state this because there is little chance that appraisers providing valuations pursuant to an agreement will achieve similar results if both are not subject to the same or similar sets of valuation standards and codes of ethics.

Because of their overall applicability to appraisers, we begin by focusing on the *Uniform Standards of Professional Appraisal Practice.* Then, because of their acceptance and the fact that this author is a member of the American Society of Appraisers, we will focus on the *ASA Business Valuation Standards.*

Uniform Standards of Professional Appraisal Practice

Quoting from the Preamble to USPAP:

> The purpose of the *Uniform Standards of Professional Appraisal Practice* (USPAP) is to promote and maintain a high level of public trust in appraisal practice by establishing requirements for appraisers. It is essential that appraisers develop and communicate their analyses, opinions, and conclusions to intended users of services in a manner that is meaningful and not misleading.
>
> The Appraisal Standards Board promulgates USPAP for both appraisers and users of appraisal services. The appraiser's responsibility is to protect the overall public trust and it is the importance of the role of the appraiser that places ethical obligations on those who serve in this capacity. USPAP reflects the current standards of the appraisal profession.
>
> USPAP does not establish who or which assignments must comply. Neither The Appraisal Foundation nor its Appraisal Standards Board is a government entity with the power to make, judge or enforce law. Compliance with USPAP is required when either the service or the appraiser is obligated to comply by law or regulation, or by agreement with the client or intended users. When not obligated, individuals may still choose to comply.[48]

---

48 *Uniform Standards of Professional Appraisal Practice*, Supra 12.

One purpose of standards is to promote public confidence in appraisal practice (and in appraisal results). USPAP provides guidance to appraisers through Definitions, Rules, Standards, Standards Rules, and Statements. USPAP is updated every year by the Appraisal Standards Board of The Appraisal Foundation.

USPAP is designed to be applicable to both real property and business appraisal. The Preamble, the Ethics Rule, the Competency Rule, the Scope of Work Rule, the Jurisdictional Exception Rule, and the Supplemental Standards Rule are applicable to both disciplines. Standards Rules 3, 9 and 10 are the specific standards applicable to business appraisal:

- *Standards Rule 3: Appraisal Review, Development and Reporting.* Standards Rule 3 is applicable to the formal review of business appraisals, both in terms of development and reporting.

- *Standards Rule 9: Business Appraisal, Development.* Standards Rule 9 provides requirements for the development of appraisal reports.

- *Standards Rule 10: Business Appraisal, Reporting.* Standards Rule 10 provides the corresponding reporting requirements, generally in parallel with the development requirements of Standards Rule 9.

Because of their importance to the business appraisal profession, the Preamble and USPAP Standards Rules 3, 9 and 10 are provided, with approval from The Appraisal Foundation, for ease of reference in Appendix C.

Business Valuation Standards of the American Society of Appraisers

The *ASA Business Valuation Standards* are applicable to all members of the American Society of Appraisers, regardless of membership status. The General Preamble of these standards is quoted below [*emphasis added* in the paragraphs below]:

I) The American Society of Appraisers, through its Business Valuation Committee, has adopted these Business Valuation Standards and Definitions ("the Standards") *in order to maintain and enhance the quality of business valuations for the benefit of the business valuation profession and users of business valuations.*

II) The American Society of Appraisers, in its *Principles of Appraisal Practice and Code of Ethics,* and The Appraisal Foundation, in its

Uniform Standards of Professional Appraisal Practice ("USPAP"), have established authoritative principles and a code of professional ethics. These Standards incorporate the *Principles of Appraisal Practice and Code of Ethics* and the relevant portions of USPAP, either explicitly or by reference, and are designed to clarify them and provide additional requirements specifically applicable to the valuation of businesses, business ownership interests, and securities.

III) These Standards incorporate all relevant business valuation standards adopted by the American Society of Appraisers through its Business Valuation Committee.

IV) *These Standards provide minimum criteria to be followed by business appraisers in developing and reporting the valuation of businesses, business ownership interests, and securities.*

V) If, in the opinion of the appraiser, the circumstances of a specific business valuation assignment dictate a departure from any provision of any Standard, such departure must be disclosed and will apply only to the specific provision.

VI) *These Standards are designed to provide guidance to ASA members and to provide a structure for regulating the development and reporting of business valuations through uniform practices and procedures.* Deviations from the Standards are not intended to form the basis of any civil liability and should not create any presumption or evidence that a legal duty has been breached. Moreover, compliance with these Standards does not create any special relationship between the appraiser and any other person.

Because of their importance to the business appraisal profession, the *ASA Business Valuation Standards* are provided in their entirety in Appendix D, with permission from the Business Valuation Committee of the American Society of Appraisers.

Members of the American Society of Appraisers, whether candidates, Accredited Members (AM designation), Accredited Senior Appraisers (ASA designation), or Fellows of the American Society of Appraisers (FASA designation), are required to follow the *ASA Business Valuation Standards*, and therefore, USPAP by reference, in the conduct of appraisals subject to the Standards. For specific information on allowable departures from the Standards in specific assignments, see

AO-1 Financial Consultation and Advisory Services, which addresses the subject of Advisory Opinions.[49]

Why Standards Should Be Specified

The specification of the standards to be followed is an essential requirement for defining the appraisal mechanism for buy-sell agreements. If the standards are not specified, there is no requirement for individuals selected as appraisers who are not members of one of the national appraisal organizations to follow any set of standards or code of ethics.

The first three defining elements of valuation for buy-sell agreements are the standard of value, the level of value, and the "as of" date for the appraisal. These elements are a portion of the requirements for identifying or specifying an appraisal under USPAP Standards Rule 9-2, which are noted below in outline form (excluding comments):

a. Identify the client and other intended users;
b. Identify the intended use of the appraiser's opinions and conclusions;
c. Identify the standard (type) [that's our standard of value requirement] and definition of value and the premise of value [that's our level of value];
d. Identify the effective date of the appraisal [that's our "as of" date];
e. Identify the characteristics of the subject property that are relevant to the standard (type) and definition of value and intended use of the appraisal, including:
    i. The subject business enterprise or intangible asset, if applicable;
    ii. The interest in the business enterprise, equity, asset, or liability to be valued [again, this is forcing a specification of the level of value called for in the appraisal];
    iii. All buy-sell and option agreements, investment letter stock restrictions, restrictive corporate charter or partnership

49 *ASA Business Valuation Standards, AO-1, Financial Consultation and Advisory Services.* This Advisory Opinion can also be reviewed in Appendix D of this book.

agreement clauses, and similar features or factors that may have an influence on value;

iv. The extent to which the interest contains elements of ownership control [this is further defining the level of value called for in the appraisal]; and

v. The extent to which the interest is marketable and/or liquid;

Our purpose in naming the first three elements above, the standard of value, the level of value, and the "as of" date is to force specific consideration of these elements by and between the parties to buy-sell agreements. If they can then agree on the qualifications of appraisers and the appraisal standards to be followed, the rest of the specification should follow naturally.

A failure to follow generally accepted business valuation standards when conducting appraisals for purposes of buy-sell agreements can foster advocacy on the part persons selected to perform appraisals. Advocacy clearly undermines the buy-sell agreement appraisal process. Even if such persons maintain their independence throughout an appraisal process, as we have shown, there can easily be the *perception of advocacy* on the part of one or both parties, which also undermines the process.

Appraisers following USPAP are required to make a number of very important certifications in each written appraisal. The relevant portions of USPAP Standard 10-3 (excluding comments) is reprinted here:[50]

> Each written appraisal report for an interest in a business enterprise or intangible asset must contain a signed certification that is similar in content to the following form:
>
> I certify that, to the best of my knowledge and belief:
>
> - the statements of fact contained in this report are true and correct.
> - the reported analyses, opinions, and conclusions are limited only by the reported assumptions and limiting conditions and are my personal, impartial, and unbiased professional analyses, opinions, and conclusions.

50 *Uniform Standards of Professional Appraisal Practice,* Standards Rule 10-3, p. 78. Supra 12. See also Appendix C.

- I have no (or the specified) present or prospective interest in the property that is the subject of this report, and I have no (or the specified) personal interest with respect to the parties involved.
- I have no bias with respect to the property that is the subject of this report or to the parties involved with this assignment.
- my engagement in this assignment was not contingent upon developing or reporting predetermined results.
- my compensation for completing this assignment is not contingent upon the development or reporting of a predetermined value or direction in value that favors the cause of the client, the amount of the value opinion, the attainment of a stipulated result, or the occurrence of a subsequent event directly related to the intended use of this appraisal.
- my analyses, opinions, and conclusions were developed, and this report has been prepared, in conformity with the Uniform Standards of Professional Appraisal Practice.
- no one provided significant business and/or intangible asset appraisal assistance to the person signing this certification. (If there are exceptions, the name of each individual providing significant business and/or intangible asset appraisal assistance must be stated.)

Appraisal standards provide the "rules of the road" for appraisal processes. Note that if both appraisers selected as the first two appraisers in a multiple appraiser process are members of the American Society of Appraisers, both will be subject to following USPAP and the *ASA Business Valuation Standards.* However, regardless of the credentials of the selected appraisers, the parties can stipulate the specific standards that they desire for the appraisers to follow.

IRS Guidance Regarding Appraisal Requirements

As this book was being finalized, new guidance was published by the Internal Revenue Service on two important terms that have bearing to our discussion of standards.[51] The first is *qualified appraisal* and the second is *qualified appraiser*. The guidance from the IRS currently relates to non-cash charitable contributions, but if history is a guide, it may become generally applicable to all gift and estate tax valuations and valuators.

This guidance is particularly significant, since it marks the first time that the IRS has advanced the following of any particular valuation standards. In addition to providing guidance regarding the meaning of qualified appraisals and qualified appraisers, this statement states that a qualified appraisal will be one that follows recognized standards like the *Uniform Standards of Professional Appraisal Practice*.

For appraisals prepared for returns filed after August 17, 2006, the new guidance applies. First, *qualified appraisal* is defined:

> Section 170(f)(11)(E)(i) provides that the term "qualified appraisal" means an appraisal that is (1) treated as a qualified appraisal under regulations or other guidance prescribed by the Secretary, and (2) conducted by a qualified appraiser in accordance with generally accepted appraisal standards and any regulations or other guidance prescribed by the Secretary.

51 *Guidance Regarding Appraisal Requirements for Noncash Charitable Contributions Notice 2006-96.* The purpose of this temporary guidance is stated at the outset:

> This notice provides transitional guidance relating to the new definitions of "qualified appraisal" and "qualified appraiser" in § 170(f)(11) of the Internal Revenue Code, and new § 6695A of the Code regarding substantial or gross valuation misstatements, as added by § 1219 of the Pension Protection Act of 2006, Pub. L. No. 109-280, 120 Stat. 780 (2006) (the "PPA").
>
> The Service and the Treasury Department expect to issue regulations under § 170(f)(11). Until those regulations are effective, taxpayers may rely on this notice to comply with the new provisions added by § 1219 of the PPA.

Note that a qualified appraisal is to be conducted by a *qualified appraiser*, which is defined next:

> Section 170(f)(11)(E)(ii) provides that the term "qualified appraiser" means an individual who (1) has earned an appraisal designation from a recognized professional appraiser organization or has otherwise met minimum education and experience requirements set forth in regulations prescribed by the Secretary, (2) regularly performs appraisals for which the individual receives compensation, and (3) meets such other requirements as may be prescribed by the Secretary in regulations or other guidance.

The new guidance includes penalties in the event that there are "substantial or gross valuation misstatements."

> Section 1219 of the PPA also adds a new penalty provision. If the claimed value of property based on an appraisal results in a substantial or gross valuation misstatement under § 6662, a penalty is imposed by new § 6695A on any person who prepared the appraisal and who knew, or reasonably should have known, the appraisal would be used in connection with a return or claim for refund.

The guidance goes into more detail as to what constitutes a qualified appraisal, and that guidance seems relevant to our discussion of the selection of appraisers for buy-sell agreements.

> An appraisal will be treated as a qualified appraisal within the meaning of § 170(f)(11)(E) if the appraisal complies with all of the requirements of § 1.170A-13(c) of the existing regulations (except to the extent the regulations are inconsistent with § 170(f)(11)), *and is conducted by a qualified appraiser in accordance with generally accepted appraisal standards.* See sections 3.02(2) and 3.03 of this notice. [*emphasis added*]

The guidance then addresses the concept of generally accepted appraisal standards:

> An appraisal will be treated as having been conducted in accordance with generally accepted appraisal standards within the meaning of

> § 170(f)(11)(E)(i)(II) if, for example, *the appraisal is consistent with the substance and principles of the Uniform Standards of Professional Appraisal Practice ("USPAP")*, as developed by the Appraisal Standards Board of the Appraisal Foundation. Additional information is available at www.appraisalfoundation.org. [*emphasis added.* See also in Appendix C of this book]

The bottom line of this important guidance, which will be followed up with new regulations, is that the bar for what constitutes a qualified appraiser and a qualified appraisal has been elevated.

Conclusion

The first five elements of the appraisal for buy-sell agreements are highlighted below in one more repetition of the chart.

1. Standard of Value	4. Qualifications of Appraisers
2. Level of Value	5. Appraisal Standards
3. The "as of" Date	6. Funding Mechanisms

Once again, we quote from the Preamble to USPAP:

> The purpose of the *Uniform Standards of Professional Appraisal Practice* (USPAP) is to promote and maintain a high level of public trust in appraisal practice by establishing requirements for appraisers. It is essential that appraisers develop and communicate their analyses, opinions, and conclusions to intended users of services in a manner that is meaningful and not misleading.

The purpose of appraisal mechanisms in buy-sell agreements should be to specify an appraisal processes that that will provide *reasonable, consistent,* and *believable* valuation results. Remember, when buy-sell agreements are signed, no one knows who will be selling, i.e., who will die, retire, or have another significant change in life, and who will be buying. Many buy-sell agreements actually call for the company to purchase interests of selling shareholders. When this happens, the rest of the shareholders are, in effect, the buyers, since they benefit from pro rata increases in their ownership positions.

The appraisal process is critical to the operation of process buy-sell agreements and should be discussed thoughtfully and developed with care so that the parties understand what will happen when trigger events occur. When the business agreements are clearly understood, counsel can then translate them into effective legal language in the buy-sell agreements.

CHAPTER 21

Defining Element #6: Funding Mechanisms

Overview of Funding Mechanisms

A buy-sell agreement is no better than its funding mechanism, which is necessary to ensure its workability from the viewpoints of both future buyers and sellers.

1. Standard of Value	4. Qualifications of Appraisers
2. Level of Value	5. Appraisal Standards
3. The "as of" Date	**6. Funding Mechanisms**

Astute readers will recognize that this element is not actually necessary to define the engagement for valuation purposes and has nothing to do with appraisal standards or qualifications. What the funding mechanism does, however, is provide that the agreed upon value will first, be affordable to the company, and second, realizable by the selling shareholder. The funding mechanism, then, is an essential business element of buy-sell agreements.

There is a natural tension between the buyer and seller in buy-sell situations. This tension is illustrated in Figure 15.

BUYER - SELLER TENSIONS

	Buyer (Company)	Seller (Shareholder)
Price	Low	High
Terms	**Lenient** *Long Term* *Deferred Payments* *Low Interest Rate* *No Security*	**Cash Now** *or Short Term* *Rapid Payments* *High Interest Rate* *Full Security*

FIGURE 15

Sellers want the highest possible price and stringent terms. Buyers, on the other hand, desire the lowest possible price and the most lenient terms. It is necessary to bridge this tension in order to balance the interests of the buyer and seller(s) in possible future transactions. This is why a central theme of this book has been to reach agreement at the outset on as many aspects of future transactions as possible.

Many buy-sell agreements which are not funded by life insurance provide for payment over a term of years. We have seen payment terms as short as two or three years and as long as ten years. Other agreements call for lump sum payments, often funded by life insurance.

There are many funding structures for buy-sell agreements. The following list will provide an idea of the variety of possibilities and serve as a stimulus for discussion.

- *Life insurance.* Some agreements are funded, in whole or in part, by life insurance on the lives of the individual shareholders. Life insurance is a tidy solution for funding when it is available and affordable. However, it is important to think through the implications of life insurance.

  The proceeds of a life insurance policy owned by a company naturally flow to the company. A critical question immediately arises: should the insurance proceeds be added to the value (as a non-operating asset) before reaching a conclusion of value for the buy-sell agreement? Arguably, the life insurance proceeds could be considered as an asset to be included in the calculation of value for the deceased shareholder's shares. Arguably, as well, the life insurance proceeds could be considered as a separate asset for the purposes of the buy-sell agreement, and not included in the determination of value.

This is a subject that warrants discussion and agreement while all parties are alive. It is a difficult question to address when one party is dead. Absent specific instructions in the buy-sell agreement, the appraisers may have to decide. What they decide will almost certainly disappoint one or both sides. (See the further discussion below regarding the treatment of life insurance proceeds for valuation purposes.)

- *Cash.* There are several potential sources of cash for buy-sell redemptions of stock, including:

    - *Life insurance.* See the comment above.

    - *Corporate assets.* Depending on the size of the required redemption, there may be sufficient corporate assets, which may have been accumulated in excess of operating requirements over time to accomplish the purchase. However, these assets would have to be accumulated during the selling shareholder's ownership period(s) and would likely be included in the valuation.

    - *External Borrowings.* Depending on the financial condition and outlook for the company, it may be able to borrow sufficient funds to pay the purchase price.

- *Selling Shareholder Notes.* Some buy-sell agreements call for the company to issue a note for the amount of the required stock redemption. If this is the case, the terms of the note should be specified clearly in the agreement. Cash payments are usually preferable to sellers because their risk associated with the buying company is relieved. However, notes are often necessary in order to facilitate orderly transactions.

- *Combinations of Cash and Shareholder Notes.* Whether in the form of a down payment or as the first payment on an extended note, some agreements call for a portion of the purchase price to be paid at closing. Once again, it is easier to negotiate these terms at the outset than for either party to have to worry about the financing aspects following a trigger event.

Any time shareholder notes are used to finance a buy-sell repurchase, it is necessary to ensure that the transaction does not impair the capital of the business. In many states, state law prohibits corporations from engaging in transactions that could impair capital or raise questions of insolvency. Your legal counsel will have to advise you regarding this issue and ensure that the language of your agreement protects the company and selling shareholders to the extent necessary and appropriate.

There are a number of possible structures for notes (or cash down plus notes) that might be considered for buy-sell agreement redemptions. Figure 16 provides a starting point for discussion of this important issue.

Potential Areas for Agreement	Installment Notes	Equal Principal Amortization	Interest Only
Potential Terms	2 - 5 years or more	2 - 5 years or more	1 - 5 years
Down Payment	a. % lump sum possible b. First payment at closing c. Nothing at closing	Same	a. % lump sum possible b. Nothing at closing
Payment Schedule	a. Annual b. Quarterly c. Monthly	Same	Same
Principal Reduction	Amortizing	Equal periodic principal payments	None
Balloon	No	No	Yes
Rate	a. Fixed b. Floating c. Adjustable	Same	Same
Priority in capital structure	Must specify position in capital structure	Same	Same
Security	a. Name b. General creditor c. Unsecured	Same	Same
Right to Pre-Pay	Company usually desires	Same	Same
Events of Default/ Rights of Holder/ Ability of Company to Cure	a. Seller desires protection b. Company desires flexibility	Same	Same
Other Terms per Counsel	As recommended & agreed	Same	Same

FIGURE 16

Absent specific agreement on the funding mechanism, the value of a buy-sell agreement as a vehicle to repurchase shares from departed shareholders may be lessened significantly. Even with a stated funding mechanism, the economic, or present value of any redemption price set by the agreement can be significantly reduced because of excessive risk to be borne by the selling shareholder.

Everyone is familiar with the old saying, "You can name the price if I can name the terms." Weak terms in a funding mechanism diminish the value of the agreement from the viewpoint of future sellers. On the other hand, terms that are too strong can make it difficult for companies to perform in circumstances calling for substantial repurchases.

We hope it is clear by now that it is essential that you or your clients agree on funding mechanisms when creating buy-sell agreements.

Treatment of Life Insurance Proceeds in Valuation

The overview indicated that there are two opposing treatments of life insurance proceeds in valuations for purposes of buy-sell agreements.

- *Treatment 1 – Proceeds Are Not a Corporate Asset.* One treatment would not consider the life insurance proceeds as a corporate asset for valuation purposes. This treatment would recognize that life insurance was purchased on the lives of shareholders for the specific purpose of funding a buy-sell agreement. Under this treatment, life insurance proceeds, if considered as an asset in valuation, would be offset by the company's liability to fund the purchase of shares. Logically, under this treatment, the expense of life insurance premiums on a deceased shareholder would be added back into income as a non-recurring expense.

- *Treatment 2 – Proceeds Are a Corporate Asset.* Another treatment would consider the life insurance proceeds as a corporate asset for valuation purposes. In the valuation, the proceeds would be treated as a non-operating asset of the company. This asset, together with all other net assets of the business, would be available to fund the purchase of shares of a deceased shareholder. Again, under this treatment, the expense of life insurance premiums on a deceased shareholder would be added back into income as a non-recurring expense.

The choice of treatment of life insurance proceeds can have a significant, if not dramatic, effect on the resulting position of a company following the receipt of life insurance proceeds and the repurchase of shares of a deceased shareholder. The choice of treatment also has an impact on the resulting position of any remaining shareholders. Consider the following hypothetical example (which is not really so hypothetical since it was prompted by a real world experience):

- Harry and Sam own 50% interests of High Point Software, and have been partners for many years.

- The buy-sell agreement states that the company will purchase the shares of stock owned by either Harry or Sam in the event of the death of either. The agreement is silent with respect to the treatment of life insurance proceeds. The agreement calls for the company to be appraised by Mercer Capital (wishful thinking, perhaps, but this is our example).

- The company owns term life insurance policies on the lives of Harry and Sam in the amount of $6 million each. Assume for simplicity that there are no corporate income taxes due or that this figure is net of income taxes.

- Now assume that Harry is killed in an accident. Assume that the company is worth $10 million based on Mercer Capital's appraisal prior to consideration of the proceeds of term life insurance owned by the company on the lives of Harry and Sam, and that earnings have been normalized in the valuation to adjust for the expense of the term policies.

- Before finalizing our appraisal, we carefully review the buy-sell agreement for direction on the treatment of life insurance proceeds. It is silent on the issue. We call a meeting of Sam and the executor of Harry's estate to discuss the issue, because we know that the choice of treatment will make a significant difference to Harry's estate, the company, and to Sam personally as the remaining shareholder.

The valuation impact of each treatment is developed below in the context of the High Point Software example.

Treatment 1 – Proceeds Are Not a Corporate Asset

Figure 17 summarizes the pre- and post-life insurance values and positions for High Point Software, Harry's estate and Sam if life insurance proceeds *are not considered* as a corporate asset in valuation.[52]

PROCEEDS ARE NOT A CORPORATE ASSET

		Company	Harry (Estate)	Sam
1	Stock Ownership (Shares)	100.0	50.0	50.0
2	Stock Ownership (%)	100.0%	50.0%	50.0%
3	Pre and Post Life Insurance Value ($m)	**$10,000.0**	**$5,000.0**	**$5,000.0**
4	Life Insurance Proceeds	$6,000.0		
5	Repurchase Liability	($5,000.0)		
6	Post-Life-Insurance Value	**$11,000.0**		
7	Repurchase Stock	($5,000.0)	$5,000.0	
8	Retire / Give Up Stock	(50.0)	(50.0)	
9	Remaining Stock	50.0	0.0	50.0
10	New Stock Ownership (%)	100.0%	0.0%	100.0%
11	Post-Life Insurance Value of Co.	$11,000.0	$0.0	**$11,000.0**
12	Post Life Insurance Proceeds		**$5,000.0**	
13	Net Change in Value from Repurchase	**$1,000.0**		

FIGURE 17

On Line 3, we see that High Point Software is worth $10 million before consideration of life insurance, and both Harry and Sam have 50% of this value, or $5 million each. Upon Harry's death, the company receives $6 million of life insurance and recognizes the liability of $5 million to repurchase Harry's stock. The post-life insurance value is $11 million (Lines 4-6).

Lines 7-10 reflect the repurchase and retirement of Harry's shares. The remaining company value, after repurchasing Harry's shares for $5 million, is $11 million. Since Sam owns all 50 shares now outstanding, his post-transaction value is $11 million. Harry's estate has received the $5 million of life insurance proceeds from the sale of 50 shares for $5 million.

---

[52] Caveat: These examples assume no decrement to value due to the loss of a 50% partner.

Treatment 2 – Proceeds Are a Corporate Asset

Figure 18 summarizes the pre- and post-life insurance values and positions for High Point Software, Harry's estate and Sam if life insurance proceeds *are considered* as a corporate asset in valuation.

PROCEEDS ARE A CORPORATE ASSET

		Company	Harry (Estate)	Sam
1	Stock Ownership (Shares)	100.0	50.0	50.0
2	Stock Ownership (%)	100.0%	50.0%	50.0%
3	Pre-Life Insurance Value ($m)	**$10,000.0**	**$5,000.0**	**$5,000.0**
4	Life Insurance Proceeds ($m)	$6,000.0	$3,000.0	$3,000.0
5	Post-Life Insurance Value ($m)	$16,000.0	**$8,000.0**	$8,000.0
6	Repurchase Liability	($8,000.0)		
7	Post-Life-Insurance Value	**$8,000.0**		
8	Repurchase Stock	($8,000.0)	$8,000.0	
9	Retire / Give Up Stock	(50.0)	(50.0)	
10	Remaining Stock	50.0	0.0	50.0
11	New Stock Ownership (%)	100.0%	0.0%	100.0%
12	Post-Life Insurance Value of Co.	$8,000.0	$0.0	**$8,000.0**
13	Post Life Insurance Proceeds		**$8,000.0**	
14	Net Change in Value from Repurchase	**($2,000.0)**		

FIGURE 18

Line 3 shows the same pre-life insurance value of $10 million as in the treatment where life insurance is not a corporate asset. Now, however, the $6 million of proceeds is treated as a non-operating asset and is added to value, raising the post-life insurance value to $16 million, and the interests of Harry's estate and Sam to $8 million each (Lines 4-5). After recognizing the repurchase liability of Harry's shares ($8 million), the post-life insurance value of High Point Software is $8 million (Lines 6-7).

The shares are repurchased and new ownership positions are calculated on Lines 9-11. Harry's ownership goes to zero, and Sam's rises to 100% of the now 50 shares outstanding. This result is the same as above. However, Harry's estate receives $8 million as result of the purchase of his shares, rather than $5 million. Note that the company's value has been reduced from the pre-death value of $10 million to a post-death value of $8 million. The decrease in value is the result of Harry's value of $8 million, which is in excess of the life insurance proceeds of $6 million, suggesting that the company had to issue a note to Harry's estate for the remaining $2 million. So the company is in a more leveraged position as result of the buy-sell transaction than it was before. Sam, on the other hand, owns 100% of the remaining value, or $8 million, rather than $11 million in the prior treatment.

Further Discussion

It should be clear that the decision to treat life insurance as a corporate asset or not is an important one for all parties. Which treatment is the most "fair?" That depends on what the parties decide. Is it fair for Sam to end up with $11 million in value while Harry's estate only receives $5 million if life insurance is not a corporate asset? Sam and the company receive a windfall, but Harry's estate got precisely the amount that Harry would have received had he and Sam decided to sell the company prior to his death.

On the other hand, despite the increase in value to Sam when it is treated as a corporate asset, is it fair to saddle the company with repurchase debt at the moment of its greatest vulnerability, the death of one of its key owner-managers? The answers to these questions may not be immediately clear.

What is clear from this example, however, is that the issue of valuation treatment of life insurance proceeds is far too important not to be addressed in your buy-sell agreement.

TAKE AWAY THOUGHT

If you have a process agreement funded by life insurance, the amount to be paid for the stock is likely uncertain. Issues related to the treatment of life insurance have suddenly become more important. If you have such an agreement, we strongly urge you to review it promptly to be certain that valuation-related issues will not arise.

SECTION FIVE

WAR STORIES

CHAPTER 22

War Stories

This chapter is devoted to a number of "war stories" derived from our years of experience valuing buy-sell agreements. We have, of course, altered the specific facts of each situation to ensure confidentiality. Nevertheless, the stories reflect problems that can be avoided with your buy-sell agreement.

As we were drafting this chapter, Mercer Capital's analytical staff identified potential valuation issues in buy-sell agreements informed by our years of experience. Some of these issues we have seen in our client base and others we are waiting to see. The significant issues we identified in our limited, non-scientific sampling were surprising, to say the least. Some of the problems created uncertainty, others created delays, and still others generated significant dissatisfaction on the part of one or all the parties. Further, some resulted in litigation. Finally, some of the identified problems have not yet been fixed, and remain as ticking time bombs. This list, presented in Figure 19, is by no means complete but should be thought-provoking.

SIGNIFICANT BUY-SELL AGREEMENTS ISSUES

Buy-Sell agreements	**1**	New owners not added over time
	2	Applicable parties not defined
	3	Not specified if voluntary or mandatory
	4	Failure to update with changing circumstances
	5	Trigger events not defined
Fixed-price agreements	**6**	Failure to specify alternate mechanism if the formula is out-of-date
	7	Unrealistically high price set
	8	Unrealistically low price set
	9	Improper use of price for estate tax purposes
Formula agreements	**10**	Book value not clearly defined
	11	Litigation when formula not accepted
	12	Failure to update formula
	13	Failure to define "earnings" and adjustments
	14	"Management" of earnings to influence result
	15	Provision allows any party "unhappy" with formula result to select an appraiser, whose conclusion is binding on all parties
Multi-appraiser agreements	**16**	Shock and dismay at expense and time
	17	Appraisal timelines not specified
Standard of value	**18**	Not specified
Level of value	**19**	Not specified
	20	Confusion whether "fair market value" relates to interest or enterprise
The "as of" date	**21**	Not specified
Appraiser qualifications	**22**	Not specified
Appraisal standards	**23**	Not specified
Funding mechanism	**24**	Payment terms not specified
	25	Specification of interest rate unclear
	26	Failure to identify collateral or other protections
	27	No instructions for treatment of life insurance proceeds for valuation purposes

FIGURE 19

Fixed Price Leads to Over-Valuation

The board of directors of a services firm prepared an initial valuation and updated it annually for purposes of the buy-sell agreement. The genesis of the original valuation methodology was unclear. Examination of historical valuations indicated that they were prepared at the strategic control level of value, i.e., as the company would be if purchased by a strategic buyer at each valuation date.

Perhaps this high level of valuation was impressive on the personal financial statements of the shareholders, all of whom were relatively young at the time (under 55 or so). The shareholders, like many of us, probably never gave a serious thought to the fact that one of them might die.

A shareholder did die, quite unexpectedly, in a strange accident. His death invoked the shareholders' agreement, which called for his estate to be paid his pro rata share of the latest valuation. We were retained by the estate's representative to examine the buy-sell agreement and the latest valuations to determine if, in our opinion, the valuation was fair from a financial point of view. The representative wanted to be sure there were no lurking problems with under-valuation.

There were no under-valuation problems. We found that the valuation per the shareholders' agreement was significantly in excess of the true pro rata value of the company's equity. We opined that the mandatory sale by the estate to the company was fair to the estate.

Keep in mind that if you insist on having a fixed price buy-sell agreement, make sure that the value is reasonable – both to the selling shareholder(s) and to the company. Had this company retained Mercer Capital of another qualified appraisal firm to conduct an annual appraisal for purposes of the shareholders' agreement, the valuation issue would have come to light.

Equal Going In, Not Equal Going Out?

Many years ago, a group of individuals acquired 100% of the stock of a small company. Although the ownership of the business was not equal among them, there was no controlling shareholder and each individual put up his proportionate share of the original financing.

The shareholders entered into a buy-sell agreement which called for a valuation to be conducted following any trigger event. The agreement called for the selected appraiser to determine "the fair market value of the interest" owned by a deceased shareholder.

During the next ten years, the company grew and was profitable. As a result, the value per share increased about 800% over the period. At this point, a shareholder who owned about 25% of the stock died unexpectedly.

Mercer Capital was retained as the single appraiser to provide the valuation to be determinative of value. Early in the engagement, after reviewing a number of documents from the time of acquisition, we informed the company and the estate that there was a conflict between the language defining valuation in the buy-sell agreement and what appeared to be the intent of the parties:

- The buy-sell agreement called for the appraiser to determine "the fair market value of the interest." We were dealing with a 25% minority interest, which would have indicated that we should develop the valuation on a nonmarketable minority basis. This would have meant that we would have applied a marketability discount to a marketable minority level of value.

- Other documents from the acquisition period made it clear that the shareholders were "going into the deal equally, and would leave the deal equally."

The estate's representative was not pleased with this news. The company was surprised at the language in the buy-sell agreement, but felt some responsibility to abide by the document.

We requested, and the parties agreed, to adjust our assignment to provide opinions at both the marketable minority and the nonmarketable minority levels of value. Our valuation report provided these two opinions. We know that the matter settled without litigation, but not the actual price at which it did settle. Suffice it to say that a routine valuation matter turned into a very anxiety-provoking experience for the remaining shareholders and the beneficiaries of the deceased shareholder's estate.

It is always a good idea to have valuation-related language in a buy-sell agreement reviewed by a qualified business appraiser. Problems such as the misspecification of the level of value like in this example can thus be avoided.

Last Minute Buy-Sell Agreement

A shareholder of a company who was a non-resident alien for tax purposes and a company entered into an agreement to sell the shareholder's 20% interest to the company. The shareholder was not eligible to be a shareholder of an S corporation, and the other shareholders of the company desired to be taxed under Subchapter S of the Internal Revenue Service Code.

The decision to make the S election was made late in December that year, and a Stock Purchase Agreement was signed on December 31st. The agreement called for payment of a fixed dollar amount, to be adjusted according to an appraisal process. The company hired one appraiser and the shareholder, another. The Stock Purchase Agreement called for the two appraisers to attempt to agree on a value after they rendered their appraisals. In the event that they could not agree, they were to agree on a third appraiser. They did not agree on a value.

The Stock Purchase Agreement called for the conclusion of the third appraiser to be determinative of value for purposes of the transaction.

With some editing to disguise things, the relevant portion of the agreement read as follows:

> XYZ shall be valued as a going concern as of December 31, 19xx immediately prior to the shareholder redemption, without giving effect to any subsequent reorganization or structural change within the entity. "Going concern" shall be determined as the value of XYZ as an operating business (as distinct from the value of its assets to another company or individual). The appraisal shall at a minimum include consideration of the following: company background, industry and economic background, nature of business, evaluation of services, earnings history, stability and diversity of revenue base, comparable businesses, similar industry businesses, earning capacity, goodwill or intangible value, appropriate capitalization rate, liquidity discount on the total enterprise value (discount not to exceed 15%), interviews with company personnel, and potential acquisition premium (if any). There will be no minority discount considered in connection with the appraisal.

First of all, note that there is no mention of the term *fair market value* (or any other standard of value) in the paragraph. Furthermore, reading the language today, it seems fairly clear that the kind of value called for is a control value, perhaps even a strategic control value. There were two interpretations of this language in the reports of the two appraisers.

- *Nonmarketable minority level of value.* The appraiser retained by the company interpreted this language as defining the fair market value of the 20% interest. In so doing, he referred not only to the "words on the page," but also to some case law in the state in which the company was domiciled.

The conclusion presented in the appraiser's report was at the nonmarketable minority level of value. The appraisal began with a *marketable minority value* indication and then subtracted a significant *marketability discount* – never mind that the language stated that any "liquidity discount" on the total enterprise would not exceed 15%. The result was a nonmarketable minority conclusion of value. The report did not apply any minority interest discount, although such a discount was clearly implicit in the conclusion.

- *Strategic control level of value.* The appraiser retained by the shareholder interpreted the language to mean a *strategic control value* of the equity of the business applied pro rata to the 20% interest. The appraiser did not use the term strategic control level in the report, because, at the time, the distinction between financial control and strategic control was only beginning to be discussed in the appraisal literature. Nevertheless, his conclusion was at the strategic control level.

The two appraisals were obviously far apart. With such disparate conclusions with respect to the required level of value, the parties were unable to reach agreement as to value. They then engaged Mercer Capital.

The non-resident alien was, well, non-resident at the time, but the appraiser he retained did not hesitate to suggest that the appropriate level of value was obvious. Alternatively, the company's management made it clear that we were definitely dealing with a minority interest and that everyone knew that such interests were valued at less than pro rata enterprise value.

There were fewer than 140 words in the defining language. We wrote more than 1,500 words in analyzing the paragraph, examining four separate charts and tables related to the levels of value. The analysis consumed seven pages of text.

Our conclusion was to determine the *fair market value* of the 20% interest of the company at the *controlling interest level of value.*

Suffice it to say that our final conclusion was considerably higher than the nonmarketable minority value, and lower than the strategic value. Our conclusion, however, was binding on all parties, and the shareholder was paid that amount by the company.

Regardless of how tight the timeframe, always discuss the definition of value in buy-sell agreements with a qualified business appraiser. Had we been there at the outset, we would have pulled out the then-prevalent three-level level of value chart (see Chapter 17) and required that the parties agree on one of the levels on the chart.

Corporate Joint Venture Dissolution

Two companies in the same industry combined forces in a joint venture to capture distribution in a portion of the country where neither of them had physical locations. The venture was owned 50% each by the partners. The joint venture operated for a number of years, growing to nearly $100 million in sales. The joint venture called for the right of a party to put its stock to the other party in the event that the other was sold.

In accordance with the joint venture agreement, each party retained an appraiser. One company (the seller) hired an experienced business appraiser with significant appraisal qualifications and experience. The other (the buyer) retained an investment banker. The appraisers went through their procedures and issued reports.

- *Appraiser Retained by the Buyer.* The investment banker prepared a discounted cash flow analysis. Since the buying party was a significant supplier to the joint venture, the investment banker assumed that this source of supply would be denied to the company following the valuation date, and that sales would decline. His valuation conclusion was quite low as a result. Call it a 3 on a scale of 1 to 10.

- *Appraiser Retained by the Seller.* The business appraiser valued the business using, among other methods, a discounted cash flow method. He employed the most recent projections prepared by management of the joint venture in his appraisal. His valuation conclusion was substantially higher than that of the banker. Call it a 10 on a scale of 1 to 10.

The appraisal conclusions were far apart, and the appraisers could not reach a consensus conclusion. In accordance with the agreement, the two appraisers selected a third, which was Mercer Capital.

In the final analysis, we concluded that the agreement called for valuing the company as if the parties were attempting to market it jointly, with each attempting to maximize proceeds. There was ample evidence, both in the wording of the definition of value in the agreement and from related transactions involving the parties, that this was a reasonable assumption. Our conclusion was in between the two appraisals. Call it an 8 on a scale of 1 to 10.

The final buy-out price per the agreement was the average of the three appraisals. After some further debate between the parties, the matter was resolved at or very near the average price.

This was a case of the investment banker (industry expert) versus the qualified, independent appraiser. The appraiser valued the company higher than we did. But a significant portion of the difference was accounted for by information that became known after he rendered his report. There was some confusion regarding the valuation date in this assignment, which was simply too complicated for this short summary. The investment banker did not consider the *Uniform Standards of Professional Appraisal Practice* to be a matter for his concern. Had he been, he would have disclosed that he had rendered a hypothetical appraisal, by assuming substantive facts not present.

Be sure that your buy-sell agreement describes the qualifications and experience of the appraisers to be selected.

Ticking Time Bomb

A company's shareholders elected to be taxed as an S corporation. In connection with the S election, the shareholders signed a shareholder agreement to update the existing buy-sell agreement to provide that no shareholder would be able to break the S election through a transfer to a non-qualifying shareholder.

The agreement incorporated a right of first refusal which gave the corporation the right to purchase shares in the event that a shareholder received an offer to purchase shares from any non-shareholder. The agreement gave the company the right, and required that the shareholder(s) agree, to purchase the shares on the same terms and conditions and price in the third party offer. In addition, the company had the right to assign the purchase right to any qualifying (to be an S shareholder) person that it chose. Finally, the agreement required that any purchaser of the offered shares become subject to the same agreement. This type of ROFR (right of first refusal) is not unusual.

The agreement specified a number of circumstances, including the death of a shareholder, in which the buy-sell agreement would be invoked. At first blush, the pricing appeared to be a formula.

1. Calculate the book value of the company, as adjusted for earnings, distributions, taxes and a couple of other items (per the company's accountant).
2. Calculate a weighted average of earnings, which weighted average is to be multiplied by a fixed multiple.
3. The buy-sell price is the average of the two figures: adjusted book value and capitalized earnings.

That was fairly straightforward. The problem was that either the selling shareholder or the company could make another choice. There were other issues as well:

- *What is an independent appraiser?* Either party could elect to choose an "independent appraiser" to provide an appraisal. This appraiser must follow the non-specific guidelines in an "appraisal overview" described in the agreement in preparing any appraisal. The appraised value was then binding upon both the shareholder and the company, regardless of which party retained the appraiser. There were no further instructions to define the meaning of "independent appraiser."

- *Who gets to pick the appraiser?* There were no guidelines regarding which party could select an appraiser. Presumably, the first party to select an appraiser was the only party who could make such a selection. So it could be a race to see who could make the selection first. There was no provision for both parties to select appraisers. Suffice it to say, there was potential for confusion and disagreement regarding the selection of the appraiser.

- *What kind of value?* There was considerable confusion regarding the definition of value and regarding the appraisal standards to be followed. There was no requirement that the appraiser submit a fully-documented valuation report. In addition, there was no provision for the parties to see a draft report prior to the submission of the binding conclusion. The agreement did mention that a party could contest the conclusion of the appraiser, but there were no provisions to indicate how that process would work.

It would be easy to discuss other business and valuation problems that might eventually arise from this buy-sell agreement, but hopefully, we have discussed enough to indicate the magnitude of potential problems.

The parties to this buy-sell agreement would do well to engage in "audits" of their agreement from legal, business and valuation perspectives.

Terminated Expert Suffers from Self-Medicating

Mercer Capital was approached by a minority shareholder who was embroiled in litigation with the controlling ownership (his partners) of a business. Events had transpired that resulted in the minority shareholder's abrupt departure from company management. This triggered a buy-sell agreement put in place by all of the owners but which was primarily drafted by the minority shareholder upon his joining the business in a senior management capacity some years before.

The business was a distributorship with features similar to those of many dealers and franchisees that sell and/or provide an exclusive product or service in a designated territory. Many corporate managers of franchiser and/or manufacturing concerns find themselves eventually attracted to joining the ranks of their respective dealer/franchisee networks. One might expect that a seasoned corporate professional in such a circumstance would be well acquainted with the intricacies of the franchisee network and the financial underpinnings of the value of such a business. Such was presumed to be the case in this scenario. In fact, the expertise of the former corporate-turned-private owner inspired a highly detailed formula for determining value in the buy-sell agreement among the shareholders. After all, who should know better concerning the value of a franchise than someone who had formerly managed his company's franchise network and regularly addressed issues of ownership succession and transactions within the network?

The highly detailed formula price left little room for conflicting interpretations of value. Unfortunately, the formula was clearly biased to favor the buyer given the high performance of the company. The formula value limited the valuation to a consideration of tangible assets and ignored the goodwill value of the business. This was bitter medicine and highly ironic given that this in-the-know expert, out of a desire for protection from the very circumstance he was in, had boxed himself into a clearly lower value than might otherwise have been developed in an arms' length valuation process.

An audit of the buy-sell agreement and a first run on the valuation prescribed by the formula would have alerted the parties to modify the agreement.

Franchise Dealers / Wholesalers Unwind Estate Plans and Reconsolidate Ownership

We regularly see companies involved in various franchise, distribution, and wholesale activities. Some are multi-product line or multi-service line businesses but many companies are contractually married to a primary or sole corporate concern (manufacturer or franchiser) which has significant power over their business practices and ownership structures. Exclusivity of territory and/or brand affiliation often comes with relatively rigorous operational and ownership mandates and prohibitions. The manufacturer or franchiser is concerned that its product or service be represented and supported in a consistent fashion across geographical markets.

Wholesale/franchise agreements are often quite explicit concerning the requirements and limitations on the transfer of ownership interests relating to the distribution channel. Increasingly, manufacturers are pressuring their dealer networks (i.e., franchisees) to consolidate ownership to eliminate minority shareholders. This change runs contrary to many owners' needs and who are well down the road of spreading ownership to family.

Some of these owners are faced with redeeming or directly purchasing interests from family members that were gifted or sold not too long ago. When minority ownership is allowed, ownership by non-employees is increasingly discouraged. Requirements that business owners be directly and actively involved in day-to-day operations as well as own controlling stakes in their business are now almost the norm. In appeasement to corporate pressures, many such distributors are busy reconsolidating their ownership. The ability of a buy-sell agreement to properly define the valuation while simultaneously gaining the approval of corporate is critical.

In one assignment, we were asked to render a fair market value opinion at the nonmarketable minority interest level of value. The sellers were numerous family members, some inside the business and some as passive owners, who had come into their ownerships via a deliberate pattern of gift activity over multiple generations. The potential for a disconnect between the parties was very real despite relatively good relations. The valuations at which the sellers came into their interests was also based the nonmarketable minority interest level of value. It would seem to make sense that a valuation for the purchases should also be based on the same level of value. However, there was concern that the original intent of the historical ownership plan was to place equal value in the hands of numerous siblings. Some debated that the buyer would end up with control and thus enjoy the opportunity for higher value realization in a future sale or other activity than the sellers were being provided in the transaction. Perhaps so, but in the interim, the buyer would also bear the risk of financing a significant purchase.

After much consideration, in which we played an advisory role, the parties agreed to adopt the nonmarketable minority valuation as the deal price.

SECTION SIX

Action Items

CHAPTER 23

Buy-Sell Audits & Buy-Sell Audit Checklist

Audits are performed annually by certified public accountants for many thousands of companies each year. There are, in fact, expectations on the part of lenders, suppliers, customers, boards of directors and, perhaps, managements that companies will have an annual audit.

The concept of a financial audit is obviously well-known. We are introducing the parallel concept of the *Buy-Sell Audit* in this book.

> The purpose of the *Buy-Sell Audit* is to enable a business owner(s), with the assistance of accountants, attorneys, business consultants, and appraisers, as necessary and appropriate, to express the opinion that his company's buy-sell agreement(s) fairly reflect the wishes and desires of the owners subject to it, in accordance with good business practices and common sense. All the shareholders and the company itself rely on this "audit" in their personal and corporate planning.

Unlike a traditional audit performed by a CPA which is backward-looking, the *Buy-Sell Audit* is forward-looking and addresses questions like the following:

- Is there a reasonable probability that the agreement will operate to effectuate a reasonable transaction when trigger events occur?

- Are all shareholders who should be subject to the agreement parties to it?

- Do the shareholders who are parties to the agreement understand how the agreement will operate to determine prices and terms for future transactions?

- Has the agreement been reviewed by legal counsel to ensure compliance with applicable laws and statutes?

- Are the six defining elements of value as developed in this book clearly specified?

- Will the pricing mechanism provide a reasonable value if and when trigger events occur in the future?

- Is the funding mechanism in place and workable?

Because we are in uncharted territory with the *Buy-Sell Audit*, we recommend that you meet with your accountant, other shareholders, corporate attorney, corporate business consultant, and financial planner, if appropriate, to review the buy-sell agreement. This team will enable you to discuss the business and legal aspects of your agreement in detail.

In addition, you should obtain competent advice regarding valuation aspects of the agreement. The valuation expert should be able to identify issues related to the expected operation of the agreement from a valuation viewpoint and make suggestions to modify the text to correct identified issues.

Mercer Capital's Buy-Sell Audit Checklist

This checklist has been prepared to assist shareholders, corporate officers and their advisors in negotiating business and valuation issues relating to buy-sell agreements. The checklist is not a substitute for competent legal advice or for the advice of other professionals regarding taxation, estate planning, and other areas of shareholder or corporate concern.

ITEMS TO CONSIDER WHEN DRAFTING OR REVIEWING A BUY-SELL AGREEMENT	✓	COMMENTS
NATURE, SIZE AND OWNERSHIP OF ENTITY		
1. Parties to consider in discussions about the buy-sell agreement ▪ The company ▪ Employee shareholders ▪ Non-employee shareholders » Active » Passive ▪ Remaining shareholders who may not be subject to the agreement		
2. Is the entity an S corporation? [It may be appropriate to restrict stock ownership to eligible classes of shareholders.]		
3. Are there multiple classes of stock or ownership? ▪ Are all classes of ownership subject to the agreement? ▪ If the agreement is applicable to only a certain class or classes of stock, what is the impact on other classes of ownership?		

NATURE, SIZE AND OWNERSHIP OF ENTITY (Continued)	✓	

4. Are there two or only a few shareholders?
   - Should all shareholders be subject to the buy-sell agreement?
   - What happens or should happen if shares subject to the agreement are transferred?
     - » If within family units, are they required to remain subject to the buy-sell agreement?
     - » If not within family units, are they required to remain subject to the buy-sell agreement?

   [A cross-purchase agreement may be appropriate, where the shareholders can purchase life insurance to acquire the shares of deceased shareholders.

   If there are numerous shareholders, or if there are other reasons, it may be appropriate to have the company act as the purchaser for required buy-sell transactions.

   If the entity is of large value, even with a small number of shareholders, it may be appropriate to have the entity act as purchaser for required buy-sell transactions.]

5. Are there groups of shareholders where it is important to maintain relative ownership between groups?

   [Family groups may desire to have provisions to maintain relative family ownership, but to have freedom to transfer shares within the group.

   There may be a control group. It may be necessary to have provisions to ensure that this group maintains control in the event of buy-sell transactions.]

Mercer Capital's Buy-Sell Audit Checklist – This checklist has been prepared to assist shareholders, corporate officers and their advisors in negotiating business and valuation issues relating to buy-sell agreements. The checklist is not a substitute for competent legal advice or for the advice of other professionals regarding taxation, estate planning, and other areas of shareholder or corporate concern.

NATURE, SIZE AND OWNERSHIP OF ENTITY (Continued)	✓	
6. Are there older shareholders in the group of owners? [Life insurance may not be available. It may be necessary to allow for purchase of their shares with a term note and to have agreement for this up front. If there are older shareholders, they will likely retire or die relatively sooner. Consider provisions to account for these eventualities.] 7. Are there shareholders who will be employees and others who will be passive owners, even if on the board? ▪ What distinctions should be made between employee owners and passive owners in the buy-sell agreement? ▪ If a passive owner dies, should employee owners be allowed to purchase all or a portion of the shares directly, if they are capable? [If so, they can increase their relative ownership if this is desirable.] » Should the employee owner purchases be pro rata to all employee owners, or is it desirable to have one or more particular employee owners make the purchases? » Should the company assist with such transactions? » If employee owners cannot make the transactions, should passive shareholders have the option to purchase the shares before the company acquires them? » With such purchases, individually or cumulatively over time, should there be provisions to maintain control of the company in any particular fashion?		

NATURE, SIZE AND OWNERSHIP OF ENTITY (Continued)	✓	
8. Are there state laws that will impact the ability of the company to redeem shares? [If so, counsel will have to advise how to draft the agreement to ensure maximum flexibility for the company and minimum likelihood for problems with insolvency as result of operation of the buy-sell agreement. Counsel will also have to draft provisions to protect the company in the event that insolvency becomes an issue as result of buy-sell transactions.] 9. Are there restrictions under loan agreements that could be triggered by buy-sell transactions? [Such restrictions need to be anticipated, and provisions drafted to ensure compliance with the agreements and maximum flexibility to engage in buy-sell transactions. The lender(s) may have to approve these provisions in the buy-sell agreement.] 10. Will there be a right of first refusal agreement (ROFR), either as a separate agreement or to be incorporated as part of the buy-sell agreement? [ROFRs may be appropriate if there is a desire to ensure approval of any new/additional shareholders] ▪ What will be the terms of the ROFR agreement? Some considerations include: » Must there be a bona fide offer, in writing, from a buyer of proven financial capacity? [If so, the right of first refusal may provide the ability for the company to purchase the shares on the same terms and conditions as in the bona fide offer.]		

NATURE, SIZE AND OWNERSHIP OF ENTITY (Continued)	✓	
» When such an offer is presented to the company, how long will the company have to consider the offer? (30 days? 60 days? Longer?) » If the company does not purchase the shares, will the shares be offered to the remaining shareholders for their purchase? ◊ In any particular order of ownership? ◊ Pro rata to their ownership percentages? ◊ How long with the shareholders have to make their decision? (30 days? 60 days? Longer?) » If the shareholders do not purchase some or all of the offered shares, will the company have a "last look" to purchase the shares? ◊ If so, how long will the company have to make its decision? » If neither the company nor the shareholders purchase the offered shares, will the purchaser of the shares be required to become a party to the ROFR?		

TRIGGER EVENTS FOR CONSIDERATION	✓	
1. *Quits.* Is quitting employment a trigger event for employee shareholders? ▪ Will the agreement make a distinction between employee owners who quit to seek unrelated employment and those who quit and enter into competition with the company? ▪ Should there be a penalty in valuation for those who compete within a specified period of time? (3 months? 6 months? One year?) » Penalty in valuation if competition begins immediately? » Withholding of a portion of proceeds for the specified period of time? ▪ Should the terms of repurchase be more lenient for the company in the event that an employee shareholder quits? 2. *Fired.* Is being fired a trigger event for employee shareholders? ▪ Will the agreement make a distinction between employee owners who are terminated for cause relative to those terminated not for cause? ▪ Should there be a penalty in valuation for those who are terminated for cause? » What should be the magnitude of the penalty relative to the buy-sell agreement price? » If a percentage, should that percentage be impacted by the amount the employee owner has invested in his or her shares? » Should this percentage penalty vary with length of employment?		

TRIGGER EVENTS FOR CONSIDERATION (Continued)	✓	
▪ Should the terms of repurchase be made more lenient for the company in the event that an employee shareholder is terminated? » If for cause, how so? » If not for cause, how so? 3. *Retires*. Is retirement a trigger event for employee shareholders? ▪ Should the retiree be allowed to elect not to sell shares upon retirement, but otherwise remain subject to the agreement? ▪ Should retirement be a mandatory trigger event? 4. *Disabled*. Is disability a trigger event for employee shareholders? ▪ What is the definition of disability for purposes of the agreement (period of time unable to work)? ▪ Is disability of the employee-shareholder a mandatory trigger event? » Can the company, at its election, defer the purchase from a disabled shareholder? If so, for how long? » Can the shareholder elect to defer the purchase? If so, for how long?		

TRIGGER EVENTS FOR CONSIDERATION (Continued)	✓	
5. *Dies.* Is the death of a shareholder a trigger event for the buy-sell agreement? ▪ Is the buy-sell agreement price binding for estate tax purposes? ▪ Is the buy-sell agreement funded by life insurance on the life of all shareholders? Or key shareholders? 6. What other events should be trigger events for the buy-sell agreement? ▪ *Divorce.* If a party divorces and the value of his or her ownership is required to be split in order to settle the marital estate, should it be mandatory that the shares (or sufficient shares such that the party can retain ownership of the remainder) be repurchased by the company or other shareholder(s) in order to prevent ownership from being shifted to the ex-spouse? ▪ *Bankruptcy.* In the event of the personal bankruptcy or insolvency of an employee shareholder, should it be mandatory that the shares be repurchased by the company or other shareholder(s) in order to prevent ownership from being shifted as result of the settlement of the bankruptcy estate? ▪ Are there other events particular to this situation that should be considered as trigger events for the buy-sell agreement?		

FIXED PRICE AGREEMENTS

✓

1. Will the agreement be a fixed price agreement? If so, how will the price be set initially?
    - What will be the amount for the valuation of the company? or per share?
    - What process will be utilized to set the price?
2. How will the price be updated?
    - Will there be an agreement to update the price annually?
    - What process will be utilized to establish the new price each year?
3. What will happen in the event that the price is not updated for one or more years and then there is a trigger event?
    - Will there be a requirement that the price be updated to a current price? [strongly advised]
    - What are the steps in updating the price?
        - » Will the parties have an opportunity to agree on a current price? How long will that period last?
        - » What happens if the parties cannot reach agreement? Will the agreement provide for a valuation process to establish the new price?

          [If a valuation process is called for, see Section Three, "Process Buy-Sell Agreements," for things to consider in specifying the updating process.]

Mercer Capital's Buy-Sell Audit Checklist – This checklist has been prepared to assist shareholders, corporate officers and their advisors in negotiating business and valuation issues relating to buy-sell agreements. The checklist is not a substitute for competent legal advice or for the advice of other professionals regarding taxation, estate planning, and other areas of shareholder or corporate concern.

FORMULA AGREEMENTS	✓	
1. Will the agreement be a formula agreement? How will the formula be established? 2. Will all the terms be specifically defined? 3. Will the formula be specified algebraically? 4. Will all adjustments to financial performance indicators (income, expense, balance sheet) called for by the formula be specified? 5. Will a calculation of the formula be included as part of the agreement? 6. Will a recalculation of the formula be required each year? ▪ Who will perform the recalculation? ▪ Will the recalculation become the current price for purposes of the agreement? » What happens if the recalculation indicates problems, such as a valuation that is significantly different from prior calculations? » What if additional adjustments are required to the formula? » What if the formula result cannot be adjusted to reach a reasonable result? 7. Will there be a provision for an appraisal process in the event of disputes regarding the formula result if a trigger event occurs?		

Mercer Capital's Buy-Sell Audit Checklist – This checklist has been prepared to assist shareholders, corporate officers and their advisors in negotiating business and valuation issues relating to buy-sell agreements. The checklist is not a substitute for competent legal advice or for the advice of other professionals regarding taxation, estate planning, and other areas of shareholder or corporate concern.

DEFINING VALUE FOR PURPOSES OF PROCESS (APPRAISAL) AGREEMENTS	✓	
There are six defining elements that must be specified clearly if a process buy-sell agreement will work as expected. Each should be the subject of specific negotiation and agreement when a process buy-sell agreement is initiated or reviewed. 1. *Standard of Value.* What is the standard of value for the required appraisal to determine price? ▪ *Fair Market Value.* This standard is the most frequently used standard of value for buy-sell agreements. It is a "willing buyer, willing seller" standard of value. [If fair market value is the concluded standard of value, it is a good idea to either incorporate the precise definition into the agreement or to provide a specific reference to the desired definition in the agreement. For example: » Definition per Revenue Ruling 59-60 found at page ______ » Definition per *ASA Business Valuation Standards* found at page ____] ▪ *Fair Value.* This standard of value appears in numerous buy-sell agreements. When it is used without further definition, it can give rise to confusion. » Is *statutory fair value* in the state of incorporation of the company the desired standard of value? [If so, the agreement should specify the appropriate statute for reference. If the statute does not define fair value, consider the agreement referring future appraisers to then-current judicial interpretations of fair value in the state, and specify a law firm to interpret the meaning of fair value for appraiser(s) in a manner they can translate into operative valuation approaches and methods.		

DEFINING VALUE FOR PURPOSES OF PROCESS (APPRAISAL) AGREEMENTS (Cont.)	✓	
Consider specifying in the agreement that all appraisers providing appraisals pursuant to the agreement will use the same definition of fair value determined just above as the standard of value for their appraisals.] » Is accounting *fair value* is the desired standard of value? [If so, the agreement should specify the appropriate accounting rules or regulations that define the kind of value that is meant by fair value. Consider specifying in the agreement that all appraisers providing appraisals pursuant to the agreement will use the same rules and regulations as the basis for their determinations of statutory fair value.] ▪ *Investment Value.* This standard suggests a value to a unique buyer or type of buyer. » If the agreement specifies investment value as the appropriate standard of value: ◊ There should be a definition of what investment value means. ◊ The specific buyer or the specific type of buyer should be defined. ◊ Consider specifying in the agreement that all appraisers providing appraisals pursuant to the agreement will use the same definition of investment value and the same specified buyer(s) in their appraisals.		

DEFINING VALUE FOR PURPOSES OF PROCESS (APPRAISAL) AGREEMENTS (Cont.)	✓	
▪ *Going Concern Value*. Often, parties desire to specify that the valuation shall be of the company as a "going concern." Specifications like "going concern value" or "value of the company as a going concern" are not, however, adequate to specify a workable standard of value. [If it is the desire of the parties that the valuation be specified as a going concern value (as opposed to, for example, a liquidation value) this modifier should be included with another selected standard of value (see above). Note that the standard of value of fair market value of a business presumes that the business is a going concern unless the analyst determines that a liquidation value would yield a higher resulting valuation (see USPAP).] ▪ *Other Standards*. If some other standard of value than those above is selected, make certain that the standard is clearly defined and that all parties understand it. In addition, make certain that business appraisers are able to make a similar interpretation. 2. *Level of Value*. What will be the level of value specified for purposes of the appraisal? [This specification is particularly critical and relates to whether the buy-sell price will represent a pro rata share of the value of the enterprise, or the value of a particular, perhaps minority, interest of the enterprise. We suggest reading Chapter 17 before discussing this specification for your buy-sell agreement.]		

DEFINING VALUE FOR PURPOSES OF PROCESS (APPRAISAL) AGREEMENTS (Cont.)	✓	
▪ *Strategic Control.* Is the appropriate level of value for the agreement that of "strategic control?" [This level reflects the value of the enterprise considering strategic or synergistic benefits available to certain buyers, but not generally available to the company or to its shareholders. If this level of value is deemed appropriate, the agreement should probably specify that no discounts related to lack of marketability or lack of liquidity be considered by the appraisers. There is no market evidence of such discounts and such discounts are not considered by qualified buyers of companies.] ▪ *Financial Control / Marketable Minority.* Is the appropriate level that of "financial control," which is also considered synonymous with the "marketable minority" level of value? [This level of value reflects the value of the enterprise based on normalized earnings of the enterprise as it operates, with existing ownership and management. In other words, value at this level would not include the benefit of expected synergies for synergistic or strategic purchasers of the business. If this level of value is deemed appropriate, the agreement should probably specify that no discounts related to lack of marketability or lack of liquidity be considered by the appraisers. There is no market evidence of such discounts and such discounts are not considered by qualified buyers of companies.]		

DEFINING VALUE FOR PURPOSES OF PROCESS (APPRAISAL) AGREEMENTS (Cont.)	✓	

- *Nonmarketable Minority.* Is the appropriate level of value for the agreement that of "nonmarketable minority?"

  [This level of value reflects the value of a minority interest in the company, taking into account its lack of marketability.

  If this level of value is deemed appropriate, the agreement should specify that the appraiser(s) should consider minority interest and marketability discounts, to the extent appropriate in the valuation of the interest.]

- General Levels of Value Issues.

  [We recommend that buy-sell agreements specify the selected level of value. We also recommend that agreements reference a "levels of value" chart indicating the selected level of value, such as the chart below, reproduced for ease of reference. The agreement might also reference the text discussing the levels of value surrounding the chart.]

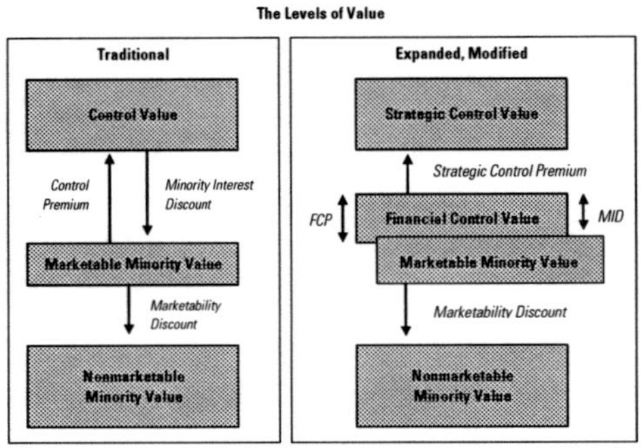

Mercer Capital's Buy-Sell Audit Checklist – This checklist has been prepared to assist shareholders, corporate officers and their advisors in negotiating business and valuation issues relating to buy-sell agreements. The checklist is not a substitute for competent legal advice or for the advice of other professionals regarding taxation, estate planning, and other areas of shareholder or corporate concern.

DEFINING VALUE FOR PURPOSES OF PROCESS (APPRAISAL) AGREEMENTS (Cont.)	✓	
3. *The "as of" Date.* [The "as of" or "effective date" is the date as of which available information pertaining to a valuation should be considered by appraisers. It should be specified. Values of companies change over time based on in such things as the national economy, interest rates or regulations, the industries in which the companies operate, regional or area economic activity, as well as changes within companies themselves. In the operation of process buy-sell agreements, it is necessary to fix the point in time at which appraisals are conducted and prices are determined. See Chapter 18.] Possible "as of" dates for consideration include: ▪ *The exact date of the trigger event.* » This may be the most understandable and agreeable date in many instances, but others may be considered appropriate by the parties. ▪ *Date determined by availability of financial statements.* » The date of the monthly financial statements immediately preceding the trigger event (which might be published after the trigger event). » The date of the quarterly financial statements immediately preceding the trigger event. » The date of the financial statements for the month during which the trigger event occurs. » The date of the quarterly financial statements for the quarter during which the trigger event occurs.		

DEFINING VALUE FOR PURPOSES OF PROCESS (APPRAISAL) AGREEMENTS (Cont.)	✓	
▪ *Date determined by the appraisal process.* » The date the initial appraiser(s) is (are) selected and hired. » The date that the appraisal report(s) is (are) submitted by the appraisers. Note that any subsequent appraiser(s) would have to use this same date. ▪ *Other date, as agreed upon by the parties.* 4. *Appraiser Qualifications.* Appraisers render appraisal opinions, but most appraisers work for appraisal firms. The issue of qualifications can, therefore, relate both to qualifications of firms and individual appraisers. ▪ Appraisal firms can be considered based on a number of criteria, including but not limited to: » Size » Longevity » Scope of business » "Convenience" factors ◊ *Location.* With today's transportation facilities and communications abilities, location may not be much more than a psychological factor for many appraisal processes.		

DEFINING VALUE FOR PURPOSES OF PROCESS (APPRAISAL) AGREEMENTS (Cont.)	✓	
◊ *Price.* Appraisal costs (prices) are not a subject for mention in buy-sell agreements; however, price is often a consideration in the selection of appraisers, even when it should not be. Keep in mind that cheaper is not necessarily the best factor on which to base a decision for products or professional services (less expensive, other things all being equal may be a factor, but not absolute cost alone). Alternatively, more expensive does not necessarily mean better. When looking for an appraisal firm, look for the best combination of quality of service, reputation, and price. ▪ Appraisers can be selected based on a number of objective criteria, including: » Education » Valuation training » Valuation experience » Industry experience » Continuing education » Publications » Credentials » Expert testimony experience » Compliance with professional standards » Public speaking on valuation issues » Other considerations relevant to the parties		

DEFINING VALUE FOR PURPOSES OF PROCESS (APPRAISAL) AGREEMENTS (Cont.) ✓

5. *Appraisal Standards.* The agreement should specify which appraisal standards should be followed by all appraisers providing appraisals pursuant to the buy-sell agreement.

   [It is critical that all appraisers follow the same, or at least similar, appraisal standards. It is even more critical that all appraisers attest in their reports that they have conducted their appraisals in accordance with applicable (to your agreement) business valuation standards. Chapter 20 discusses the *Uniform Standards of Professional Appraisal Practice* (USPAP) and the *ASA Business Valuation Standards* at some length and mentions other relevant business valuation standards.]

   - *Uniform Standards of Professional Appraisal Practice (USPAP).* USPAP Standards Rules 3, 9 and 10 are reproduced in Appendix C. SR 3 relates to appraisal reviews. SR 9 and SR 10 relate to the development and reporting, respectively, of business appraisals.

   - *ASA Business Valuation Standards.* These standards are required to be followed by all appraisers who are members of the American Society of Appraisers and are reproduced in Appendix D. In addition, members of the American Society of Appraisers are required to follow USPAP in their appraisals.

   - Other relevant business appraisal standards. See Chapter 20 for references to these standards.

DEFINING VALUE FOR PURPOSES OF PROCESS (APPRAISAL) AGREEMENTS (Cont.)	✓	
6. *Funding Mechanism.* As stated in Chapter 21, the funding mechanism is not generally necessary to define the valuation, but it is so important to the operation of buy-sell agreements that it is mentioned specifically in this "audit." [The primary funding mechanisms in buy-sell agreements are life insurance (in the event of the death of a shareholder), corporate assets, external borrowings, and selling shareholder notes. Combinations of the above are also possible.] Considerations related to the funding mechanism include the following: ▪ *Life insurance.* » Will the agreement be funded, in whole or in part, by life insurance? ◊ Will the insurance be whole life insurance or term insurance? ◊ What happens if one or more shareholders are uninsurable or not insurable at reasonable cost? » *Valuation issue.* Will life insurance proceeds (net of applicable corporate taxes) be considered by the appraisers as a corporate asset in their appraisals, or should it be considered to be a funding mechanism only, and not be additive to value)? [See Chapter 21 for a discussion of valuation issues related to life insurance.]		

DEFINING VALUE FOR PURPOSES OF PROCESS (APPRAISAL) AGREEMENTS (Cont.)	✓	
▪ *Corporate assets.* There may be sufficient corporate assets to fund particular required redemptions. » Should the available corporate assets be considered in the valuation as an excess asset and included in the valuation for purposes of the buy-sell agreement? » If there are not sufficient corporate assets to finance a repurchase, there may be sufficient assets to support external borrowings. ▪ *Selling shareholder notes.* Many agreements call for financing buy-sell agreement transactions through the issuance of corporate notes. [If this is the funding mechanism decided upon for an agreement, the following table provides an overview of considerations for inclusion in the agreement regarding the structure of shareholder notes. See Figure 16 in Chapter 21.]		

PROCESS BUY-SELL AGREEMENTS: MULTIPLE APPRAISER OPTIONS	✓	
Multiple appraiser agreements call for the selection of two or more appraisers to engage in a process that will develop one, two, or three appraisals whose conclusions form the basis for the prices. For more information on each multiple appraiser process, see Chapters 11 and 12. 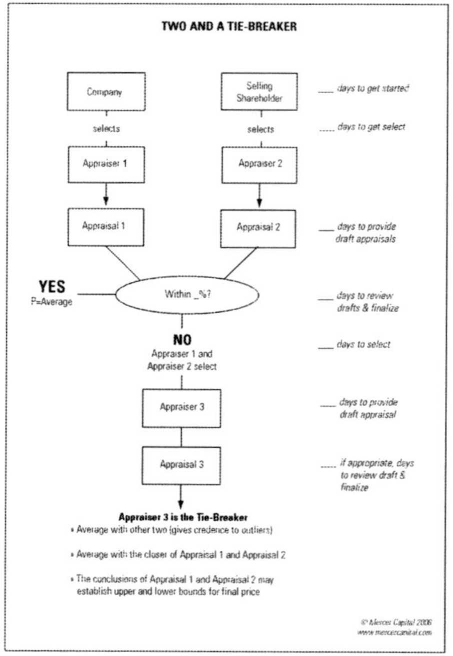		

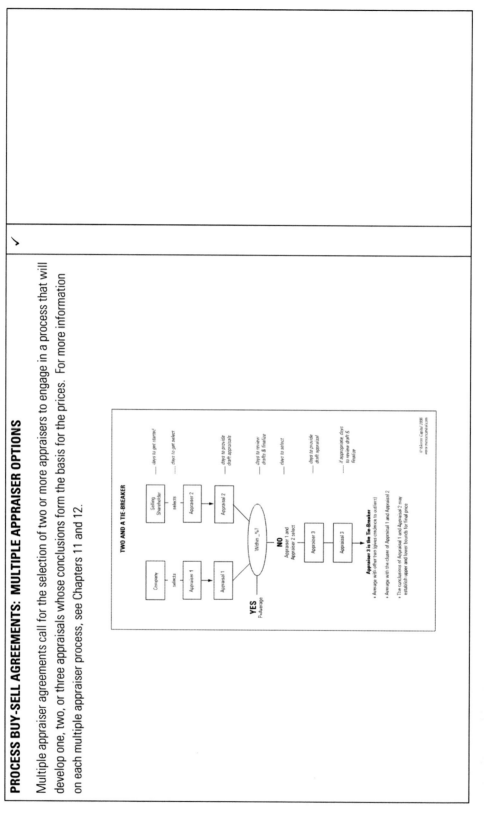

PROCESS BUY-SELL AGREEMENTS: MULTIPLE APPRAISER OPTIONS (Continued)

✓

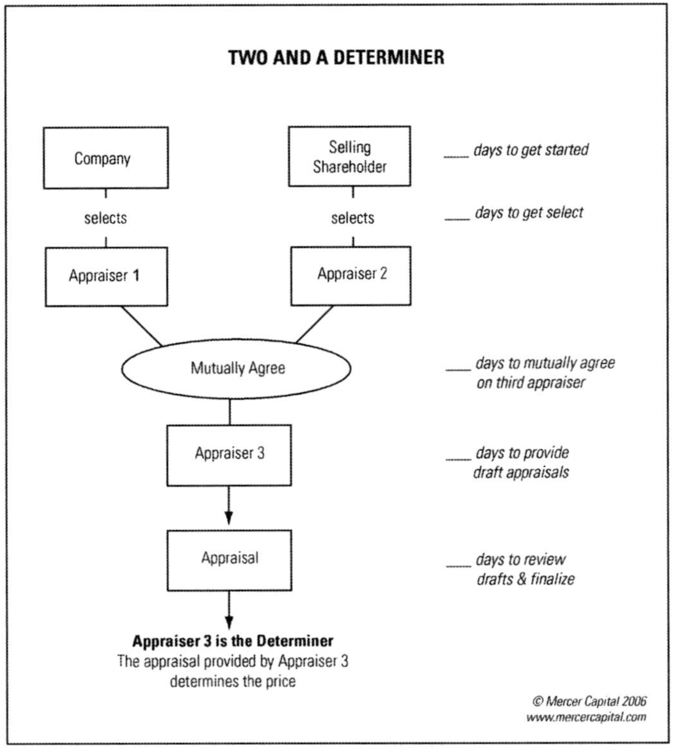

Mercer Capital's Buy-Sell Audit Checklist – This checklist has been prepared to assist shareholders, corporate officers and their advisors in negotiating business and valuation issues relating to buy-sell agreements. The checklist is not a substitute for competent legal advice or for the advice of other professionals regarding taxation, estate planning, and other areas of shareholder or corporate concern.

PROCESS BUY-SELL AGREEMENTS: MULTIPLE APPRAISER OPTIONS (Continued)

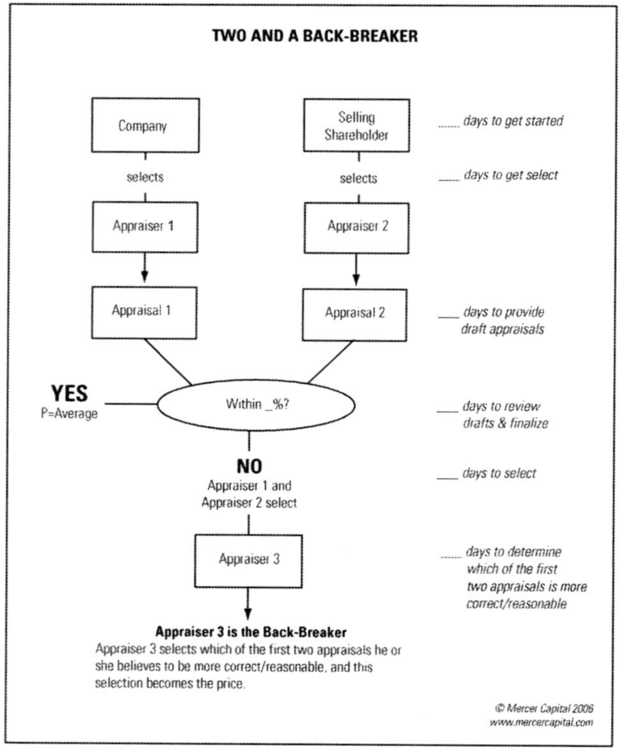

	✓	

Mercer Capital's Buy-Sell Audit Checklist – This checklist has been prepared to assist shareholders, corporate officers and their advisors in negotiating business and valuation issues relating to buy-sell agreements. The checklist is not a substitute for competent legal advice or for the advice of other professionals regarding taxation, estate planning, and other areas of shareholder or corporate concern.

PROCESS BUY-SELL AGREEMENTS: MULTIPLE APPRAISER OPTIONS (Continued)

✓

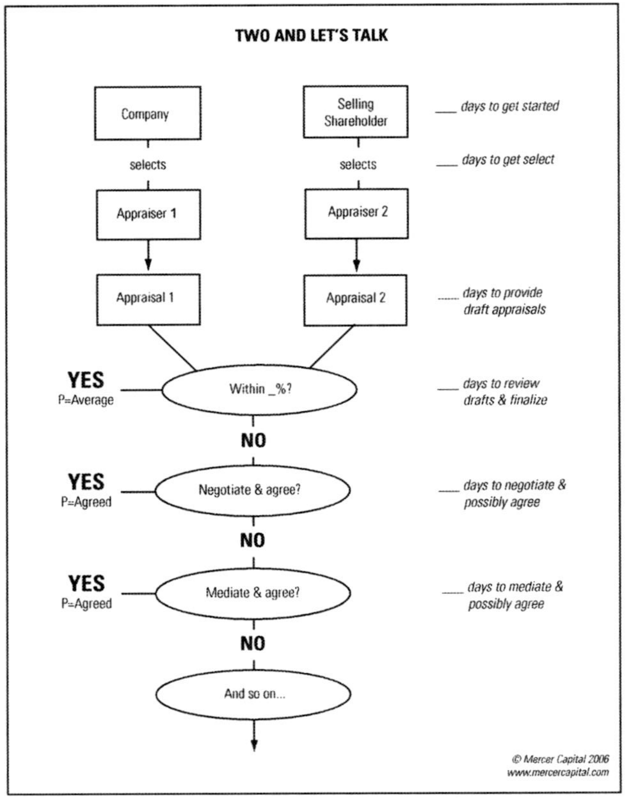

Mercer Capital's Buy-Sell Audit Checklist – This checklist has been prepared to assist shareholders, corporate officers and their advisors in negotiating business and valuation issues relating to buy-sell agreements. The checklist is not a substitute for competent legal advice or for the advice of other professionals regarding taxation, estate planning, and other areas of shareholder or corporate concern.

PROCESS BUY-SELL AGREEMENTS: SINGLE APPRAISER OPTIONS	✓	
Single appraiser agreements call for the selection of one appraiser who provides an appraisal for purposes of the agreement – the conclusion of which becomes the price. For more information, see Chapters 11 and 13. 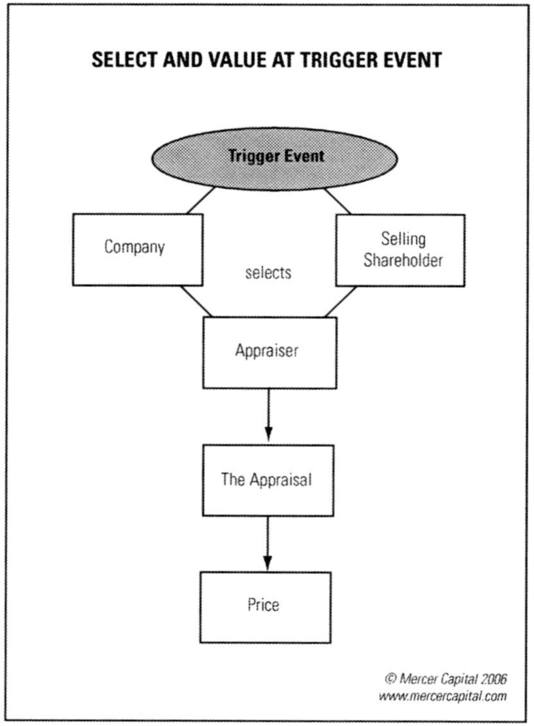		

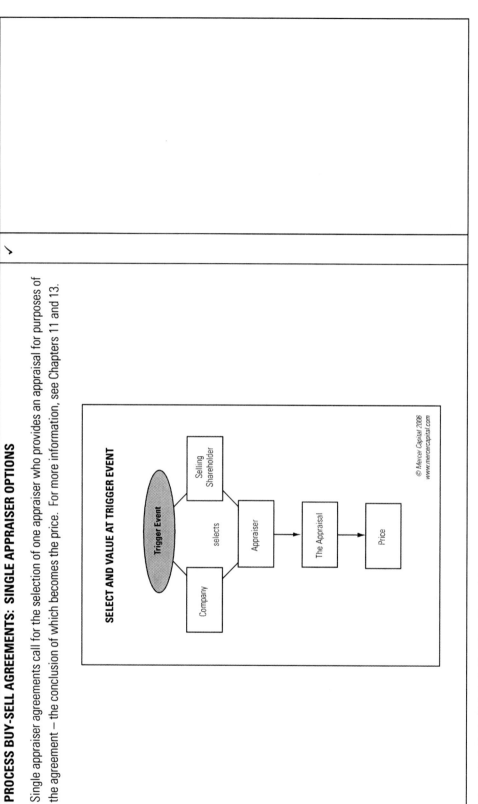

Mercer Capital's Buy-Sell Audit Checklist – This checklist has been prepared to assist shareholders, corporate officers and their advisors in negotiating business and valuation issues relating to buy-sell agreements. The checklist is not a substitute for competent legal advice or for the advice of other professionals regarding taxation, estate planning, and other areas of shareholder or corporate concern.

PROCESS BUY-SELL AGREEMENTS: SINGLE APPRAISER OPTIONS (Continued)	✓	
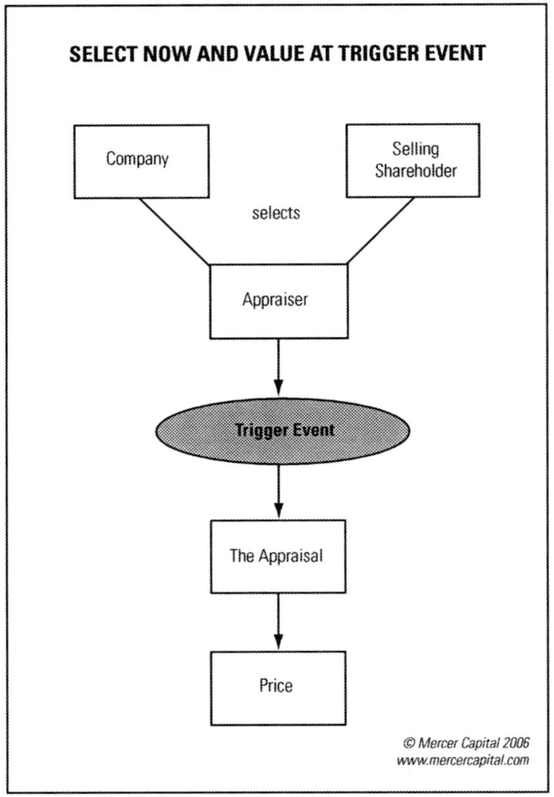		

Mercer Capital's Buy-Sell Audit Checklist – This checklist has been prepared to assist shareholders, corporate officers and their advisors in negotiating business and valuation issues relating to buy-sell agreements. The checklist is not a substitute for competent legal advice or for the advice of other professionals regarding taxation, estate planning, and other areas of shareholder or corporate concern.

PROCESS BUY-SELL AGREEMENTS: SINGLE APPRAISER OPTIONS (Continued)

✓

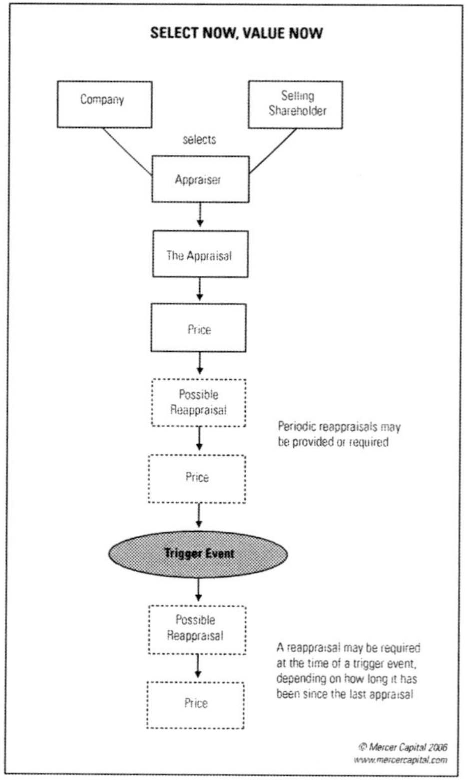

Mercer Capital's Buy-Sell Audit Checklist – This checklist has been prepared to assist shareholders, corporate officers and their advisors in negotiating business and valuation issues relating to buy-sell agreements. The checklist is not a substitute for competent legal advice or for the advice of other professionals regarding taxation, estate planning, and other areas of shareholder or corporate concern.

PROCESS BUY-SELL AGREEMENTS: SINGLE APPRAISER AGREEMENT WITH MULTIPLE APPRAISER OPTIONS – *APPRAISAL REVIEW*

✓

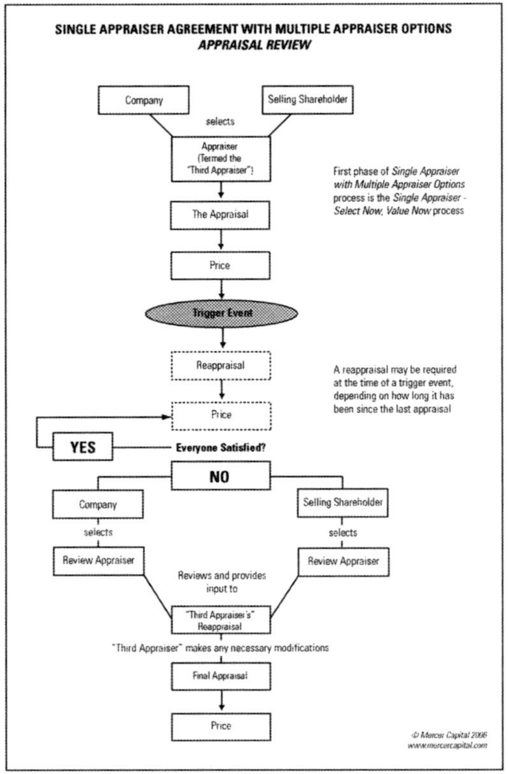

Mercer Capital's Buy-Sell Audit Checklist – This checklist has been prepared to assist shareholders, corporate officers and their advisors in negotiating business and valuation issues relating to buy-sell agreements. The checklist is not a substitute for competent legal advice or for the advice of other professionals regarding taxation, estate planning, and other areas of shareholder or corporate concern.

PROCESS BUY-SELL AGREEMENTS: SINGLE APPRAISER AGREEMENT WITH MULTIPLE APPRAISER OPTIONS – *ADDITIONAL APPRAISALS*

✓

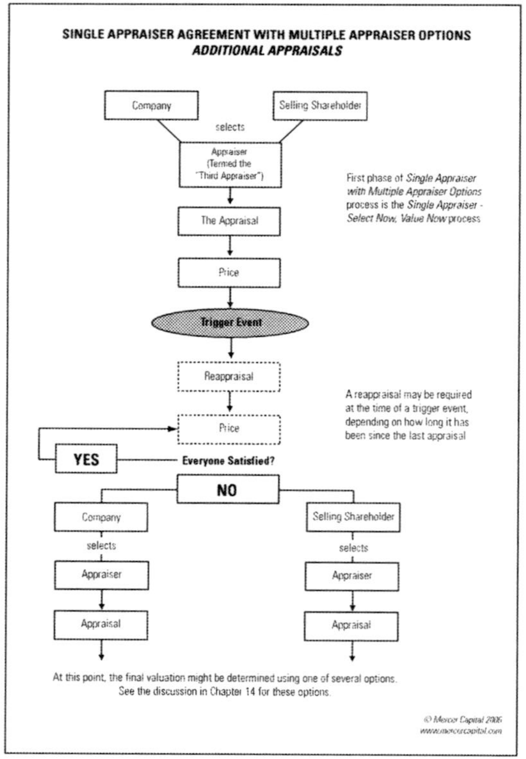

FINANCIAL STATEMENTS TO BE USED	✓	
Once the "as of" date for the appraisal is selected, the appraisers must decide which financial statements should be used in the appraisal. See the discussion in Chapter 15. 1. *Trailing 12-months ending the fiscal quarter-end immediately prior to the "as of" date.* [This choice is fairly common and necessary for companies that do not prepare monthly financial statements in the level of detail available for quarters.] 2. *Trailing 12-months ending the month-end immediately prior to the "as of" date.* [This can also be a good choice, if the quality of the monthly financials is good.] 3. *If the "as of" date is close to the fiscal year-end.* [It may be desirable to agree to use the year-end financial statements, either internally prepared or audited, if available. Waiting for the audit results can delay the valuation process, but the additional clarity and certainty provided by the year-end statements (adjusted for end-of-year adjustments) and/or the audit may offset the inconvenience.]		

PROCESS TIMETABLES	✓	
Each stage of the appraisal process takes time. Agreement on the basic timelines is a good idea. Note that one or more of the following stages may not be applicable to the process, whether multiple appraiser or single appraiser, that is agreed upon. 1. *Time to get started:* _____ days. [It is a good idea to allow some time to get an appraisal process underway. Depending on the trigger event, a relatively shorter or longer start-up may be indicated.] 2. *Time to select appraiser(s):* _____ days. [Particularly for shareholders who may never have been involved with an appraisal process, it can take considerable time to identify, talk with, and to select an appraiser. The company may have more experience, but it can still take time.] ▪ *Independence.* [In the event of a multiple appraiser process, it may be a good idea to preclude appraisers who have previously worked for the company, or at least, to require acceptance of such an appraiser by the side not selecting him or her.] 3. *Time to prepare appraisals:* _____ days. The major steps in an appraisal process are outlined below to help establish an appropriate timeline for your particular process: ▪ *Engagement letter phase.* [Once selected, the company (for a single appraiser process) or the company and the shareholder, will need to enter into engagement agreements with the appraiser(s).]		

PROCESS TIMETABLES (Continued)	✓	
▪ *Information gathering phase:* ______ days. [Each selected appraiser will provide an information checklist to the company. It will take some time for the company to respond to these requests.] » *Assurance of completeness.* [It is a good idea for the company to provide all information requested (by either or both appraisers) to both appraisers. It is important that all appraisers have access to the same information base. This rule applies to initial information requests as well as all subsequent questions raised by any appraiser.] ▪ *Due diligence visits:* ______ days. [The appraiser(s) will almost always visit the company. It is a good idea to schedule the visits simultaneously. By following this procedure, you will be assured that both appraisers hear the same information from the same representatives of management. There is the added benefit that neither side can use the visit as a reason for delay.] » *Discussions with shareholder or his representatives.* [In many cases, a selling shareholder will desire to have the opportunity to talk with the appraiser(s). Consider whether this is desirable for your particular agreement.] » *Subsequent questions.* [Quite often, appraisers have post-visit questions for management. You may specify that they e-mail a designated management representative with any questions. Management can then respond by e-mail to both appraisers. Note that this procedure keeps pressure on all parties to maintain the momentum of the process.]		

PROCESS TIMETABLES (Continued)	✓	
▪ *Initial Drafting phase:* ______ days. [It takes time for the appraiser(s) to draft their reports. 30 days from the date of the visit is a good target time for drafting. This would have to be extended, of course, if management were slow in responding to subsequent questions.] ▪ *Initial Draft review and finalization phase:* ______ days. [You may desire to allow some time, perhaps a week or two, for review of draft reports and for the appraisers to finalize their reports.] ▪ *Process completion check.* [If the two appraisals are within ___% of each other (you pick), then the price for the buy-sell agreement might be the average of the two appraisals. If the two conclusions are apart by more than ___% (you pick), the second phase of the process will begin.] ▪ *Specifying the base for calculating the desired percentage of difference.* [To avoid confusion, it is a good idea to specify one or the other of the two appraisals, perhaps the lower of the two, as the base to determine whether the percentage difference test is met.]		

PROCESS TIMETABLES (Continued)	✓	
4. *Time to select the third appraiser:* _____ days. [It will take some time for the first two appraisers to identify and agree upon the selection of the third appraiser.] ▪ *Specify what happens if the first two appraisers cannot agree on the third appraiser.* [If agreement cannot be reached, there has to be a mechanism for resolving the selection. One possibility would be to name a specific person or institution (like a bank trust department) in the agreement that would, in this event, be called upon to name the third appraiser. An arbitrator could also be selected at this point for the sole purpose of identifying and naming the third (neutral) appraiser.] ▪ *Specify whether the third appraiser will have access to the appraisal reports prepared by the first two appraisers as well as to the appraisers themselves* (preferably together). 5. *Time to prepare the third appraisal:* _____ days. [The third appraiser must go through his processes, including data gathering, visiting with management, and drafting the report.] ▪ The agreement should specify whether the third appraiser is to provide a draft report for review by the parties or whether the report should be issued in final form, without review by the parties.		

PROCESS TIMETABLES (Continued)	✓	
▪ The third appraisal should at this point be definitive of value, depending on the agreement of the parties: » Average of the third appraisal with the closest of the first two appraisals, or » Average of the third appraisal with both of the first two appraisals, or » Setting the first two appraisals as the upper and lower bound for the final price, or » The third appraisal's conclusion determines the price, or » Other, as the parties agree.		

WHO BEARS THE COST OF THE APPRAISAL(S)?	✓	
1. *Company pays for appraisals.* [The parties can agree that the company will pay for the cost of all appraisals in the process.] ▪ *Agreed upon budgets.* [The company and the selling shareholder should have similar budgets for the appraisal process.] 2. *Parties pay their own respective appraisal costs.* [Some agreements call for the company to retain and pay for its appraiser and for the selling shareholder to retain and pay for its appraiser. If a third appraisal is required, those agreements often call for its cost to be shared by the parties. For reasons discussed in Chapter 15, this may not be reasonable for selling shareholders, particularly those with relatively small (in dollar value) positions.] ▪ *Transaction costs.* [When the company is ultimately sold, there will be transaction costs, including some or all of the following: legal fees, accounting fees, consulting fees, and investment banking or brokerage fees.] ▪ *Transaction fee.* [The parties could agree on a transaction fee of ____% of the value based on the conclusion of the appraisal process for the interest under consideration. This would represent a transaction fee that places all shareholders who sell on the same fee-adjusted basis.] ▪ *Legal fees.* [The agreement should specify who pays legal or other professional fees in the event that there is litigation during the appraisal process.]		

WHO BEARS THE COST OF THE APPRAISAL(S)? (Continued)	✓	
3. *What rights does the triggering of the buy-sell agreement create?* [When the buy-sell agreement is triggered, an appraisal process is set into motion (for process agreements). Many buy-sell agreements consider that the selling shareholder owns stock until it is purchased. It is possible for the shares to be converted into a right to receive the value determined by the appraisal process.] ▪ *Continuing ownership interest.* [There are a number of potential issues for consideration if the shares represent a continuing interest in the company.] ▪ *Interest.* [The parties should agree on whether the value of the shares will bear interest from the trigger date until the price is determined. If interest is to be paid, the interest rate should be determined or defined in relationship to a known index rate.] ▪ *Vote.* Are the shares entitled to vote following the trigger event, but prior to their purchase? ▪ *Dividends of distributions.* Is the company bound to maintain its historical distribution policies between the trigger date and final resolution? ▪ *Tax pass-through payments.* Is the company required to make an additional payment upon purchase of the shares to account for the shares' pro rata portion of applicable state and federal income taxes accruing from the trigger event until the purchase?		

Mercer Capital's Buy-Sell Audit Checklist – This checklist has been prepared to assist shareholders, corporate officers and their advisors in negotiating business and valuation issues relating to buy-sell agreements. The checklist is not a substitute for competent legal advice or for the advice of other professionals regarding taxation, estate planning, and other areas of shareholder or corporate concern.

WHO BEARS THE COST OF THE APPRAISAL(S)? (Continued)	✓	
▪ *Right to receive value as of the "as of" date.* [If the shares turn into a right to receive value, the shareholder would, in effect, cease to be a shareholder upon the occurrence of a trigger event. This would be analogous to the rights of a dissenting shareholder who perfects the right to dissent to a corporate transaction giving rise to the right to dissent.] » *Interest.* [If the shares convert to a right to receive value, interest should, in all likelihood, be paid between the "as of" date and the end of the appraisal process. If interest is to be paid, the interest rate should be determined or defined in relationship to a known index rate.]		

TAX PASS-THROUGH ENTITY APPRAISAL ISSUES	✓	
There are a number of issues related to the treatment of S corporations in the valuation process. Many appraisers consider S corporations and other tax pass-through entities to be C corporation equivalent in value *at the enterprise level of equity.* Others believe that it is appropriate to consider a "premium" in value related to the "additional value" of an S corporation relative to a C corporation. 1. *Have an appraiser explain the various positions to you.* [If all the parties are not familiar with the various arguments related to S corporation valuation, have a qualified appraiser explain the differences to you.] 2. *State the preferred valuation method for the agreement.* [Based on the appraiser's explanations, the parties should decide, for purposes of the agreement, how the issue of S corporation status (or other pass-through entity) should be treated for purposes of valuation.] ▪ *As-if-C corporation.* [The tax pass-through entity is to be valued as if it were a C corporation at the enterprise level (whether marketable minority, financial control, or strategic control is the desired level of value).] ▪ *S corporation benefits.* [The tax pass-through entity is to be valued in such a way to provide a valuation premium for the future benefit of expected total tax savings from being a tax pass-through entity.]		

CHAPTER 24

The One-Percent Solution

What is the solution to funding buy-sell agreements and financing the expenditures necessary to manage the wealth tied up in closely held businesses? The solution is so obvious that we mostly overlook it, thinking that such activities either are too expensive, too time-consuming, or worse, are not even a high priority. For owners of closely held businesses, the solution lies in the decision to treat their ownership interests as an investment. We term this *The One Percent Solution.*

Let us ask a few important questions about current American investing habits:

- *What do the very wealthy in America do with their money?* The very wealthy quite often establish what are called "family offices" through which investments are handled and a variety of personal or family planning activities are administered. By and large, these family offices hire staffs responsible to the family for distributing their assets among a variety of investment funds and strategies, seeking diversification, satisfactory (or superior) returns, and reduction in volatility, or risk. The very wealthy place their assets across a variety of investment classes, ranging from Treasuries, to fixed income securities, to market portfolios bearing numerous names representing their "strategies," to private equity funds, and even to hedge funds. And then, there are investments in land, timber and developed real estate, either through REITs or more directly, through proprietary funds, and even direct investments. In addition, the very wealthy are continually investigating tax-efficient ways in which to preserve their wealth and to pass it to subsequent generations, or, increasingly, to give it away (like Bill and Melinda Gates, Warren Buffet, and many others).

- *What do the merely wealthy in America do with their money?* In many respects, the merely wealthy do the same thing as the very wealthy, except they may outsource the investment decisions to a trust department of a bank or to a variety of investment managers. Quite often, the merely wealthy will spend considerable time and money seeking tax and legal advice to accomplish their objectives of intergenerational wealth transfers as well as their charitable objectives.

- *What do the affluent in America do with their money?* Most affluent Americans place all, or at least large portions of their liquid assets, into a variety of mutual funds, or place their assets with other investment intermediaries who, in turn, place collective assets into some of the same funds used by the very wealthy.

- *What do the rest of Americans do with their money?* Many Americans who may have virtually no liquid assets nevertheless have assets invested on their behalf through their retirement plans at work. The fiduciaries of these plans, who deal with growing pools of assets over time, are charged with the duty to invest our retirement funds, and they do so through the same vehicles as do the very wealthy or merely wealthy.

What do all of these investments, by the very wealthy, the merely wealthy, the affluent, and the rest of us in America, have in common? The common denominator of the investing habits of most Americans is that our assets are treated like investments, and they are placed in the custody of capable investment managers who handle the direct investment activities and periodic changes to our portfolios. In other words, there are structures in place to facilitate decisions regarding asset allocation, diversification, risk profiles, return monitoring, and also, wealth preservation and transfer activities.

Now, let's ask another important question. *What do many business owners do to manage the wealth tied up in their closely held business?* For many business owners, the answer to the last questions is "not much."

A Top Ten list of questions to ask yourself to determine if you are treating your business as an important investment is included at the end of this chapter for your information.

The eleventh question is a bonus added here: How can anyone answer the first ten questions or get others to help answer them? The answer lies in making one simple decision – to treat your investments in closely held businesses as the important investments they are. We pay significant fees to the people who manage our wealth. We do so because we treat our wealth as an investment.

The One Percent Solution is based on the premise that owners of closely held businesses should treat their ownership interests just the same way – as important *investments.*

The One Percent Solution in Action

The One Percent Solution suggests allocating a *percentage of value* for the illiquid assets *under management* to provide the budget necessary to manage wealth. If the wealth were liquid wealth, that budget would be one percent of assets under management, plus or minus, depending on the asset category of investment. For illiquid wealth, we suggest a budget for investment management of one to two percent of value for businesses with values of $20 million or less, as indicated in the following table. The management fee can scale down in percentage terms as business value increases.

The One Percent Solution for Managing Wealth in Closely Held Businesses					
Assumed Pre-Tax Income ($m)	**Assumed Valuation Multiple**	**Estimated Value of Business ($m)**	**Management Fee as % of Value**	**Budget for Investment Management ($m)**	**Management Fee as % of Earnings**
$1,250	4.0	$5,000	2.00%	$100	8.0%
$2,222	4.5	$9,999	1.50%	$150	6.8%
$4,000	**5.0**	**$20,000**	**1.00%**	**$200**	**5.0%**
$8,333	6.0	$49,998	0.75%	$375	4.5%
$14,286	7.0	$100,002	0.50%	$500	3.5%
$62,500	8.0	$500,000	0.25%	$1,250	2.0%

Assume a private business is worth $20 million, as highlighted above. *The One Percent Solution* would suggest a budget of *one percent of value*, or $200 thousand *per year* to be dedicated to managing that block of illiquid wealth. This $200 thousand investment management budget amounts to 5% of pre-tax earnings in the example. What would that budget be spent on? There are a number of possibilities:

- *Annual appraisals.* Liquid assets are valued every day, and portfolio performance reports are made at least quarterly for most portfolios. Annual appraisal is the best way of tracking investment performance over time, and for reporting to shareholders about a company's return performance relative to itself and to other asset categories.

- *Buy-sell agreements.* Annual appraisals can establish the value for buy-sell agreements. The investment management budget would include the expense of an annual review of the buy-sell agreement by legal counsel and business advisors.

- *Life insurance funding.* The budget could certainly include the cost of life insurance purchased on the lives of key shareholders to fund buy-sell agreements. The annual appraisal can establish the amount of life insurance needed, and be a prompt for necessary adjustments to the amounts purchased as value changes over time.

- *Estate planning.* Tax counsel could be retained to provide ongoing advice regarding estate planning issues for shareholders. The annual appraisal, if it includes a valuation conclusion at the nonmarketable minority basis, can be used by the shareholders in their personal estate planning.

- *Financial planning.* Key owners and shareholders could retain personal financial advisors to assist with their personal financial planning. The annual appraisal will assist financial planners in advising with respect to asset allocation decisions for non-business assets.

- *Audited financial statements.* While an audit might be considered a normal business expense, many private companies do not obtain an annual audit. It is a fact that having audited financial statements enhances the marketability of companies, so part of investment management expenses could include the annual audit – or at least make it easier to make the decision to obtain an audit.

- *Annual legal review.* It is often helpful to have legal counsel review a company's board of directors' minutes and other legal documents and contracts on a periodic basis. This practice helps to identify and eliminate issues that, left alone, can create potential problems in the future.

- *Other "make-ready" projects.* Most businesses can be sold – at some price. Businesses that are "ready for sale," however, tend to sell more readily and for better prices. They are more attractive to larger pools of potential buyers, and their sales processes are less frequently caught in snags from surprises with inventories, accounts receivable, fixed assets, information shortfalls, and the like. If there are known issues at a company, it can be helpful to consider funding their correction with the investment management budget.

There's No Such Thing as a Free Lunch

While there is no such thing as a free lunch, the investment management budget for closely held firms may be at least partially free. Any dollar spent is certainly not available for distribution or reinvestment, so investment management expenses are definitely not free. However, dollars spent on annual appraisals, life insurance policies, estate planning, financial planning, and even some one-time consulting projects are often added back to earnings by buyers in their normalizing processes. We would certainly add them back when preparing a company for sale.

While the dollars spent on investment management activities do reflect real expenses, they may be capitalizable at the time of the ultimate sale of a business, and are therefore partially "free."

Conclusion

The One Percent Solution reflects a conscious way of thinking about the wealth held in closely held businesses as an *investment*. It then provides a conceptual way to create a budget for investment management activities and expenses related to the *investment nature* of ownership in a business.

DO YOU TREAT YOUR BUSINESS AS AN INVESTMENT? TOP TEN QUESTIONS

1. How much is your company worth? Has it been appraised in the last three years?
2. What has been your shareholders' rate of return on their investment over the last one, two, three, four, or five years or more? How does this rate of return performance compare with other alternative investments?
3. What portion of your net worth is tied up in your business ownership interest?
4. Is your wealth adequately diversified to avoid the risk of major loss from adverse events with any of your assets, including your business?
5. Does your business make distributions in excess of those necessary to pay taxes? If not, is the return on your reinvestment of earnings into fixed assets or working capital sufficient to warrant the investments?
6. Are you reinvesting distributions in assets in a plan to diversify your wealth? If not, why not?
7. What is the plan to obtain liquidity from your ownership of your business? And for your other shareholders, if any, to obtain liquidity from their investments? Is this plan realistic? Is it documented? And is it workable in the event something adverse happens to you or to another key owner/manager?
8. Is your business "ready for sale?" In other words, not that you want to sell it today, but should you make that decision, is the business positioned to be attractive to a range of prospective purchasers?
9. Are there things you know that need to done and that take time to begin to get the business in a position to be "ready for sale?"
10. What is the plan to transfer ownership and/or management to other members of your family? Is this plan realistic? Is it documented?

Bonus Question: How can anyone answer the first ten questions or get others to help answer them?

Bonus Answer. ***The One Percent Solution***

APPENDICES

APPENDIX A

The "Valuation Professional" vs. the "Industry Expert"

One of the most frequent issues addressed when talking with attorneys, accountants and business owners relates to the valuation expertise that may be appropriate for specific business appraisal requirements. The basic question often boils down to: Should we hire an *industry expert* for this engagement, or is it preferable to hire a *valuation professional*? The question is certainly an important one for current assignments. It is equally important when deciding upon the selection of appraisers in a buy-sell agreement.

An Example of the Wrong Decision?

Let us relate a composite story. An attorney called who had been retained in a matter involving a significant dispute with the Internal Revenue Service. An appraisal had been rendered for the client by an investment banking firm. At this point, the ox was in the ditch and the attorney was looking for valuation assistance.

She noted that in arriving at the report's conclusion, several valuation methods had been used, including the guideline company method using similar publicly traded companies, the discounted cash flow method, and a "mergers and acquisitions" method, which capitalized a company's earnings using comparative change of control transactions.

The attorney asked what "level of value" the valuation reflected. Since a) the guideline company method is a *marketable minority interest method*; and b) the discounted cash flow is likely a *marketable minority interest method* or can be a *controlling interest method* depending upon how it was applied; and c) the "mergers and acquisitions" method was definitely a *controlling interest method,* it was entirely unclear whether the valuation reflected a marketable minority interest method or a controlling interest method.

Upon further discussion, we learned that the appraisal had been used as the basis for a charitable gift of a significant *nonmarketable minority interest* of a privately owned company.

Why was the investment banking firm retained to value this company? Because one of its bankers was well known in the company's industry. In fact, he had been selected over two well-qualified business appraisal experts who had some knowledge of the specific industry, but who could not claim industry expertise.

What's wrong with this story? The investment banker, who was an industry specialist, provided a valuation of the company, but not the appraisal that was needed. The appraisal was, in fact, inappropriate for use as a basis for a charitable gift appraisal, creating overvaluation issues for the client. He had determined some form of value, perhaps *investment value,* for the private company, but his conclusion had absolutely nothing to do with the *fair market value* of the gifted interest.

Readers of Mercer Capital publications will recognize that we are dealing once again with the familiar "levels of value" that we talk about so frequently. For a quick review of the basic levels of value chart, see below. It shows the traditional, three-level chart on the left, and the modified chart on the right, which distinguishes between financial control and strategic control levels.

The Levels of Value

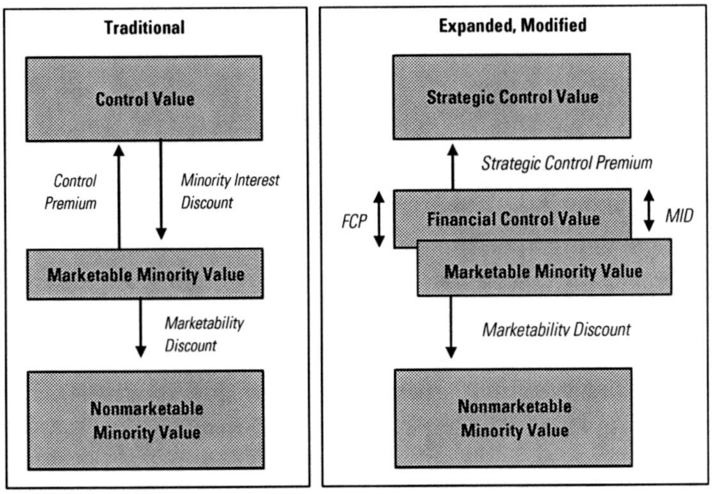

The business owner and his original advisors asked themselves: Do we need a valuation professional or an industry expert for this appraisal of the charitable gift? Unfortunately, they made the wrong decision. The *industry expert* lacked even a basic understanding of the concept of fair market value of a nonmarketable minority interest of a private company in the context of a charitable tax matter. In retrospect, the client should have hired one of the two well-qualified *valuation experts.*

Industry Expertise vs. Valuation Expertise

There are literally hundreds of industry categories and subcategories. There are, in fact, more industry categories than there are corresponding industry valuation specialists. Many, if not most, industry subcategories do not have "industry specialists." There simply aren't enough businesses in these categories to enable specialization by valuation professionals, investment bankers, or business brokers. From a business perspective, being the leading valuation expert in an industry with only 50 companies may be a sure strategy for starvation! In small industries or industry subcategories, business owners are likely to be referred to business valuation professionals.

If an industry is large, it is often possible to find several industry experts. These large industries each have thousands of companies. Frequently, the industry experts focus only on transactions-type valuations and know very little about the elements of expertise developed by the *valuation expert.*

The lesson from our composite is this: When selecting an *industry expert* to perform business appraisals, be sure that the expert also has *valuation expertise.*

Valuation Expertise

Valuation expertise is learned over years of study and practice. Business appraisers become knowledgeable about valuation methods and techniques, business appraisal standards and documentation requirements. In addition, appraisers must understand the relevant literature and the cases applicable to minority interest appraisals, as well as other tax-related and institutional matters that influence valuation. Valuation expertise also includes a working knowledge of financial theory and valuation methods. This enables the valuation expert to learn quickly about new industries and to develop credible appraisals of companies across a broad range of industries.

For example, at Mercer Capital, we have provided valuations in more than 500 industry categories and subcategories. We have applied valuation expertise and knowledge and developed credible appraisals in each and every new industry assignment. Along the way, we have developed specific expertise in a number of industries, including financial institutions, auto dealerships, construction-related companies, service companies, and certain areas of health care.

We, like other business appraisers, must be quick studies of new industries. Most *valuation professionals* are just that – quick studies of new industries. Based on many years of valuation experience, we can say that *valuation expertise* combined with a broad base of industry experience is a preferable experience set than purely industry expertise. If a referring professional or a direct client can obtain both sets of qualifications in one firm, so much the better.

So, in choosing an appraiser, it is a good idea to check *appraisal qualifications* as well as *industry qualifications* before making a selection. Courts are seldom misled by "experts" who know little about valuation when it comes to deciding valuation issues. Do not be swayed by the *industry experts* who plan to pick up valuation experience at your or your client's expense. The lessons learned can prove very costly!

Business appraisers who are members of the American Society of Appraisers are required to perform appraisals in conformity with the *Business Valuation Standards* and the *Principles of Appraisal Practice and Code of Ethics* of the American Society of Appraisers. They are also required to prepare valuation reports in accordance with the requirements of the *Uniform Standards of Professional Appraisal Practice* (promulgated by The Appraisal Foundation). Unfortunately, many *industry experts*, like the investment banker in the composite story above, do not feel bound by the prevailing industry valuation standards. And we do not say this in a derogatory way. Most of their work simply does not involve the determination of the fair market value of anything. If fair market value is the appropriate standard of value, clients may be well-served finding a valuation professional to provide the required valuation opinions.

Conclusion

We believe you should expect your business appraiser to be a valuation professional and to have knowledge of a broad base of industries. Anything less will probably result in an unsatisfactory valuation result. Given valuation expertise and broad industry perspective, specific industry expertise provides an element of comfort. However, in most independent valuation situations, industry expertise alone is simply an inadequate level of qualification unless supplemented by valuation knowledge and breadth of industry experience.

APPENDIX B

Business Valuation Professional Credentials Chart

Note: The CFA, or Chartered Financial Analyst, designation, offered by the CFA Institute is not listed in the table. Individuals who have completed a three-year program of study and examination in finance, investments and related disciplines can earn the CFA designation. This designation is the primary professional designation in the money management and investment banking fields. The CFA designation is also considered to be an excellent credential for business appraisal.

Organization	Certification	Prerequisites	Course/Exam	Reports	Experience/Other
American Institute of Certified Public Accountants (AICPA)	ABV – Accredited in Business Valuation	AICPA certificate or member with current CPA License	8-Hour Multiple Choice Exam	None	Substantial involvement in at least 10 business valuation engagements. Provide evidence of 75 hours of continuing professional education related to the business of valuation body of knowledge
American Society of Appraisers (ASA)	AM – Accredited Member	Four-year college degree or equivalent	Completion of 4 courses of 3 days each with successful completion of 1 half day exam following each course or successful completion of 1 all-day challenge exam and USPAP exam	Submission of 2 actual reports from within the last 2 years to satisfaction of board examiners	Two years full time or equivalent (e.g. 5 years of 400 hours business appraisal work per year equals one year full time equivalent). One full year of requirement is granted to anyone who has a CPA, CFA or CBI designation with five years of practice in the field
	ASA – Accredited Senior Appraiser	Met AM requirements			Five years of full time or equivalent experience including 2 years for AM
	FASA – Fellow of American Society of Appraisers	Met ASA requirements, plus voted into College of Fellows on the basis of technical leadership and contribution to the profession of the Society			

Source: Business Valuation Resources (www.bvresources.com)

Organization	Certification	Prerequisites	Course/Exam	Reports	Experience/Other
Institute of Business Appraisers (IBA)	AIBA – Accredited by IBA	Four year college degree or equivalent; Possess business appraisal designation from AICPA, ASA or NACVA or complete IBA 8-day Appraisal Workshop.	Comprehensive written exam	Submit 1 report for peer review	Provide 4 references of character and fitness
	CBA – Certified Business Appraiser	Four year college degree or equivalent	6 hour exam; applicants may be exempt from the exam if they hold he ASA designation, ABV designation, CVA designation or AVA designation	Submit 2 business appraisal reports showing professional competence	Successful completion of 90 hours of upper level business valuation course work (at least 24 hours from IBA) or 5 years full-time active experience as a business appraiser
	BVAL – Business Valuator Accredited for Litigation	Business appraisal designation from IBA, AICPA, ASA, NACVA or CVA candidate who has passed the exam.	5 day Expert Witness Skills Workshop and 4 hour exam.	None	Letters of reference from 2 attorneys OR complete 16 hours of education in the area of law the appraiser will testify in
	MCBA – Master Certified Business Appraiser	Four-year college degree and 2 year post graduate degree or equivalent. Held CBA designation for at least 5 years and hold one other designation (ASA, CVA or ABV)			10 years full time practice. Provide 3 references from MCBAs with personal knowledge of applicant's work
	FIBA – Fellow of the Institute of Business Appraisers	Met all CBA requirements, plus voted into College of Fellows on basis of technical leadership and contribution to the profession and the Institute			

Source: Business Valuation Resources (www.bvresources.com)

Organization	Certification	Prerequisites	Course/Exam	Reports	Experience/Other
National Association of Certified Valuation Analysts (NACVA)	AVA – Accredited Valuation Analyst, includes prior GVA designation	Business degree and/or an MBA or higher; Member in good standing of NACVA	5-day course; 4 hour exam. Additional 8 hour exam for applicants without accounting fundamentals background	Case study for exam	2 years full time or equivalent business valuation or related experience OR 10 or more business valuations. Provide 3 personal references and 3 business references and a minimum of 1 letter of recommendation from an employer or another CPA
	CVA – Certified Valuation Analyst	College degree, CPA and member in good standing of NACVA	5 day course; 4 hour proctored exam	Case study for exam	2 years experience as a CPA. Provide personal and 3 business references
	CFFA - Certified Financial Forensic Analyst	Possess one of the following designations: CVA, AVA, AM, ASA, CBA, CBV, CFA, CMA, CPA or CA. Hold advanced degree in economics, accounting or finance OR undergraduate degree and MBA	2 week course, 8 hour exam	Case study report under Fed. Rule 26 OR report admitted into evidence within the last 3 years	Provide 1 business and 2 legal references. Substantial experience in 10 litigation matters, including 5 in which a deposition or testimony was given
Canadian Institute of Chartered Business Valuators (CICBV)	CBV – Chartered Business Valuator	College degree or equivalent: accounting or finance encouraged	Successful completion of 6 courses, including assignments and exams for each course plus the required experience, followed by the writing of the Membership Entrance Exam. Writing of exam can be challenged without successful completion of courses if applicant has at least 5 years full-time experience in business valuations	None	2 years full-time experience or the equivalent of part-time obtained over a 5 year period, attested to by a sponsoring CICBV member
	FCBV – Fellow of the Canadian Institute of Chartered Business Valuators	Members who have rendered outstanding service to the business valuation profession or whose achievements in their professional lives or in the community have earned them distinction and have brought honor		None	2 years full-time experience or the equivalent of part-time obtained over a 5 year period, attested to by a sponsoring CICBV member

Source: Business Valuation Resources (www.bvresources.com)

APPENDIX C

Uniform Standards of Professional Appraisal Practice

UNIFORM STANDARDS OF PROFESSIONAL APPRAISAL PRACTICE and ADVISORY OPINIONS 2006 EDITION

APPRAISAL STANDARDS BOARD

THE APPRAISAL FOUNDATION

Authorized by Congress as the Source of Appraisal Standards and Appraiser Qualifications

Published in the United States of America.

EFFECTIVE:

July 1, 2006

PREAMBLE

The purpose of the *Uniform Standards of Professional Appraisal Practice* (USPAP) is to promote and maintain a high level of public trust in appraisal practice by establishing requirements for appraisers. It is essential that appraisers develop and communicate their analyses, opinions, and conclusions to intended users of their services in a manner that is meaningful and not misleading.

The Appraisal Standards Board promulgates USPAP for both appraisers and users of appraisal services. The appraiser's responsibility is to protect the overall public trust and it is the importance of the role of the appraiser that places ethical obligations on those who serve in this capacity. USPAP reflects the current standards of the appraisal profession.

USPAP does not establish who or which assignments must comply. Neither The Appraisal Foundation nor its Appraisal Standards Board is a government entity with the power to make, judge, or enforce law. Compliance with USPAP is required when either the service or the appraiser is obligated to comply by law or regulation, or by agreement with the client or intended users. When not obligated, individuals may still choose to comply.

USPAP addresses the ethical and performance obligations of appraisers through DEFINITIONS, Rules, Standards, Standards Rules, and Statements.

- The DEFINITIONS establish the application of certain terminology in USPAP.
- The ETHICS RULE sets forth the requirements for integrity, impartiality, objectivity, independent judgment, and ethical conduct.
- The COMPETENCY RULE presents pre-assignment and assignment conditions for knowledge and experience.
- The SCOPE OF WORK RULE presents obligations related to problem identification, research and analyses.
- The JURISDICTIONAL EXCEPTION RULE preserves the balance of USPAP if a portion is contrary to law or public policy of a jurisdiction.
- The SUPPLEMENTAL STANDARDS RULE provides the means for government agencies, government sponsored enterprises, and other entities that establish public policy to augment USPAP.
- The ten Standards establish the requirements for appraisal, appraisal review, and appraisal consulting service and the manner in which each is communicated.
    - STANDARDS 1 and 2 establish requirements for the development and communication of a real property appraisal.
    - STANDARD 3 establishes requirements for the development and communication of an appraisal review.
    - STANDARDS 4 and 5 establish requirements for the development and communication of a real property appraisal consulting assignment.
    - STANDARD 6 establishes requirements for the development and communication of a mass appraisal.
    - STANDARDS 7 and 8 establish requirements for the development and communication of a personal property appraisal.
    - STANDARDS 9 and 10 establish requirements for the development and communication of a business or intangible asset appraisal.
- Statements on Appraisal Standards clarify, interpret, explain, or elaborate on a Rule or Standards Rule.
- Comments are an integral part of USPAP and have the same weight as the component they address. These extensions of the DEFINITIONS, Rules, and Standards Rules provide interpretation and establish the context and conditions for application.

STANDARD 3: APPRAISAL REVIEW, DEVELOPMENT AND REPORTING

In performing an appraisal review assignment, an appraiser acting as a reviewer must develop and report a credible opinion as to the quality of another appraiser's work and must clearly disclose the scope of work performed.

Comment: Appraisal review is the act or process of developing and communicating an opinion about the quality of all or part of the work of another appraiser that was performed as part of an appraisal, appraisal review, or appraisal consulting assignment. The reviewer's opinion about quality must encompass the completeness, adequacy, relevance, appropriateness, and reasonableness of the work under review, developed in the context of the requirements applicable to that work.

The COMPETENCY RULE applies to the reviewer, who must correctly employ those recognized methods and techniques necessary to develop credible appraisal review opinions and also avoid material errors of commission or omission. A misleading or fraudulent appraisal review report violates the ETHICS RULE.

Appraisal review requires the reviewer to prepare a separate report setting forth the scope of work performed and the results of the appraisal review.

Appraisal review is distinctly different from the cosigning activity addressed in Standards Rules 2-3, 5-3, 6-9, 8-3, and 10-3. To avoid confusion between these activities, a reviewer performing an appraisal review must not sign the work under review unless he or she intends to accept the responsibility of a cosigner of that work.

Standards Rule 3-1

In developing an appraisal review, the reviewer must:

(a) identify the reviewer's client and intended users, the intended use of the reviewer's opinions and conclusions, and the purpose of the assignment;[37]

Comment: The intended use is in the context of the client's use of the reviewer's opinions and conclusions; examples include, without limitation, quality control, audit, qualification, or confirmation. The purpose of the assignment relates to the reviewer's objective; examples include, without limitation, to evaluate compliance with relevant USPAP requirements, with a client's requirements, or with applicable regulations.

A reviewer must ascertain whether the assignment includes the development of his or her own opinion of value about the subject property of the work under review.

If the assignment includes the reviewer developing his or her own opinion of value about the subject property of the work under review, that opinion is an appraisal whether it:

- concurs with the opinion of value in the work under review, as of the date of value in that work or a different date of value; or
- differs from the opinion of value in the work under review, as of the date of value in that work or a different date of value.

37 See Statement on Appraisal Standards No. 9, *Identification of Intended Use and Intended Users*. See also Advisory Opinion 20, *An Appraisal Review Assignment That Includes the Reviewer's Own Opinion of Value.* References to Advisory Opinions are for guidance only and do not incorporate Advisory Opinions into USPAP.

(b) identify the:

(i) subject of the appraisal review assignment,

(ii) effective date of the review,

(iii) property and ownership interest appraised (if any) in the work under review,

(iv) date of the work under review and the effective date of the opinion or conclusion in the work under review, and

(v) appraiser(s) who completed the work under review, unless the identity was withheld;

<u>Comment</u>: The subject of an appraisal review assignment may be all or part of a report, a workfile, or a combination of these, and may be related to an appraisal, appraisal review, or appraisal consulting assignment.

(c) determine the scope of work necessary to produce credible assignment results in accordance with the SCOPE OF WORK RULE;[38]

<u>Comment</u>: In making the scope of work decision, the reviewer must identify any extraordinary assumptions necessary in the assignment. An extraordinary assumption may be used in an appraisal review assignment only if:

- it is required to properly develop credible opinions and conclusions;
- the reviewer has a reasonable basis for the extraordinary assumption;
- use of the extraordinary assumption results in a credible analysis; and
- the reviewer complies with the disclosure requirements set forth in SR 3-2(d) for extraordinary assumptions.

The appraisal review must be conducted in the context of market conditions as of the effective date of the opinion in the work being reviewed. Information available to the reviewer that could not have been available to the appraiser as of or subsequent to the date of the work being reviewed must not be used by a reviewer in the development of an opinion as to the quality of the work under review.

When the reviewer's scope of work includes developing his or her own opinion of value, the following apply:

- The reviewer's scope of work in developing his or her own opinion of value may be different from that of the work under review.

- The effective date of the reviewer's opinion of value may be the same or different from the date of the work under review.

[38] See Advisory Opinion 28, *Scope of Work Decision, Performance, and Disclosure*, and Advisory Opinion 29, *An Acceptable Scope of Work*. References to Advisory Opinions are for guidance only and do not incorporate Advisory Opinions into USPAP.

- The reviewer is not required to replicate the steps completed by the original appraiser. Those items in the work under review that the reviewer concludes are credible and in compliance with the applicable development Standard (STANDARD 1, 3, 4, 6, 7, or 9) can be extended to the reviewer's value opinion development process on the basis of an extraordinary assumption by the reviewer. Those items not deemed to be credible or in compliance must be replaced with information or analysis by the reviewer, developed in conformance with STANDARD 1, 3, 4, 6, 7, or 9, as applicable, to produce a credible value opinion.

- The reviewer may use additional information available to him or her that was not available to the original appraiser in the development of his or her value opinion; however, the reviewer must not use such information as the basis to discredit the original appraiser's opinion of value.

(d) develop an opinion as to the completeness of the material under review, given the reviewer's scope of work;

Comment: The reviewer is required to develop an opinion as to the completeness of the work under review within the context of the requirements applicable to that work.

(e) develop an opinion as to the apparent adequacy and relevance of the data and the propriety of any adjustments to the data, given the reviewer's scope of work;

Comment: When reviewing a mass appraisal report and considering the propriety of any adjustment to value for isolated differences in data, the reviewer must develop an opinion as to the use of the coefficients from decomposition of a statistical model.

(f) develop an opinion as to the appropriateness of the appraisal methods and techniques used, given the reviewer's scope of work, and develop the reasons for any disagreement; and

(g) develop an opinion as to whether the analyses, opinions, and conclusions are appropriate and reasonable, given the reviewer's scope of work, and develop the reasons for any disagreement.

Comment: When reviewing a mass appraisal report, the reviewer must develop an opinion as to the standards of accuracy and adequacy of the mass appraisal testing performed and develop the reasons for any disagreement.

Standards Rule 3-2

In reporting the results of an appraisal review, the reviewer must:

(a) state the identity of the client, by name or type, and intended users; the intended use of the assignment results; and the purpose of the assignment;[39]

(b) state the information that must be identified in accordance with Standards Rule 3-1(b);

Comment: If the identity of the appraiser(s) in the work under review was withheld, state that fact in the review report.

[39] See Statement on Appraisal Standards No. 9, *Identification of Intended Use and Intended Users.* See also Advisory Opinion 20, *An Appraisal Review Assignment That Includes the Reviewer's Own Opinion of Value.* References to Advisory Opinions are for guidance only and do not incorporate Advisory Opinions into USPAP.

(c) state the scope of work used to develop the appraisal review;[40]

Comment: Because intended users' reliance on an appraisal review may be affected by the scope of work, the report must enable them to properly informed and not misled. Sufficient information includes disclosure of research and analyses performed and might also include disclosure of research and analyses not performed.

When any portion of the work involves significant appraisal, appraisal review, or appraisal consulting assistance, the reviewer must state the extent of that assistance. The signing reviewer must also state the name(s) of those providing the significant assistance in the certification, in accordance with SR 3-3.

(d) state the opinions, reasons, and conclusions required in Standards Rule 3-1(d–g), given the reviewer's scope of work;

Comment: When the reviewer's scope of work includes expressing his or her own opinion of value, the reviewer must:

1. state which information, analyses, opinions, and conclusions in the material under review that the reviewer accepted as credible and used in developing the reviewer's opinion of value;

2. summarize any additional information relied on and the reasoning and basis for the reviewer's opinion of value;

3. state all assumptions and limiting conditions; and

4. clearly and conspicuously:

    - state all extraordinary assumptions and hypothetical conditions connected with the reviewer's opinion of value; and
    - state that their use might have affected the assignment results.

The reviewer may include his or her own value opinion within the appraisal review report itself without preparing a separate appraisal report. However, data and analyses provided by the reviewer to support a different value conclusion must match, at a minimum, the reporting requirements for a Summary Appraisal Report for a real property appraisal (SR 2-2(b)) and a personal property appraisal (SR 8-2(b)), an appraisal consulting report for real property appraisal consulting (SR 5-2), a mass appraisal report for mass appraisal (SR 6-8), and an Appraisal Report for business appraisal (SR 10-2(a)).

(e) include all known pertinent information; and

Comment: The reviewer must provide sufficient information to enable the client and intended users to understand the rationale for the reviewer's opinions and conclusions.

(f) include a signed certification in accordance with Standards Rule 3-3.

[40] See Advisory Opinion 28, *Scope of Work Decision, Performance, and Disclosure,* and Advisory Opinion 29, *An Acceptable Scope of Work.* References to Advisory Opinions are for guidance only and do not incorporate Advisory Opinions into USPAP.

<u>Standards Rule 3-3</u>

Each written appraisal review report must contain a signed certification that is similar in content to the following form:

I certify that, to the best of my knowledge and belief:

— the facts and data reported by the reviewer and used in the review process are true and correct.

— the analyses, opinions, and conclusions in this review report are limited only by the assumptions and limiting conditions stated in this review report and are my personal, impartial, and unbiased professional analyses, opinions, and conclusions.

— I have no (or the specified) present or prospective interest in the property that is the subject of the work under review and no (or the specified) personal interest with respect to the parties involved.

— I have no bias with respect to the property that is the subject of the work under review or to the parties involved with this assignment.

— my engagement in this assignment was not contingent upon developing or reporting predetermined results.

— my compensation is not contingent on an action or event resulting from the analyses, opinions, or conclusions in this review or from its use.

— my analyses, opinions, and conclusions were developed and this review report was prepared in conformity with the *Uniform Standards of Professional Appraisal Practice.*

— I have (or have not) made a personal inspection of the subject property of the work under review. (If more than one person signs this certification, the certification must clearly specify which individuals did and which individuals did not make a personal inspection of the subject property of the work under review.)

— no one provided significant appraisal, appraisal review, or appraisal consulting assistance to the person signing this certification. (If there are exceptions, the name of each individual(s) providing appraisal, appraisal review, or appraisal consulting assistance must be stated.)

<u>Comment</u>: A signed certification is an integral part of the appraisal review report. A reviewer who signs any part of the appraisal review report, including a letter of transmittal, must also sign this certification.

Any reviewer(s) who signs a certification accepts full responsibility for all elements of the certification, for the assignment results, and for the contents of the appraisal review report.

When a signing reviewer(s) has relied on work done by others who do not sign the certification, the signing reviewer is responsible for the decision to rely on their work.

The signing reviewer(s) is required to have a reasonable basis for believing that those individuals performing the work are competent and that their work is credible.

The names of individuals providing significant appraisal, appraisal review, or appraisal consulting assistance who do not sign a certification must be stated in the certification. It is not required that the description of their assistance be contained in the certification, but disclosure of their assistance is required in accordance with SR 3-2(c).

For reviews of business or intangible asset appraisal reports, the inspection portion of the above certification is not applicable.

Standards Rule 3-4

To the extent that it is both possible and appropriate, an oral appraisal review report must address the substantive matters set forth in Standards Rule 3-2.

Comment: See the Record Keeping section of the ETHICS RULE for corresponding requirements.

STANDARD 9: BUSINESS APPRAISAL, DEVELOPMENT

In developing an appraisal of an interest in a business enterprise or intangible asset, an appraiser must identify the problem to be solved, determine the scope of work necessary to solve the problem, and correctly complete the research and analyses necessary to produce a credible appraisal.

Comment: STANDARD 9 is directed toward the substantive aspects of developing a credible appraisal of an interest in a business enterprise or intangible asset.

Standards Rule 9-1

In developing an appraisal of an interest in a business enterprise or intangible asset, an appraiser must:

(a) be aware of, understand, and correctly employ those recognized approaches, methods and procedures that are necessary to produce a credible appraisal;

Comment: Changes and developments in the economy and in investment theory have a substantial impact on the business and intangible asset appraisal profession. Important changes in the financial arena, securities regulation, financial reporting requirements, and law may result in corresponding changes in appraisal theory and practice.

(b) not commit a substantial error of omission or commission that significantly affects an appraisal; and

Comment: An appraiser must use sufficient care to avoid errors that would significantly affect his or her opinions and conclusions. Diligence is required to identify and analyze the factors, conditions, data, and other information that would have a significant effect on the credibility of the assignment results.

(c) not render appraisal services in a careless or negligent manner, such as by making a series of errors that, although individually might not significantly affect the results of an appraisal, in the aggregate affect the credibility of those results.

Comment: Perfection is impossible to attain, and competence does not require perfection. However, an appraiser must not render appraisal services in a careless or negligent manner. This Standards Rule requires an appraiser to use due diligence and due care.

Standards Rule 9-2

In developing an appraisal of an interest in a business enterprise or intangible asset, an appraiser must:

(a) identify the client and other intended users;[89]

(b) identify the intended use of the appraiser's opinions and conclusions;[90]

Comment: An appraiser must not allow the intended use of an assignment or a client's objectives to cause the assignment results to be biased.

(c) identify the standard (type) and definition of value and the premise of value;

---

89 See Statement on Appraisal Standards No. 9, *Identification of Intended Use and Intended Users.*

90 See Statement on Appraisal Standards No. 9, *Identification of Intended Use and Intended Users.*

(d) identify the effective date of the appraisal;

(e) identify the characteristics of the subject property that are relevant to the standard (type) and definition of value and intended use of the appraisal, including:

(i) the subject business enterprise or intangible asset, if applicable;

(ii) the interest in the business enterprise, equity, asset, or liability to be valued;

Comment: The interest to be valued may represent all ownership rights or a subset of those rights, such as a specific right to use the asset.

(iii) all buy-sell and option agreements, investment letter stock restrictions, restrictive corporate charter or partnership agreement clauses, and similar features or factors that may have an influence on value;

(iv) the extent to which the interest contains elements of ownership control; and

Comment: The elements of control in a given situation may be affected by law, distribution of ownership interests, contractual relationships, and many other factors.

(v) the extent to which the interest is marketable and/or liquid;

Comment on (i)-(v): An appraiser must identify the attributes of the interest being appraised, including the rights and benefits of ownership.
The information used by an appraiser to identify the property characteristics must be from sources the appraiser reasonably believes are reliable.

(f) identify any extraordinary assumptions necessary in the assignment;

Comment: An extraordinary assumption may be used in an assignment only if:
it is required to properly develop credible opinions and conclusions;
the appraiser has a reasonable basis for the extraordinary assumption;
use of the extraordinary assumption results in a credible analysis; and
the appraiser complies with the disclosure requirements set forth in USPAP for extraordinary assumptions.

(g) identify any hypothetical conditions necessary in the assignment; and

Comment: A hypothetical condition may be used in an assignment only if:
use of the hypothetical condition is clearly required for legal purposes, for purposes of reasonable analysis, or for purposes of comparison;
use of the hypothetical condition results in a credible analysis; and
the appraiser complies with the disclosure requirements set forth in USPAP for hypothetical conditions.

(h) determine the scope of work necessary to produce credible assignment results in accordance with the SCOPE OF WORK RULE.[91]

Standards Rule 9-3

In developing an appraisal of an equity interest in a business enterprise with the ability to cause liquidation, an appraiser must investigate the possibility that the business enterprise may have a higher value by liquidation of all or part of the enterprise than by continued operation as is. If liquidation of all or part of the enterprise is the indicated premise of value, an appraisal of any real property or personal property to be liquidated may be appropriate.

Comment: This Standards Rule requires the appraiser to recognize that continued operation of a business is not always the best premise of value because liquidation of all or part of the enterprise may result in a higher value. However, this typically applies only when the business equity being appraised is in a position to cause liquidation. If liquidation of all or part of the enterprise is the appropriate premise of value, the scope of work may include an appraisal of real property or tangible personal property. If so, competency in real property appraisal (STANDARD 1) or tangible personal property appraisal (STANDARD 7) is required.

Standards Rule 9-4

In developing an appraisal of an interest in a business enterprise or intangible asset, an appraiser must collect and analyze all information necessary for credible assignment results.

(a) An appraiser must develop value opinion(s) and conclusion(s) by use of one or more approaches that are necessary for credible assignment results.

(b) An appraiser must, when necessary for credible assignment results, analyze the effect on value, if any, of:

(i) the nature and history of the business enterprise or intangible asset;

(ii) financial and economic conditions affecting the business enterprise or intangible asset, its industry, and the general economy;

(iii) past results, current operations, and future prospects of the business enterprise;

(iv) past sales of capital stock or other ownership interests in the business enterprise or intangible asset being appraised;

(v) sales of capital stock or other ownership interests in similar business enterprises;

(vi) prices, terms, and conditions affecting past sales of similar ownership interests in the asset being appraised or a similar asset; and

(vii) economic benefit of tangible and intangible assets.

Comment on (i)-(vii): This Standards Rule directs the appraiser to study the prospective and retrospective aspects of the business enterprise and to study it in terms of the economic and industry environment within which it operates.

[91] See Advisory Opinion 28, *Scope of Work Decision, Performance, and Disclosure,* and Advisory Opinion 29, *An Acceptable Scope of Work.* References to Advisory Opinions are for guidance only and do not incorporate Advisory Opinions into USPAP.

(c) An appraiser must, when necessary for credible assignment results, analyze the effect on value, if any, of buy-sell and option agreements, investment letter stock restrictions, restrictive corporate charter or partnership agreement clauses, and similar features or factors that may influence value.

(d) An appraiser must, when necessary for credible assignment results, analyze the effect on value, if any, of the extent to which the interest appraised contains elements of ownership control and is marketable and/or liquid.

Comment: An appraiser must analyze factors such as holding period, interim benefits, and the difficulty and cost of marketing the subject interest.

Equity interests in a business enterprise are not necessarily worth the pro rata share of the business enterprise interest value as a whole. Also, the value of the business enterprise is not necessarily a direct mathematical extension of the value of the fractional interests. The degree of control, marketability and/or liquidity or lack thereof depends on a broad variety of facts and circumstances that must be analyzed when applicable.

Standards Rule 9-5

In developing an appraisal of an interest in a business enterprise or intangible asset, an appraiser must:

(a) reconcile the quality and quantity of data available and analyzed within the approaches, methods, and procedures used; and

(b) reconcile the applicability or relevance of the approaches, methods and procedures used to arrive at the value conclusion(s).

Comment: The value conclusion is the result of the appraiser's judgment and not necessarily the result of a mathematical process.

STANDARD 10: BUSINESS APPRAISAL, REPORTING

In reporting the results of an appraisal of an interest in a business enterprise or intangible asset, an appraiser must communicate each analysis, opinion, and conclusion in a manner that is not misleading.

Comment: STANDARD 10 addresses the content and level of information required in a report that communicates the results of an appraisal of an interest in a business enterprise or intangible asset developed under STANDARD 9.

STANDARD 10 does not dictate the form, format, or style of business or intangible asset appraisal reports, which are functions of the needs of intended users and appraisers. The substantive content of a report determines its compliance.

Standards Rule 10-1

Each written or oral appraisal report for an interest in a business enterprise or intangible asset must:

(a) clearly and accurately set forth the appraisal in a manner that will not be misleading;

(b) contain sufficient information to enable the intended user(s) to understand the report; and

(c) clearly and accurately disclose all assumptions, extraordinary assumptions, hypothetical conditions, and limiting conditions used in the assignment.

Standards Rule 10-2

Each written appraisal report for an interest in a business enterprise or intangible asset must be prepared in accordance with one of the following options and prominently state which option is used: Appraisal Report or Restricted Use Appraisal Report.

Comment: When the intended users include parties other than the client, an Appraisal Report must be provided. When the intended users do not include parties other than the client, a Restricted Use Appraisal Report may be provided.

The essential difference between these options is in the content and level of information provided. The appropriate reporting option and the level of information necessary in the report are dependent on the intended use and intended users.

An appraiser must use care when characterizing the type of report and level of information communicated upon completion of an assignment. An appraiser may use any other label in addition to, but not in place of, the label set forth in this Standard for the type of report provided.

The report content and level of information requirements set forth in this Standard are minimums for both types of report.

A party receiving a copy of an Appraisal Report or Restricted Use Appraisal Report does not become an intended user of the appraisal unless the appraiser identifies such party as an intended user as part of the assignment.

(a) The content of an Appraisal Report must be consistent with the intended use of the appraisal and, at a minimum:

(i) state the identity of the client and any other intended users, by name or type;[92]

Comment: An appraiser must use care when identifying the client to ensure a clear understanding and to avoid violations of the Confidentiality section of the

ETHICS RULE. In those rare instances when the client wishes to remain anonymous, an appraiser must still document the identity of the client in the workfile but may omit the client's identity in the report.

(ii) state the intended use of the appraisal;[93]

(iii) summarize information sufficient to identify the business or intangible asset and the interest appraised;

<u>Comment</u>: The identification information must include property characteristics relevant to the type and definition of value and intended use of the appraisal.

(iv) state the extent to which the interest appraised contains elements of ownership control, including the basis for that determination;

(v) state the extent to which the interest appraised lacks elements of marketability and/or liquidity, including the basis for that determination;

(vi) state the standard (type) and definition of value and the premise of value and cite the source of the definition;

<u>Comment</u>: Stating the definition of value also requires any comments needed to clearly indicate to the intended users how the definition is being applied.

(vii) state the effective date of the appraisal and the date of the report;

<u>Comment</u>: The effective date of the appraisal establishes the context for the value opinion, while the date of the report indicates whether the perspective of the appraiser on the market or property as of the effective date of the appraisal was prospective, current, or retrospective.

(viii) summarize the scope of work used to develop the appraisal;[94]

<u>Comment</u>: Because intended users' reliance on an appraisal may be affected by the scope of work, the report must enable them to be properly informed and not misled. Sufficient information includes disclosure of research and analyses performed and might also include disclosure of research and analyses not performed.

When any portion of the work involves significant business and/or intangible asset appraisal assistance, the appraiser must summarize the extent of that assistance. The signing appraiser must also state the name(s) of those providing the significant business and/or intangible asset appraisal assistance in the certification, in accordance with SR 10-3.

---

92 See Statement on Appraisal Standards No. 9, *Identification of Intended Use and Intended Users.*

93 See Statement on Appraisal Standards No. 9, *Identification of Intended Use and Intended Users.*

94 See Advisory Opinion 28, *Scope of Work Decision, Performance, and Disclosure,* and Advisory Opinion 29, *An Acceptable Scope of Work.* References to Advisory Opinions are for guidance only and do not incorporate Advisory Opinions into USPAP.

(ix) summarize the information analyzed, the appraisal procedures followed, and the reasoning that supports the analyses, opinions, and conclusions; exclusion of the market approach, asset-based (cost) approach, or income approach must be explained;

Comment: An Appraisal Report must include sufficient information to indicate that the appraiser complied with the requirements of STANDARD 9. The amount of detail required will vary with the significance of the information to the appraisal.

The appraiser must provide sufficient information to enable the client and intended users to understand the rationale for the opinions and conclusions, including reconciliation in accordance with Standards Rule 9-5.

(x) clearly and conspicuously:

- state all extraordinary assumptions and hypothetical conditions; and
- state that their use might have affected the assignment results; and

(xi) include a signed certification in accordance with Standards Rule 10-3.

(b) The content of a Restricted Use Appraisal Report must be consistent with the intended use of the appraisal and, at a minimum:

(i) state the identity of the client, by name or type;[95] and state a prominent use restriction that limits use of the report to the client and warns that the appraiser's opinions and conclusions set forth in the report may not be understood properly without additional information in the appraiser's workfile;

Comment: An appraiser must use care when identifying the client to ensure a clear understanding and to avoid violations of the Confidentiality section of the ETHICS RULE. In those rare instances when the client wishes to remain anonymous, an appraiser must still document the identity of the client in the workfile but may omit the client's identity in the report.

The Restricted Use Appraisal Report is for client use only. Before entering into an agreement, the appraiser should establish with the client the situations where this type of report is to be used and should ensure that the client understands the restricted utility of the Restricted Use Appraisal Report.

(ii) state the intended use of the appraisal;[96]

Comment: The intended use of the appraisal must be consistent with the limitation on use of the Restricted Use Appraisal Report option in this Standards Rule (i.e. client use only).

(iii) state information sufficient to identify the business or intangible asset and the interest appraised;

Comment: The identification information must include property characteristics relevant to the type and definition of value and intended use of the appraisal.

---

[95] See Statement on Appraisal Standards No. 9, *Identification of Intended Use and Intended Users.*

[96] See Statement on Appraisal Standards No. 9, *Identification of Intended Use and Intended Users.*

(iv) state the extent to which the interest appraised contains elements of ownership control, including the basis for that determination;

(v) state the extent to which the interest appraised lacks elements of marketability and/or liquidity, including the basis for that determination;

(vi) state the standard (type) of value and the premise of value, and cite the source of its definition;

(vii) state the effective date of the appraisal and the date of the report;

<u>Comment</u>: The effective date of the appraisal establishes the context for the value opinion, while the date of the report indicates whether the perspective of the appraiser on the market or property as of the effective date of the appraisal was prospective, current, or retrospective.

(viii) state the scope of work used to develop the appraisal;[97]

<u>Comment</u>: Because the client's reliance on an appraisal may be affected by the scope of work, the report must enable them to be properly informed and not misled. Sufficient information includes disclosure of research and analyses performed and might also include disclosure of research and analyses not performed.

When any portion of the work involves significant business and/or intangible asset appraisal assistance, the appraiser must state the extent of that assistance. The signing appraiser must also state the name(s) of those providing the significant business and/or intangible asset appraisal assistance in the certification, in accordance with SR 10-3.

(ix) state the appraisal procedures followed, state the value opinion(s) and conclusion(s) reached, and reference the workfile; exclusion of the market approach, asset-based (cost) approach, or income approach must be explained;

<u>Comment</u>: An appraiser must maintain a specific, coherent workfile in support of a Restricted Use Appraisal Report. The contents of the workfile must include sufficient information to indicate that the appraiser complied with the requirements of STANDARD 9 and for the appraiser to produce an Appraisal Report. The file must be available for inspection by the client (or the client's representatives, such as those engaged to complete an appraisal review), such third parties as may be authorized by due process of law, and a duly authorized professional peer review committee except when such disclosure to a committee would violate applicable law or regulation.

(x) clearly and conspicuously:

- state all extraordinary assumptions and hypothetical conditions; and
- state that their use might have affected the assignment results; and

(xi) include a signed certification in accordance with Standards Rule 10-3.

[97] See Advisory Opinion 28, *Scope of Work Decision, Performance, and Disclosure* and Advisory Opinion 29, *An Acceptable Scope f Work.* References to Advisory Opinions are for guidance only and do not incorporate Advisor Opinions into USPAP.

Standards Rule 10-3

Each written appraisal report for an interest in a business enterprise or intangible asset must contain a signed certification that is similar in content to the following form:

I certify that, to the best of my knowledge and belief:

— the statements of fact contained in this report are true and correct.

— the reported analyses, opinions, and conclusions are limited only by the reported assumptions and limiting conditions and are my personal, impartial, and unbiased professional analyses, opinions, and conclusions.

— I have no (or the specified) present or prospective interest in the property that is the subject of this report, and I have no (or the specified) personal interest with respect to the parties involved.

— I have no bias with respect to the property that is the subject of this report or to the parties involved with this assignment.

— my engagement in this assignment was not contingent upon developing or reporting predetermined results.

— my compensation for completing this assignment is not contingent upon the development or reporting of a predetermined value or direction in value that favors the cause of the client, the amount of the value opinion, the attainment of a stipulated result, or the occurrence of a subsequent event directly related to the intended use of this appraisal.

— my analyses, opinions, and conclusions were developed, and this report has been prepared, in conformity with the *Uniform Standards of Professional Appraisal Practice.*

— no one provided significant business and/or intangible asset appraisal assistance to the person signing this certification. (If there are exceptions, the name of each individual providing significant business and/or intangible asset appraisal assistance must be stated.)

<u>Comment</u>: A signed certification is an integral part of the appraisal report. An appraiser who signs any part of the appraisal report, including a letter of transmittal, must also sign this certification.

In an assignment that includes only assignment results developed by the business and/or intangible asset appraiser(s), any appraiser(s) who signs a certification accepts full responsibility for all elements of the certification, for the assignment results, and for the contents of the appraisal report. In an assignment that includes real property or personal property assignment results not developed by the business and/or intangible asset appraiser(s), any business and/or intangible asset appraiser(s) who signs a certification accepts full responsibility for the business and/or intangible asset elements of the certification, for the business and/or intangible asset assignment results, and for the business and/or intangible asset contents of the appraisal report.

When a signing appraiser(s) has relied on work done by others who do not sign the certification, the signing appraiser is responsible for the decision to rely on their work. The signing appraiser(s) is required to have a reasonable basis for believing that those individuals performing the work are competent.[98]

98 See Advisory Opinion 5, *Assistance in the Preparation of an Appraisal.* References to Advisory Opinions are for guidance only and do not incorporate Advisory Opinions into USPAP.

The names of individuals providing significant business and/or intangible asset appraisal assistance who do not sign a certification must be stated in the certification. It is not required that the description of their assistance be contained in the certification but disclosure of their assistance is required in accordance with SR 10-2(a) or (b)(vii), as applicable.

Standards Rule 10-4

To the extent that it is both possible and appropriate, an oral appraisal report for an interest in a business enterprise or intangible asset must address the substantive matters set forth in Standards Rule 10-2(a).

Comment: See the Record Keeping section of the ETHICS RULE for corresponding requirements.

APPENDIX D

Business Valuation Standards© of the American Society of Appraisers

[Reprinted with permission from the Business Valuation Committee of the American Society of Appraisers]

This release of the approved Business Valuation Standards of the American Society of Appraisers contains all standards approved through November 2005, and is to be used in conjunction with the *Uniform Standards of Professional Appraisal Practice* (USPAP) of The Appraisal Foundation and the *Principles of Appraisal Practice and Code of Ethics* of the American Society of Appraisers. Periodic updates to these Standards are posted to the Business Valuation Committee's website **www.bvappraisers.org**.

It contains the following sections, effective on the dates listed:

Item	Title	Effective Date
GENERAL PREAMBLE		September 1992 Revised January 1994 Revised February 2001 Revised August 2002 Revised January 2004

BUSINESS VALUATION STANDARDS (BVS)
(Standards provide minimum criteria for developing and reporting on the valuation of businesses, business ownership interests, or securities.)

BVS-I	General Requirements for Developing a Business Valuation Revised	January 1992 June 1993 Revised January 1994 Revised January 1996 Revised February 2001
BVS-II	Financial Statement Adjustments	September 1992 Revised January 1994 Revised February 2001

BVS-III	Asset-Based Approach to Business Valuation	January 1992 Revised January 1994 Revised February 2001 Revised August 2002
BVS-IV	Income Approach to Business Valuation	September 1992 Revised January 1994 Revised February 2001
BVS-V	Market Approach to Business Valuation	September 1992 Revised January 1994 Revised February 2001
BVS-VI	Reaching a Conclusion of Value	September 1992 Revised January 1994 Revised February 2001 Revised August 2002
BVS-VII	Valuation Discounts and Premiums	January 1996 Revised February 2001
BVS-VIII	Comprehensive Written Business Valuation Report	June 1991 Revised January 1994 Revised February 2001
GLOSSARY		January 1989 Revised September 1992 Revised June 1993 Revised January 1994 Revised February 2001 Revised June 2002 January 2004 June 2005

STATEMENTS ON BUSINESS VALUATION STANDARDS (SBVS)

(Statements clarify, interpret, explain, or elaborate on Standards. Statements have the full weight of Standards.)

SBVS-1	The Guideline Public Company Method	November 2005
SBVS-2	The Merger & Acquisition Method	January 2004

ADVISORY OPINIONS (AO)

(Advisory Opinions illustrate the applicability of Standards and Statements in specific situations, offer advice for the resolution of valuation issues, and are not binding.)

AO-1	Financial Consultation and Advisory Services	February 1997 Revised February 2001

PROCEDURAL GUIDELINES (PG)

(Procedural Guidelines suggest certain procedures that may be used in the conduct of an assignment. They are not binding.)

PG-1	Litigation support: Role of The Independent Financial Expert	July 2001

AMERICAN SOCIETY OF APPRAISERS
Business Valuation Standards

General Preamble©

I. The American Society of Appraisers, through its Business Valuation Committee, has adopted these Business Valuation Standards and Definitions ("the Standards") in order to maintain and enhance the quality of business valuations for the benefit of the business valuation profession and users of business valuations.

II. The American Society of Appraisers, in its Principles of Appraisal Practice and Code of Ethics, and The Appraisal Foundation, in its Uniform Standards of Professional Appraisal Practice ("USPAP"), have established authoritative principles and a code of professional ethics. These Standards incorporate the Principles of Appraisal Practice and Code of Ethics and the relevant portions of USPAP, either explicitly or by reference, and are designed to clarify them and provide additional requirements specifically applicable to the valuation of businesses, business ownership interests, and securities.

III. These Standards incorporate all relevant business valuation standards adopted by the American Society of Appraisers through its Business Valuation Committee.

IV. These Standards provide minimum criteria to be followed by business appraisers in developing and reporting the valuation of businesses, business ownership interests, and securities.

V. If, in the opinion of the appraiser, the circumstances of a specific business valuation assignment dictate a departure from any provision of any Standard, such departure must be disclosed and will apply only to the specific provision.

VI. These Standards are designed to provide guidance to ASA members and to provide a structure for regulating the development and reporting of business valuations through uniform practices and procedures. Deviations from the Standards are not intended to form the basis of any civil liability and should not create any presumption or evidence that a legal duty has been breached. Moreover, compliance with these Standards does not create any special relationship between the appraiser and any other person.

AMERICAN SOCIETY OF APPRAISERS
Business Valuation Standards

BVS-I General Requirements for Developing a Business Valuation©

I. Preamble

A. This Standard must be followed in all valuations of businesses, business ownership interests, and securities developed by all members of the American Society of Appraisers, be they Candidates, Accredited Members (AM), Accredited Senior Appraisers (ASA), or Fellows (FASA).

B. The purpose of this Standard is to define and describe the general requirements for developing the valuation of businesses, business ownership interests, and securities.

C. This Standard incorporates the General Preamble to the Business Valuation Standards of the American Society of Appraisers.

II. Appropriate definition of the assignment

A. Business Valuation is the act or process of determining the value of a business enterprise or ownership interest therein.

B. In developing a business valuation, an appraiser must identify and define:

1. The business, business ownership interest, or security to be valued
2. The effective date of the appraisal
3. The standard of value
4. The purpose and intended use of the valuation

C. The nature and scope of the assignment must be defined. An acceptable scope of work will generally be one of the three types detailed below. Other scopes of work should be explained and described.

1. Appraisal
   a. An Appraisal is the act or process of determining the value of a business, business ownership interest, security, or intangible asset.
   b. The objective of an appraisal is to express an unambiguous opinion as to the value of a business, business ownership interest, or security, which opinion is supported by all procedures that the appraiser deems to be relevant to the valuation.
   c. An appraisal has the following qualities:
      (1) Its conclusion of value is expressed as either a single dollar amount or a range.
      (2) It considers all relevant information as of the appraisal date available to the appraiser at the time of performance of the valuation.
      (3) The appraiser conducts appropriate procedures to collect and analyze all information expected to be relevant to the valuation.
      (4) The valuation considers all conceptual approaches deemed to be relevant by the appraiser.

2. Limited appraisal
   a. The objective of a limited appraisal is to express an estimate as to the value of a business, business ownership interest, or security. The development of this estimate excludes some additional procedures that are required in an appraisal.
   b. A limited appraisal has the following qualities:
      (1) Its conclusion of value is expressed as either a single dollar amount or a range.
      (2) It is based upon consideration of limited relevant information.
      (3) The appraiser conducts only limited procedures to collect and analyze the information that such

appraiser considers necessary to support the conclusion presented.

(4) The valuation is based upon the conceptual approach(es) deemed by the appraiser to be most appropriate.

3. Calculations

a. The objective of calculations is to provide an approximate indication of value based upon the performance of limited procedures agreed upon by the appraiser and the client.

b. Calculations have the following qualities:

(1) Their results may be expressed as either a single dollar amount or a range.

(2) They may be based upon consideration of only limited relevant information.

(3) The appraiser performs limited information and analysis procedures.

(4) The calculations may be based upon conceptual approaches agreed upon with the client.

III. Information collection and analysis

The appraiser shall gather, analyze, and adjust the relevant information necessary to perform a valuation appropriate to the scope of work. Such information shall include:

A. Characteristics of the business, business ownership interest, or security to be valued, including rights, privileges, conditions, quantity, factors affecting control, and agreements restricting sale or transfer

B. The nature, history, and outlook of the business

C. Historical financial information for the business

D. Assets and liabilities of the business

E. The nature and conditions of relevant industries that have an impact on the business

F. Economic factors affecting the business

G. Capital markets providing relevant information; for example, available rates of return on alternative investments, relevant public stock market information, and relevant merger and acquisition information

H. Prior transactions involving the subject business, an interest in the subject business, or the securities of the subject business

I. Other information deemed by the appraiser to be relevant

IV. Approaches, methods, and procedures

A. The appraiser shall select and apply appropriate valuation approaches, methods, and procedures.

B. The appraiser shall develop a conclusion of value pursuant to the valuation assignment as defined, considering the relevant valuation approaches, methods, and procedures, the information available, and appropriate premiums and discounts, if any.

V. Documentation and retention

The appraiser shall appropriately document and retain all information relied on and the work product used in reaching a conclusion.

VI. Reporting

The appraiser shall report the appraisal conclusions to the client in an appropriate written or oral format. Other than preliminary communications of results to a client, reporting on valuation calculations, or reporting on engagements that do not result in conclusions of value, the report must meet the requirements of Standard 10 of the Uniform Standards of Professional Appraisal Practice. In the event the assignment results in a Comprehensive Written Business Valuation Report, the report shall meet the requirements of BVS-VIII.

AMERICAN SOCIETY OF APPRAISERS
Business Valuation Standards

BVS-II Financial Statement Adjustments©

I. Preamble

A. This Standard must be followed in all valuations of businesses, business ownership interests, and securities developed by all members of the American Society of Appraisers, be they Candidates, Accredited Members (AM), Accredited Senior Appraisers (ASA), or Fellows (FASA).

B. The purpose of this Standard is to define and describe the requirements for making financial statement adjustments in the valuation of businesses, business ownership interests, and securities.

C. This Standard applies to appraisals and may not necessarily apply to limited appraisals and calculations as defined in BVS-I, Section II.B.

D. This Standard incorporates the General Preamble to the Business Valuation Standards of the American Society of Appraisers.

II. Conceptual framework

A. As a procedure in the valuation process, financial statements should be analyzed and, if appropriate, adjusted. Financial statements to be analyzed include those of the subject entity and any entities used as guideline companies.

B. Financial statement adjustments are modifications to reported financial information that are relevant and significant to the appraisal process. Adjustments may be appropriate for the following reasons, among others:

1. To present financial data of the subject and guideline companies on a consistent basis.
2. To adjust from reported values to current values
3. To adjust revenues and expenses to levels that are reasonably representative of continuing results

4. To adjust for non-operating assets and liabilities, and any related revenues and expenses

C. Financial statement adjustments are made for the sole purpose of assisting the appraiser in reaching a conclusion of value.

III. Documentation of adjustments

All adjustments made should be fully described and supported.

AMERICAN SOCIETY OF APPRAISERS
Business Valuation Standards

BVS-III Asset-Based Approach to Business Valuation

I. Preamble

A. This Standard must be followed in all valuations of businesses, business ownership interests, and securities developed by all members of the American Society of Appraisers, be they candidates, Accredited Members (AM), Accredited Senior Appraisers (ASA), or Fellows (FASA).

B. The purpose of this Standard is to define and describe the requirements for the use of the asset-based approach (and the circumstances in which it is appropriate) in the valuation of businesses, business ownership interests, and securities, but not the reporting thereof.

C. This Standard applies to appraisals and may not necessarily apply to limited appraisals and calculations as defined in BVS-I, Section II.B.

D. This Standard incorporates the General Preamble to the Business Valuation Standards of the American Society of Appraisers.

II. The asset-based approach

A. The asset-based approach is a general way of determining a value indication of a business, business ownership interest, or security using one or more methods based on the value of the assets net of liabilities.

B. In business valuation, the asset-based approach may be analogous to the cost approach of other disciplines.

C. Assets, liabilities, and equity relate to a business that is an operating company, a holding company, or a combination thereof (a mixed business).

1. An operating company is a business that conducts an economic activity by generating and selling, or trading in a product or service.
2. A holding company is a business that derives its revenues by receiving returns on its assets, which may include operating companies and/or other businesses.

D. The asset-based approach should be considered in valuations conducted at the enterprise level and involving:
   1. An investment or real estate holding company
   2. A business appraised on a basis other than as a going concern

Valuations of particular ownership interests in an enterprise may or may not require the use of the asset-based approach.

E. The asset-based approach should not be the sole appraisal approach used in assignments relating to operating companies appraised as going concerns unless this approach is customarily used by sellers and buyers. In such cases, the appraiser must support the selection of this approach.

AMERICAN SOCIETY OF APPRAISERS
Business Valuation Standards

BVS-IV Income Approach to Business Valuation

I. Preamble

A. This Standard must be followed in all valuations of businesses, business ownership interests, and securities developed by all members of the American Society of Appraisers, be they Candidates, Accredited Members (AM), Accredited Senior Appraisers (ASA), or Fellows (FASA).

B. The purpose of this Standard is to define and describe the requirements for the use of the income approach in the valuation of businesses, business ownership interests, and securities, but not the reporting thereof.

C. This Standard applies to appraisals and may not necessarily apply to limited appraisals and calculations as defined in BVS-I, Section II.B.

D. This Standard incorporates the General Preamble to the Business Valuation Standards of the American Society of Appraisers.

II. The income approach

A. The income approach is a general way of determining a value indication of a business, business ownership interest, or security by using one or more methods through which anticipated benefits are converted into value.

B. Both capitalization of benefits methods and discounted future benefits methods are acceptable. In capitalization of benefits methods, a representative benefit level is divided or multiplied by an appropriate capitalization factor to convert the benefit to value. In discounted future benefits methods, benefits are estimated for each of several future periods. These benefits are converted to value by applying an appropriate discount rate and using present value procedures.

III. Anticipated benefits

A. Anticipated benefits, as used in the income approach, are expressed in monetary terms.

Anticipated benefits may be reasonably represented by such items as dividends or various forms of earnings or cash flow.

B. Anticipated benefits should be estimated by considering such items as the nature, capital structure, and historical performance of the related business entity, the expected future outlook for the business entity and relevant industries, and relevant economic factors.

IV. Conversion of anticipated benefits

A. Anticipated benefits are converted to value by using procedures that consider the expected growth and timing of the benefits, the risk profile of the benefits stream, and the time value of money.

B. The conversion of anticipated benefits to value normally requires the determination of a capitalization factor or discount rate. In that determination, the appraiser should consider such factors as the level of interest rates, the rates of return expected by investors on alternative investments, and the specific risk characteristics of the anticipated benefits.

C. In discounted future benefits methods, expected growth is considered in estimating the future stream of benefits. In capitalization of benefits methods, expected growth is incorporated in the capitalization factor.

D. The capitalization factors or discount rates should be consistent with the types of anticipated benefits used. For example, pre-tax factors or rates should be used with pretax benefits, common equity factors or rates should be used with common equity benefits, and net cash flow factors or rates should be used with net cash flow benefits.

AMERICAN SOCIETY OF APPRAISERS
Business Valuation Standards

BVS-V Market Approach to Business Valuation©

I. Preamble

A. This Standard must be followed in all valuations of businesses, business ownership interests, and securities developed by all members of the American Society of Appraisers, be they Candidates, Accredited Members (AM), Accredited Senior Appraisers (ASA), or Fellows (FASA).

B. The purpose of this Standard is to define and describe the requirements for the use of the market approach in the valuation of businesses, business ownership interests, and securities, but not the reporting thereof.

C. This Standard applies to appraisals and may not necessarily apply to limited appraisals and calculations as defined in BVS-I, Section II.B.

D. This Standard incorporates the General Preamble to the Business Valuation Standards of the American Society of Appraisers.

II. The market approach

A. The market approach is a general way of determining a value indication of a business, business ownership interest, or security by using one or more methods that compare the subject to similar businesses, business ownership interests, or securities that have been sold.

B. Examples of market approach methods include the guideline company method (see SBVS-1) and the analysis of prior transactions in the ownership of the subject company.

III. Reasonable basis for comparison

A. The business, business ownership interest, or security used for comparison must serve as a reasonable basis for such comparison.

B. Factors to be considered in judging whether a reasonable basis for comparison exists include:

1. A sufficient similarity of qualitative and quantitative investment characteristics
2. The amount and verifiability of data known about the similar investment
3. Whether or not the price of the similar investment was obtained in an arm's-length transaction, or a forced or distress sale

IV. Selection of valuation ratios

A. Comparisons are normally made through the use of valuation ratios. The computation and use of such ratios should provide meaningful insight about the value of the subject, considering all relevant factors. Accordingly, care should be exercised with respect to issues such as:

1. The selection of the underlying data used to compute the valuation ratios
2. The selection of the time periods and/or the averaging methods used for the underlying data
3. The computation of the valuation ratios
4. The timing of the price data used in the valuation ratios
5. How the valuation ratio or ratios were selected and applied to the subject's underlying data

B. In general, comparisons should be made by using comparable definitions of the components of the valuation ratios. However, where appropriate, valuation ratios based on components that are reasonably representative of ongoing results may be used.

V. Rules of thumb

Rules of thumb may provide insight on the value of a business, business ownership interest, or security. However, value indications derived from the use of rules of thumb should not be given substantial weight unless they are supported by other valuation methods and it can be established that knowledgeable buyers and sellers place substantial reliance on them.

AMERICAN SOCIETY OF APPRAISERS
Business Valuation Standards

BVS-VI Reaching a Conclusion of Value©

I. Preamble

A. This Standard must be followed in all valuations of businesses, business ownership interests, and securities developed by all members of the American Society of Appraisers, be they Candidates, Accredited Members (AM), Accredited Senior Appraisers (ASA), or Fellows (FASA).

B. The purpose of this Standard is to define and describe the requirements for reaching a final conclusion of value in the valuation of businesses, business ownership interests, and securities.

C. This Standard applies to appraisals and may not necessarily apply to limited appraisals and calculations as defined in BVS-I, Section II.B.

D. This Standard incorporates the General Preamble to the Business Valuation Standards of the American Society of Appraisers.

II. General

A. The conclusion of value reached by the appraiser shall be based upon the applicable standard of value, the purpose and intended use of the valuation, and all relevant information available as of the valuation date in carrying out the scope of the assignment.

B. The conclusion of value reached by the appraiser will be based on value indications resulting from one or more methods performed under one or more appraisal approaches.

III. Selection and weighing of methods

A. The selection of and reliance on appropriate methods and procedures depends on the judgment of the appraiser and not on any prescribed formula. One or more approaches may not be relevant to a particular situation, and more than one method under an approach may be relevant.

B. The appraiser must use informed judgment when determining the relative weight to be accorded to indications of value reached on the basis of various methods, or whether an indication of value from a single method should dominate. The appraiser's judgment may be presented either in general terms or in terms of mathematical weighting of the indicated values reflected in the conclusion. In any case, the appraiser should provide the rationale for the selection or weighing of the method or methods relied on in reaching the conclusion.

C. In assessing the relative importance of indications of value determined under each method, or whether an indication of value from a single method should dominate, the appraiser should consider factors such as:
   1. The applicable standard of value
   2. The purpose and intended use of the valuation
   3. Whether the subject is an operating company, a real estate or investment holding company, or a company with substantial non-operating or excess assets
   4. The quality and reliability of data underlying the indication of value
   5. Such other factors that, in the opinion of the appraiser, are appropriate for consideration

IV. Additional factors to consider

As appropriate for the valuation assignment as defined, and if not considered in the process of determining and weighing the indications of value provided by various procedures, the appraiser should separately consider the following factors in reaching a final conclusion of value:

A. Marketability or lack thereof, considering the nature of the business, the business ownership interest, or security; the effect of relevant contractual and legal restrictions; and the condition of the markets

B. The ability of the appraised interest to control the operation, sale, or liquidation of the relevant business

C. Such other factors that, in the opinion of the appraiser, are appropriate for consideration.

AMERICAN SOCIETY OF APPRAISERS
Business Valuation Standards

BVS-VII Valuation Discounts and Premiums©

I. Preamble

A. This Standard must be followed in all valuations of businesses, business ownership interests, and securities developed by all members of the American Society of Appraisers, be they Candidates, Accredited Members (AM), Accredited Senior Appraisers (ASA), or Fellows (FASA).

B. The purpose of this Standard is to define and describe the requirements for the use of discounts and premiums whenever they are applied in the valuation of businesses, business ownership interests, and securities.

C. This Standard applies to appraisals and may not necessarily apply to limited appraisals and calculations as defined in BVS-I, Section II.B.

D. This Standard incorporates the General Preamble to the Business Valuation Standards of the American Society of Appraisers.

E. This Standard applies at any time in the valuation process, whether within a method, to the value indicated by a valuation method, or to the result of weighing or correlating methods.

II. The concepts of discounts and premiums

A. A discount has no meaning until the conceptual basis underlying the base value to which it is applied is defined.

B. A premium has no meaning until the conceptual basis underlying the base value to which it is applied is defined.

C. A discount or premium is warranted when characteristics affecting the value of the subject interest differ sufficiently from those inherent in the base value to which the discount or premium is applied.

D. A discount or premium quantifies an adjustment to account for differences in characteristics affecting the value of the subject interest relative to the base value to which it is compared.

III. The application of discounts and premiums

A. The purpose, applicable standard of value, or other circumstances of an appraisal may indicate the need to account for differences between the base value and the value of the subject interest. If so, appropriate discounts or premiums should be applied. B. The base value to which the discount or premium is applied must be specified and defined.

C. Each discount or premium to be applied to the base value must be defined.

D. The primary reasons why each selected discount or premium applies to the appraised interest must be stated.

E. The evidence considered in deriving the discount or premium must be specified.

F. The appraiser's reasoning in arriving at a conclusion regarding the size of any discount or premium applied must be explained.

AMERICAN SOCIETY OF APPRAISERS
Business Valuation Standards

BVS-VIII Comprehensive Written Business Valuation Report©

I. Preamble

A. This Standard must be followed only in the preparation of comprehensive written business valuation reports developed by all members of the American Society of Appraisers, be they Candidates, Accredited Members (AM), Accredited Senior Appraisers (ASA), or Fellows (FASA).

B. A business valuation report may be less comprehensive in content provided that the report complies with the minimum content required by Standard 10.2 of the USPAP.

C. The purpose of this Standard is to define and describe the requirements for the written communication of the results of a business valuation, analysis, or opinion, but not the conduct thereof, which may reflect the three scopes of work defined in BVS-I Section (II) B.

D. This Standard incorporates the General Preamble to the Business Valuation Standards of the American Society of Appraisers.

II. Signature and certification

A. An appraiser assumes responsibility for the statements made in the comprehensive written report and accepts that responsibility by signing the report. To comply with this Standard, a comprehensive written report must be signed by the appraiser. For the purpose of this Standard, the appraiser is the individual or entity undertaking the appraisal assignment under a contract with the client.

B. Clearly, at least one individual is responsible for the valuation conclusion(s) expressed in a report. A report must contain a certification, as required by Standard 10 of the Uniform Standards of Professional Appraisal Practice of The Appraisal Foundation, in which the individual(s) responsible for the valuation conclusion(s) must be identified.

III. Assumptions and limiting conditions

The following assumptions and/or limiting conditions must be stated:

A. Pertaining to bias. A report must contain a statement that the appraiser has no interest in the asset appraised, or other conflict that could cause a question as to the appraiser's independence or objectivity; or, if such an interest or conflict exists, it must be disclosed.

B. Pertaining to data used. Where appropriate, a report must indicate that an appraiser relied on data supplied by others, without further verification by the appraiser, as well as the sources that were relied on.

C. Pertaining to validity of the valuation. A report must contain a statement that a valuation is valid only for the valuation date indicated and for the purpose stated.

IV. Definition of the valuation assignment

The precise definition of the valuation assignment is a key aspect of the report. The following are components of such a definition and must be included in the report:

A. The business interest being valued must be clearly defined, such as "100 shares of the Class A common stock of the XYZ Corporation" or "a 20 percent limited partnership interest in the ABC Limited Partnership." The existence, rights, and/or restrictions of other classes of ownership in the subject business must also be adequately described if they are relevant to the conclusion of value.

B. The purpose and use of the valuation must be clearly stated, such as "a determination of fair market value for ESOP purposes" or "a determination of fair value for dissenters' rights purposes." If a valuation is being performed pursuant to a particular statute, the statute must be referenced.

C. The standard of value used in the valuation must be stated and defined. The premise or basis of value, such as the valuation of a minority interest or a controlling interest, must be stated.

D. The effective date and the report date must be stated.

V. Business description

A comprehensive written business valuation report must include a business description that covers relevant factual areas, such as:

A. Form of organization (corporation, partnership, etc.)
B. History
C. Products and/or services
D. Markets and customers
E. Management
F. Major assets, both tangible and intangible, and major liabilities
G. Outlook for the economy, industry, and business
H. Past transactional evidence of value
I. Sensitivity to seasonal or cyclical factors
J. Competition
K. Sources of information used
L. Such other factual information as may be required to present a clear description of the business, and the general context within which it operates

VI. Financial analysis

A. An analysis and discussion of a firm's financial statements is an integral part of a business valuation and must be included. Exhibits summarizing balance sheets and income statements for a period of years sufficient to the purpose of the valuation and the nature of the subject company must be included in the valuation report.

B. Any adjustments made to the reported financial data must be fully explained.

C. If projections of balance sheets or income statements were used in the valuation, key assumptions underlying those projections must be included and discussed.

D. If appropriate, the company's financial results in comparison to those of the industry in which it operates must be discussed.

VII. Valuation methodology

A. The valuation method or methods selected, and the reasons for their selection, must be discussed. The steps followed in the application of the method(s) selected must be described. The description of the methodology and the procedures followed must contain sufficient detail to allow the intended user of the report to understand how the appraiser reached the valuation conclusion.

B. The report must include an explanation of how any variables such as discount rates, capitalization rates, or valuation multiples were determined and used. The rationale and/or supporting data for any premiums or discounts must be clearly presented.

VIII. Comprehensive written business valuation report format

The comprehensive written business valuation report must clearly communicate pertinent information, valuation methods, and conclusions in a logical progression, and must incorporate the other specific requirements of this Standard, including the signature and certification provisions.

IX. Confidentiality of the report

No copies of the report may be furnished to persons other than the client without the client's specific permission or direction unless ordered by a court of competent jurisdiction.

AMERICAN SOCIETY OF APPRAISERS
Business Valuation Standards

Glossary

Preamble

The American Society of Appraisers, through its Business Valuation Committee, has adopted these Definitions ("Definitions") to ensure the quality of valuations by defining terms whose meanings are clear and consistently applied for the benefit of appraisers, their clientele, and other intended users.

A. These Definitions include the International Glossary of Business Valuation Terms as adopted by the following professional societies and organizations:

American Institute of Certified Public Accountants
American Society of Appraisers
National Association of Certified Valuation Analysts
The Canadian Institute of Chartered Business Valuators
The Institute of Business Appraisers

The International Glossary of Business Valuation Terms are marked with an asterisk (*)

B. In the event that the assignment requires use of definitions that materially depart from those contained herein, the appraiser should fully explain the reason for departure and the implications it may have on the valuation assignment.

C. These Definitions provide guidance to ASA members by offering uniformity and consistency in the course of applying valuation terms used in developing and reporting the valuation of businesses, business ownership interests, and securities.

D. Departure from these Definitions is not intended to form the basis of any civil liability and should not create any presumption or evidence that a legal duty has been breached. Moreover, compliance with these Definitions does not create any special relationship between the appraiser and any other person.

Definitions

Adjusted Book Value - The book value that results after asset or liability amounts are added, deleted, or changed from their respective book amounts.

Adjusted Book Value Method* – a method within the asset approach whereby all assets and liabilities (including off-balance sheet, intangible, and contingent) are adjusted to their fair market values (NOTE: In Canada on a going concern basis).

Adjusted Net Asset Method* – see Adjusted Book Value Method.

Appraisal - see Valuation.

Appraisal Approach* - see Valuation Approach.

Appraisal Date* - see Valuation Date.

Appraisal Method* - see Valuation Method.

Appraisal Procedure* - see Valuation Procedure.

Appraised Value - The appraiser's opinion or conclusion of value.

Arbitrage Pricing Theory* – a multivariate model for estimating the cost of equity capital, which incorporates several systematic risk factors.

Asset (Asset-Based) Approach* - a general way of determining a value indication of a business, business ownership interest, or security using one or more methods based on the value of the assets net of liabilities.

Beta* - a measure of systematic risk of a stock; the tendency of a stock's price to correlate with changes in a specific index.

Blockage Discount* - an amount or percentage deducted from the current market price of a publicly traded stock to reflect the decrease in the per share value of a block of stock that is of a size that could not be sold in a reasonable period of time given normal trading volume.

Book Value* - see Net Book Value.

Business* - see Business Enterprise.

Business Appraiser - A person who, by education, training, and experience, is qualified to develop an appraisal of a business, business ownership interest, security or intangible assets.

Business Enterprise* - a commercial, industrial, service, or investment entity (or a combination thereof) pursuing an economic activity.

Business Risk* - the degree of uncertainty of realizing expected future returns of the business resulting from factors other than financial leverage. See Financial Risk.

Business Valuation* - the act or process of determining the value of a business enterprise or ownership interest therein.

Capital Asset Pricing Model (CAPM)* - a model in which the cost of capital for any stock or portfolio of stocks equals a risk-free rate plus a risk premium that is proportionate to the systematic risk of the stock or portfolio.

Capitalization* - a conversion of a single period of economic benefits into value.

Capitalization Factor* - any multiple or divisor used to convert anticipated economic benefits of a single period into value.

Capitalization of Earnings Method* – a method within the income approach whereby economic benefits for a representative single period are converted to value through division by a capitalization rate.

Capitalization Rate* - any divisor (usually expressed as a percentage) used to convert anticipated economic benefits of a single period into value.

Capital Structure* - the composition of the invested capital of a business enterprise, the mix of debt and equity financing.

Cash Flow* - cash that is generated over a period of time by an asset, group of assets, or business enterprise. It may be used in a general sense to encompass various levels of specifically defined cash flows. When the term is used, it should be supplemented by a qualifier (for example, "discretionary" or "operating") and a specific definition in the given valuation context.

Common Size Statements* – financial statements in which each line is expressed as a percentage of the total. On the balance sheet, each line item is shown as a percentage of total assets, and on the income statement, each item is expressed as a percentage of sales.

Control* - the power to direct the management and policies of a business enterprise.

Control Premium* - an amount or a percentage by which the pro rata value of a controlling interest exceeds the pro rata value of a non-controlling interest in a business enterprise, to reflect the power of control.

Cost Approach* - a general way of determining a value indication of an individual asset by quantifying the amount of money required to replace the future service capability of that asset.

Cost of Capital* - the expected rate of return that the market requires in order to attract funds to a particular investment.

Debt-Free* - we discourage the use of this term. See Invested Capital.

Discount for Lack of Control* - an amount or percentage deducted from the pro rata share of value of 100% of an equity interest in a business to reflect the absence of some or all of the powers of control.

Discount for Lack of Liquidity - an amount or percentage deducted from the value of an ownership interest to reflect the relative inability to quickly convert property to cash.

Discount for Lack of Marketability* - an amount or percentage deducted from the value of an ownership interest to reflect the relative absence of marketability.

Discount for Lack of Voting Rights* – an amount or percentage deducted from the per share value of a minority interest voting share to reflect the absence of voting rights.

Discount Rate* - a rate of return used to convert a future monetary sum into present value.

Discounted Cash Flow Method* – a method within the income approach whereby the present value of future expected net cash flows is calculated using a discount rate.

Discounted Future Earnings Method* – a method within the income approach whereby the present value of future expected economic benefits is calculated using a discount rate.

Discretionary Earnings - earnings that may be defined, in certain applications, to reflect earnings of a business enterprise prior to the following items:

- Income taxes
- Nonoperating income & expenses
- Nonrecurring income & expenses
- Depreciation and amortization
- Interest expense or income
- Owner's total compensation for those services, which could be provided by a sole owner/manager.

Economic Benefits* - inflows such as revenues, net income, net cash flows, etc.

Economic Life* - the period of time over which property may generate economic benefits.

Effective Date* - see Valuation Date.

Enterprise* - see Business Enterprise.

Equity* - The owner's interest in property after deduction of all liabilities.

Equity Net Cash Flows* - those cash flows available to pay out to equity holders (in the form of dividends) after funding operations of the business enterprise, making necessary capital investments, and increasing or decreasing debt financing.

Equity Risk Premium* - a rate of return added to a risk-free rate to reflect the additional risk of equity instruments over risk free instruments (a component of the cost of equity capital or equity discount rate).

Excess Earnings* - that amount of anticipated economic benefits that exceeds an appropriate rate of return on the value of a selected asset base (often net tangible assets) used to generate those anticipated economic benefits.

Excess Earnings Method* - a specific way of determining a value indication of a business, business ownership interest, or security determined as the sum of a) the value of the assets derived by capitalizing excess earnings and b) the value of the selected asset base. Also frequently used to value intangible assets. See Excess Earnings.

Fair Market Value* - the price, expressed in terms of cash equivalents, at which property would change hands between a hypothetical willing and able buyer and a hypothetical willing and able seller, acting at arm's length in an open and unrestricted market, when neither is under compulsion to buy or sell and when both have reasonable knowledge of the relevant facts. {NOTE: In Canada, the term "price" should be replaced with the term "highest price"}

Fairness Opinion* - an opinion as to whether or not the consideration in a transaction is fair from a financial point of view.

Financial Risk* – the degree of uncertainty of realizing expected future returns of the business resulting from financial leverage. See Business Risk.

Forced Liquidation Value* - liquidation value, at which the asset or assets are sold as quickly as possible, such as at an auction.

Free Cash Flow* – we discourage the use of this term. See Net Cash Flow.

Going Concern* - an ongoing operating business enterprise.

Going Concern Value* - the value of a business enterprise that is expected to continue to operate into the future. The intangible elements of Going Concern Value result from factors such as having a trained work force, an operational plant, and the necessary licenses, systems, and procedures in place.

Going Concern Value – refers to the intangible elements that result from factors such as having a trained work force, an operational plant, and the necessary licenses, systems, and procedures in place. Also refers to the premise of value based on the concept that a business enterprise is expected to continue operations into the future.

Goodwill* - that intangible asset arising as a result of name, reputation, customer loyalty, location, products, and similar factors not separately identified.

Goodwill - that intangible asset arising as a result of elements such as name, reputation, customer loyalty, location, products, and related factors not separately identified and quantified.

Goodwill Value* - the value attributable to goodwill.

Goodwill Value - the value attributable to the elements of intangible assets above the identifiable tangible and intangible assets employed in a business.

Guideline Public Company Method* – a method within the market approach whereby market multiples are derived from market prices of stocks of companies that are engaged in the same or similar lines of business, and that are actively traded on a free and open market.

Holding Company - an entity that derives its returns from investments rather than from the sale of products or services.

Hypothetical Condition - that which is contrary to what exists but is supposed for the purpose of analysis.

Income (Income-Based) Approach* - a general way of determining a value indication of a business, business ownership interest, security, or intangible asset using one or more methods that convert anticipated economic benefits into a present single amount.

Intangible Assets* - non-physical assets such as franchises, trademarks, patents, copyrights, goodwill, equities, mineral rights, securities and contracts (as distinguished from physical assets) that grant rights and privileges, and have value for the owner.

Internal Rate of Return* - a discount rate at which the present value of the future cash flows of the investment equals the cost of the investment.

Intrinsic Value* - the value that an investor considers, on the basis of an evaluation or available facts, to be the "true" or "real" value that will become the market value when other investors reach the same conclusion. When the term applies to options, it is the difference between the exercise price or strike price of an option and the market value of the underlying security.

Invested Capital* - the sum of equity and debt in a business enterprise. Debt is typically a) all interest bearing debt or b) long-term interest-bearing debt. When the term is used, it should be supplemented by a specific definition in the given valuation context.

Invested Capital Net Cash Flows* - those cash flows available to pay out to equity holders (in the form of dividends) and debt investors (in the form of principal and interest) after funding operations of the business enterprise and making necessary capital investments.

Investment Risk* - the degree of uncertainty as to the realization of expected returns.

Investment Value* - the value to a particular investor based on individual investment requirements and expectations. {NOTE: in Canada, the term used is "Value to the Owner"}.

Key Person Discount* - an amount or percentage deducted from the value of an ownership interest to reflect the reduction in value resulting from the actual or potential loss of a key person in a business enterprise.

Levered Beta* - the beta reflecting a capital structure that includes debt.

Limited Appraisal* - the act or process of determining the value of a business, business ownership interest, security, or intangible asset with limitations in analyses, procedures, or scope.

Liquidation Value* - the net amount that would be realized if the business is terminated and the assets are sold piecemeal. Liquidation can be either "orderly" or "forced."

Liquidity* - the ability to quickly convert property to cash or pay a liability.

Liquidity - the ability to readily convert an asset, business, business ownership interest or security into cash without significant loss of principal.

Majority Control* - the degree of control provided by a majority position.

Majority Interest* - an ownership interest greater than 50% of the voting interest in a business enterprise.

Market (Market-Based) Approach* - a general way of determining a value indication of a business, business ownership interest, security, or intangible asset by using one or more methods that compare the subject to similar businesses, business ownership interests, securities, or intangible assets that have been sold.

Market Capitalization of Equity* - the share price of a publicly traded stock multiplied by the number of shares outstanding.

Market Capitalization of Invested Capital* - the market capitalization of equity plus the market value of the debt component of invested capital.

Market Multiple* - the market value of a company's stock or invested capital divided by a company measure (such as economic benefits, number of customers).

Marketability* - the ability to quickly convert property to cash at minimal cost.

Marketability - the capability and ease of transfer or salability of an asset, business, business ownership interest or security.

Marketability Discount* - see Discount for Lack of Marketability.

Merger and Acquisition Method* - a method within the market approach whereby pricing multiples are derived from transactions of significant interests in companies engaged in the same or similar lines of business.

Mid-Year Discounting* - a convention used in the Discounted Future Earnings Method that reflects economic benefits being generated at midyear, approximating the effect of economic benefits being generated evenly throughout the year.

Minority Discount* - a discount for lack of control applicable to a minority interest.

Minority Interest* - an ownership interest less than 50% of the voting interest in a business enterprise.

Multiple* - the inverse of the capitalization rate.

Net Assets - Total assets less total liabilities.

Net Book Value* - with respect to a business enterprise, the difference between total assets (net of accumulated depreciation, depletion, and amortization) and total liabilities as they appear on the balance sheet (synonymous with Shareholder's Equity). With respect to a specific asset, the capitalized cost less accumulated amortization or depreciation as it appears on the books of account of the business enterprise.

Net Cash Flows* - a form of cash flow. When the term is used, it should be supplemented by a qualifier (for example, "Equity" or "Invested Capital") and a specific definition in the given valuation context.

Net Income - Revenue less expenses and taxes.

Net Present Value* - the value, as of a specified date, of future cash inflows less all cash outflows (including the cost of investment) calculated using an appropriate discount rate.

Net Tangible Asset Value* - the value of the business enterprise's tangible assets (excluding excess assets and non-operating assets) minus the value of its liabilities. {NOTE: in Canada, tangible assets also include identifiable intangible assets}.

Non-Operating Assets* - assets not necessary to ongoing operations of the business enterprise. {NOTE: in Canada, the term used is "Redundant Assets"}.

Normalized Earnings* - economic benefits adjusted for nonrecurring, non-economic, or other unusual items to eliminate anomalies and/or facilitate comparisons.

Normalized Financial Statements* - financial statements adjusted for nonoperating assets and liabilities and/or for nonrecurring, non-economic, or other unusual items to eliminate anomalies and/or facilitate comparisons.

Operating Company - a business that conducts an economic activity by generating and selling, or trading in a product or service.

Orderly Liquidation Value* - liquidation value at which the asset or assets are sold over a reasonable period of time to maximize proceeds received.

Portfolio Discount* - an amount or percentage deducted from the value of a business enterprise to reflect the fact that it owns dissimilar operations or assets that do not fit well together.

Premise of Value* - an assumption regarding the most likely set of transactional circumstances that may be applicable to the subject valuation; e.g. going concern, liquidation.

Present Value* - the value, as of a specified date, of future economic benefits and/or proceeds from sale, calculated using an appropriate discount rate.

Price/Earnings Multiple* - the price of a share of stock divided by its earnings per share.

Rate of Return* - an amount of income (loss) and/or change in value realized or anticipated on an investment, expressed as a percentage of that investment.

Redundant Assets* - see Non-Operating Assets.

Replacement Cost New* - the current cost of a similar new property having the nearest equivalent utility to the property being valued.

Report Date* - the date conclusions are transmitted to the client.

Reproduction Cost New* - the current cost of an identical new property.

Required Rate of Return* - the minimum rate of return acceptable by investors before they will commit money to an investment at a given level of risk.

Residual Value* - the value as of the end of the discrete projection period in a discounted future earnings model.

Return on Equity* - the amount, expressed as a percentage, earned on a company's common equity for a given period.

Return on Investment* - see Return on Invested Capital and Return on Equity.

Return on Invested Capital* - the amount, expressed as a percentage, earned on a company's total capital for a given period.

Risk-Free Rate* - the rate of return available in the market on an investment free of default risk.

Risk Premium* - a rate of return added to a risk-free rate to reflect risk.

Rule of Thumb* - a mathematical formula developed from the relationship between price and certain variables based on experience, observation, hearsay, or a combination of these; usually industry specific.

Special Interest Purchasers* - acquirers who believe they can enjoy post-acquisition economies of scale, synergies, or strategic advantages by combining the acquired business interest with their own.

Standard of Value* - the identification of the type of value being used in a specific engagement; e.g. fair market value, fair value, investment value.

Sustaining Capital Reinvestment* - the periodic capital outlay required to maintain operations at existing levels, net of the tax shield available from such outlays.

Systematic Risk* - the risk that is common to all risky securities and cannot be eliminated through diversification. The measure of systematic risk in stocks is the beta coefficient.

Tangible Assets* - physical assets (such as cash, accounts receivable, inventory, property, plant and equipment, etc.)

Terminal Value* - See Residual Value

Transaction Method* - see Merger and Acquisition Method.

Unlevered Beta* - the beta reflecting a capital structure without debt.

Unsystematic Risk* - the risk specific to an individual security that can be avoided through diversification.

Valuation* - the act or process of determining the value of a business, business ownership interest, security, or intangible asset.

Valuation Approach* - a general way of determining a value indication of a business, business ownership interest, security, or intangible asset using one or more valuation methods.

Valuation Date* - the specific point in time as of which the valuator's opinion of value applies (also referred to as "Effective Date" or "Appraisal Date").

Valuation Method* - within approaches, a specific way to determine value.

Valuation Procedure* - the act, manner, and technique of performing the steps of an appraisal method.

Valuation Ratio* - a fraction in which a value or price serves as the numerator and financial, operating, or physical data serves as the denominator.

Value to the Owner* - see Investment Value.

Voting Control* - de jure control of a business enterprise.

Weighted Average Cost of Capital (WACC)* - the cost of capital (discount rate) determined by the weighted average, at market value, of the cost of all financing sources in the business enterprise's capital structure.

Working Capital - The amount by which current assets exceed current liabilities.

AMERICAN SOCIETY OF APPRAISERS
Statements on Business Valuation Standards

SBVS-1 Guideline Public Company Method©

I. Preamble

A. Statements clarify, interpret, explain, or elaborate on Standards. Statements have the full weight of Standards.

B. The purpose of this Statement is to define and describe the requirements for the use of the Guideline Public Company Method, when applicable, under Standard BVS –V Market Approach To Business Valuation.

II. Conceptual framework

A. Market transactions in securities can provide objective, empirical data for developing valuation ratios for use in business valuation.

B. The development of valuation ratios from guideline public companies should be considered in the valuation of businesses, business ownership interests, and securities, to the extent that adequate information is available.

C. Guideline public companies are those that provide a reasonable basis for comparison to the investment characteristics of the company being valued.

III. Search for and selection of guideline public companies

A. A thorough, objective search for guideline public companies is required to establish the credibility of the valuation analysis. The procedure must include criteria for screening and selecting guideline public companies.

B. Guideline public company empirical data can be found in market based valuation ratios of guideline public companies that are engaged in the same or similar lines of business, and that are actively traded on a free and open market.

IV. **Financial data of guideline public companies**

A. It is necessary to obtain and analyze financial and operating data on the guideline public companies, as available.

B. Adjustments to the financial data of the subject company and guideline public companies should be considered to minimize the difference in accounting treatments when such differences are significant. Unusual or nonrecurring items should be analyzed and adjusted as appropriate.

V. **Valuation ratios derived from guideline public companies**

A. Comparisons are made through the use of valuation ratios. The computation and use of such ratios should provide meaningful insight about the value of the subject, considering all relevant factors. Accordingly, care should be exercised with respect to issues such as:

1. The selection of the underlying data used to compute the valuation ratios
2. The selection of the time periods and/or the averaging methods used for the underlying data
3. The computation of the valuation ratios
4. The timing of the price data used in the valuation ratios
5. How the valuation ratio or ratios were selected and applied to the subject's underlying data

B. In general, comparisons should be made by using comparable definitions of the components of the valuation ratios. However, where appropriate, valuation ratios based on components that are reasonably representative of ongoing results may be used.

C. Several valuation ratios may be selected for application to the subject company. These ratios may require adjustment for differences in qualitative and quantitative factors between the guideline public companies and the subject. One or more indications of value may result.

The appraiser must consider the relative importance or weight accorded to each of the indications of value used in arriving at the opinion or conclusion of value.

VI. Other factors and considerations

Adjustments may be necessary to the ratios or values for factors relating to the subject interest, which may not have been considered earlier in the appraisal, such as:

A. Degree of control

B. Degree of marketability and liquidity

C. Strategic or investment value issues

D. Size; depth of management; diversification of markets, products and services; and, relative growth and risk

AMERICAN SOCIETY OF APPRAISERS
Statements on Business Valuation Standards

SBVS-2 Merger and Acquisition Method©

I. Preamble

A. Statements clarify, interpret, explain, or elaborate on Standards. Statements have the full weight of Standards.

B. The purpose of this Statement is to define and describe the requirements for the use of the Merger and Acquisition Method, when applicable, under Standard BVS –V Market Approach To Business Valuation.

II. Conceptual framework

A. Transactions involving the sale, merger or acquisition of businesses, business ownership interests, and securities can provide objective, empirical data for developing valuation multiples.

B. The development of valuation multiples from transactions of significant interests in guideline companies should be considered in the valuation of businesses, business ownership interests, and securities, to the extent that sufficient and relevant information is available.

C. Guideline companies are companies that provide a reasonable basis for comparison to the investment characteristics of the company being valued. Ideal guideline companies are in the same industry as the subject company. However, if there is insufficient transaction information available in that industry, it may be necessary to select other companies having an underlying similarity to the subject company in terms of relevant investment characteristics such as markets, products, growth, cyclical variability, and other salient factors.

III. Search for and selection of transactions in guideline companies

A. A thorough, objective search for transactions of significant interests in guideline companies is required to establish the credibility of The Merger and Acquisition Method. This procedure must include criteria for screening and selecting such companies.

B. Guideline company empirical data can be found in transactions involving controlling or significant minority interests in publicly traded or closely held companies.

IV. Financial data of guideline companies

A. It is necessary to obtain and analyze relevant financial and operating data of the guideline companies, as available.

B. Adjustments to the financial data of the subject company and guideline companies should be considered to minimize the difference in accounting treatments when such differences are significant. Unusual or nonrecurring items should be analyzed and adjusted, as appropriate.

V. Valuation multiples derived from guideline companies

A. Valuation multiples are derived by relating transaction prices in guideline companies to the appropriate underlying financial, operating, or physical data of the respective companies.

B. Several valuation multiples may be selected for application to the subject company. These multiples may require adjustment for differences in qualitative and quantitative factors between the guideline companies and the subject.

C. Several indications of value may result. The appraiser must consider the relative importance or weight accorded to each of the indications of value used in arriving at the opinion or conclusion of value.

VI. Other factors and considerations

Adjustments may be necessary for factors that have not been considered earlier in the appraisal, such as:

A. Degree of control

B. Degree of marketability and liquidity

C. Timing differences between market transactions and the valuation date

D. Strategic or investment value issues

E. Size, depth of management, and diversification of markets, products and services

AMERICAN SOCIETY OF APPRAISERS
Advisory Opinions

AO-1 Financial Consultation and Advisory Services©

It is the opinion of the Business Valuation Committee that the American Society of Appraisers Business Valuation Standards and the Uniform Standards of Professional Appraisal Practice of The Appraisal Foundation, as they apply to business valuation issues, are intended to apply to appraisals that are formally developed and presented opinions of value performed as the primary or ultimate objective of an appraisal engagement. These standards are not intended to apply to financial consultation or advisory services where there is no expression of value opinion or the primary or the ultimate objective is not to express an opinion of value, including but not limited to, fairness opinions, solvency opinions, pricing of securities for public offerings, feasibility studies, transfer pricing studies, lifing studies of intangibles, estate planning or estate tax services, economic damage analysis and quantification, litigation consulting, royalty rate studies for intangibles, and similar engagements.

AMERICAN SOCIETY OF APPRAISERS
Procedural Guidelines

PG-1 Litigation Support: Role of The Independent Financial Expert

I. Preamble

A. Business valuation professionals are frequently engaged as independent financial experts for purposes of assisting in dispute resolution, litigation, or potential litigation. To preserve and enhance the quality of the services of such experts, the American Society of Appraisers, through its Business Valuation Committee, has adopted this Procedural Guideline.

B. This Procedural Guideline incorporates, where appropriate, all relevant Business Valuation Standards and Statements on Standards adopted by the American Society of Appraisers through its Business Valuation Committee.

C. This Procedural Guideline suggests specific procedures that may be used by experts. It is not binding.

D. This Procedural Guideline is designed to offer guidance to ASA members providing Litigation-Support Services. Deviations from this Procedural Guideline are not designed to be or intended to be the basis of any civil liability, and should not create any presumption or evidence that a legal duty has been breached, or create any special relationship between the expert and any other person.

II. Performance of Litigation-Support Services

A. Litigation-Support Services include any professional assistance provided to a client in a matter involving pending or potential litigation or dispute resolution proceedings before a trier of fact.

B. In rendering Litigation-Support Services, the expert may be retained to provide an expert opinion on the financial effects of facts and assumptions. In addition to forming an expert opinion, the expert may value a business, project future financial results, analyze the performance of a business operation, interpret financial data, opine on an impaired stream of earnings, or render other similar types of professional services.

C. In providing Litigation-Support Services, an independent financial expert may play a role as:
1. Expert — One who is qualified by knowledge, skill, experience, training, or education in performing business valuation services and/or related financial analyses.
2. Expert Witness — An expert who is engaged to explain technical, scientific, or specialized knowledge in order to assist the trier of fact in understanding evidence.
3. Arbitrator — An expert who serves as a trier of fact in an alternative dispute resolution context.
4. Court-Appointed Expert — An expert who is engaged by the court to assist the trier of fact.
5. Consulting or Advisory Expert — An expert who is engaged to review another expert's work product or who is engaged to advise the client, lawyer or another expert witness about technical matters relating to the subject litigation, but who will not be called to testify at trial, may or may not be independent. Accordingly, this Procedural Guideline may not apply to such an expert.

D. The expert should obtain a clear understanding of the scope of the assignment.

E. When planning the scope of work for a particular engagement, the expert should obtain a sufficient understanding of the nature of the dispute, the events giving rise to the claim, as well as the economic context and industry outlook impacting the business and/or individual central to the assignment.

F. The expert should obtain sufficient relevant data to afford a reasonable basis for the conclusions reached and/or recommendations made.

G. Sufficient information and documentation should be gathered by such means as inspection, inquiry, computation and analysis to ensure that the expert's analysis and conclusion are properly supported. The expert should exercise professional judgment in determining the extent of the information and documentation necessary to support the conclusion.

H. The expert witness, arbitrator or court-appointed expert should maintain integrity, objectivity and independence.

I. The following examples represent some of the many types of cases in which an expert may provide Litigation-Support Services in the area of business valuation and related financial analysis:

1. Business Valuation

   a. Determination of "fair value" of minority shares in dissenting stockholder and oppression suits.
   b. Income, property, gift tax, and estate tax issues, including the determination of fair market value in non-arm's length transactions, allocation of purchase price among different categories of assets, corporate reorganizations, rollovers, stockholder benefits, deemed dispositions, gifts and bequests, capital gains, etc.
   c. Valuation of shares held by an Employee Stock Ownership Plan.
   d. Separation and divorce.
   e. Partner/shareholder disputes.
   f. Business valuations.
   g. Buy-sell agreements.

2. Quantification of Financial Loss or Damages

   a. Breach of contract and tort, including:
      (1) measuring damages for lost profits and loss of goodwill,
      (2) defining relevant markets and calculating market share,
      (3) restating or reconstructing financial records,
      (4) developing profit and cost relationships,
      (5) creating pro-forma financial statements.

   b. Personal injury and fatality claims, including the quantification of impaired earnings.
   c. Insurance claims, including business interruption and disturbance losses.
   d. Condemnation/Expropriation of business or property.
   e. Trespass and conversion.
   f. Professional malpractice.
   g. Anti-trust/unfair competition.
   h. Intellectual property-infringement damages.
   i. Bankruptcy and reorganization.

III. Conducting the Assignment

A. In performing the engagement, the expert should consider the appropriate method(s) to be adopted and procedures to be applied.

B. The expert should consider key assumptions and hypothetical conditions, determining the reasonableness and appropriateness thereof. The use of unwarranted assumptions may impair the objectivity — actual or perceived — of the expert.

C. The expert should consider the necessity of relying on the work of a specialist. When there is such reliance, the expert may wish to consider the specialist's independence and competency. If the expert relies upon a specialist, the conclusions drawn should be documented. Any written opinion or report from a specialist should be retained on file.

D. Work performed in the course of an engagement should be documented and files should be maintained in an organized manner. The form and extent of work papers should suit the circumstances and needs of the engagement for which they are prepared.

E. The expert should evaluate the necessity of obtaining a client representation letter and, if possible and applicable, a representation letter from management or other representatives of the underlying business.

F. The expert should either retain on file, or have access to, all information relied upon.

G. When the expert has determined that an engagement letter is required, the engagement letter should be retained on file. When no engagement letter has been received, the expert's file should include a summary of the nature and function of the assignment.

H. When the expert has determined that a client representation letter and/or a management representation letter is necessary, this (these) letter(s) should be retained on file.

I. The method(s) selected by the expert should be documented along with the reasons for selection. In addition, the specific procedures should be documented along with the reasons for selection. The expert should document key areas considered and significant assumptions made. A copy of calculations, explanations, and documentation supporting the final conclusion should be retained in the file.

J. The expert should follow the rules of the applicable jurisdiction.

IV. Preparation of an Expert Report

A. An expert report is often considered to constitute any communication, written or oral (and not in draft or preliminary form) that is prepared by an expert and that contains a conclusion pertaining to a review, analysis, or quantification of business value, damages, or economic loss and that is to be used in litigation or arbitration proceedings.

B. It is recommended that the individual(s) responsible for the preparation of the expert report be identified.

C. To the extent that it is both possible and appropriate, an expert report should contain, as a minimum, the following information:

1. **Identity of Client**

   The expert's client(s) should be clearly identified.

2. **Description of Assignment**

   The expert report should contain a clear description as to the specific nature of the expert's assignment.

3. **Effective Date(s) or Effective Time Period(s)**

   Value(s) or damages should be expressed as of a specific date or time period. In damage claims, the damages may relate to past, present and/or future economic losses.

4. **Intended Use**

   If not already included in the description of the nature of the assignment, the intended use of the expert report should be clearly stated, and use for other purposes should be precluded.

5. **Definitions**

   The expert report should contain the expert's definition of key terms not commonly defined. The expert should define or explain terms such as (but not limited to) "damages," "economic loss," "loss of profits," "lost contribution margin."

6. **Documents and Information**

The expert report should identify significant documents and information relied upon, and, if applicable, those reviewed but not relied upon.

7. **Limitations**

If the expert was unable to obtain, or was otherwise denied access to, documents, information, and/or interviews, or where the information provided was incomplete, this limitation should be clearly disclosed in the expert report. It may also be appropriate to disclose the reasons for this limitation. To the extent that such limitation would restrict the ability of the expert to form an opinion, it may be necessary to express a qualified opinion, a disclaimer, or a denial of an opinion, depending on the specific circumstances.

8. **Relevant Chronology**

When relevant, the expert report should summarize the chronology of events giving rise to the claim(s) in the litigation. The chronology of events, as set out in the expert report, should be consistent with the effective date or time period.

9. **Relevant Context and Financial Analysis**

When relevant, the expert report should include an appropriate description of factors such as those listed in BVS VIII, paragraph V, and a financial analysis such as the one described in BVS VIII, paragraph VI.

10. **Methodology**

The expert report should contain a description of the method(s) adopted and the reason(s) for their use.

11. Analysis

The expert report should provide adequate description in clear terms of how the expert determined value, quantified economic losses, damages, etc.

12. Assumptions

The expert report should clearly state, and identify the basis of, all assumptions, hypothetical conditions, and limiting conditions that affected the analyses, opinions, and conclusions (see USPAP 10-2(a)(viii)).

13. Conclusion

The expert report should clearly state the conclusions of the expert.

14. Report Date

The expert report should be dated as of the day on which it is completed or issued.

15. Exhibits, Appendices, Graphs, Charts, Schedules, and Tables

The use of visual aids in the body of, or appending, the expert report should be made in an objective, unbiased, and professional manner, so that they can be properly interpreted by the trier of fact and others connected with the litigation or arbitration.

V. Retention of Work Papers and Report

A. The expert should retain fully-documented work papers for each engagement, whether in hard copy or electronic copy. The expert should also retain summaries of oral reports or testimony (or a transcript of testimony) and all other data, information and documentation necessary to support the expert's opinions and conclusions. Summaries of key meetings, discussions and correspondence should be retained on file.

B. The expert should maintain custody of the work papers, or make appropriate retention, access, and retrieval arrangements with the party having custody of those work papers. The expert should retain the work papers for a period of at least five (5) years after preparation, or at least two (2) years after final disposition of any judicial proceeding (including arbitration) in which testimony was given, whichever period expires last.

C. A copy of the final issued expert report should be retained on file for a period of at least five (5) years after preparation, or at least two (2) years after final disposition of any judicial proceeding (including arbitration) in which testimony was given, whichever period expires last.

A

B

C

D

E

F

G

H

I

L

M

N

O

P

Q

R

S

T

U

V

W

Z

About the Author – Z. Christopher Mercer, ASA, CFA

Z. Christopher Mercer is founder and chief executive officer of Mercer Capital, one of the leading independent business valuation and investment banking firms in the country. Mercer Capital, founded in 1982, provides services to a national and international clientele.

Chris began his valuation career in the late 1970s. He has prepared, overseen, or contributed to hundreds of valuations for purposes related to M&A, litigation, and tax, among others. He is a prolific author on valuation-related topics. He has written four books and contributed to numerous others, and has written hundreds of articles on business valuation and business topics. Chris is a member of the National Speakers Association and is one of the most sought after speakers on business valuation issues for national professional associations and other business and professional groups.

He is an Accredited Senior Appraiser (ASA) of the American Society of Appraisers and holds the Chartered Financial Analyst (CFA) professional designation from the CFA Institute. Chris holds a bachelor's degree in economics from Stetson University and a master's degree in economics from Vanderbilt University.

Chris has held numerous leadership positions with the American Society of Appraisers and the ESOP Association. He has served on the boards of several companies and currently serves on the board of Klumb Lumber Company, Point Clear, Alabama.

Chris lives in Memphis with his wife, Ashley, the minor four of his five children, two cats and a dog. He writes a blog, MERCER ON VALUE (www.merceronvalue.com), where he drafted numerous sections of this book and displays his latest thinking in early form.

Chris welcomes your comments on the information found in this book. Feel free to contact him at:

Mercer Capital
5860 Ridgeway Center Parkway, Suite 400
Memphis, TN 38120
901.685.2120
www.mercercapital.com
mercerc@mercercapital.com (Chris's e-mail address)

If you would like Chris to speak to your company or organization about buy-sell agreements, business valuation, building business value, or the seminal question "Is your business ready for sale?," contact him or Barbara Price at 901.685.2120.

About Mercer Capital

Mercer Capital Management, Inc. (Mercer Capital) is an employee-owned independent business valuation and investment banking firm. Since our founding in 1982, Mercer Capital has provided over 6,000 sound, well-documented financial analyses and valuation opinions for corporations large and small located throughout the world.

We offer a broad range of services including valuation for financial statement reporting purposes as well as tax compliance, M&A advisory, fairness and solvency opinions, ESOP and ERISA valuation services, and litigation support.

Industry experience includes, but is not limited to, automotive, consumer products, distribution, energy, financial services, health care, industrial products, manufacturing, media and entertainment, pharmaceuticals, technology, telecommunications and utilities. (For a more complete listing of industry experience, visit our website at www.mercercapital.com.)

For over 20 years, Mercer Capital has been bringing uncommon professionalism, intellectual rigor, technical expertise, and superior client service to a broad range of public and private companies and financial institutions.

To learn more about Mercer Capital, please visit us at www.mercercapital.com or call any of our senior professionals below at 901.685.2120.

Z. Christopher Mercer, ASA, CFA (Chris)
mercerc@mercercapital.com

Kenneth W. Patton, ASA (Ken)
pattonk@mercercapital.com

Matthew R. Crow, ASA, CFA (Matt)
crowm@mercercapital.com

Timothy R. Lee, ASA (Tim)
leet@mercercapital.com

Andrew K. Gibbs, CFA, CPA/ABV (Andy)
gibbsa@mercercapital.com

James E. Graves, ASA, CFA (Jim)
gravesj@mercercapital.com

Travis W. Harms, CFA, CPA/ABV
harmst@mercercapital.com

Jean E. Harris, CFA
harrisj@mercercapital.com

Nicholas J. Heinz (Nick)
heinzn@mercercapital.com

Wendy S. Ingalls, CPA/ABV, CBA, ASA
ingallsw@mercercapital.com

Brent A. McDade, CBA, BVAL
mcdadeb@mercercapital.com

Barbara Walters Price
priceb@mercercapital.com

Notes

Notes

Notes

Notes

Notes

Notes

Notes

Printed in the United States
90655LV00001B/7-54/A